# ADHD DOES NOT EXIST

# ADHD

The Truth About

# DOES

Attention Deficit and Hyperactivity Disorder

# NOT

RICHARD SAUL, MD

# EXIST.

**HARPER** WAVE

www.harperwave.com

ADHD DOES NOT EXIST. Copyright © 2014 by Richard Saul, MD. All rights reserved. Printed in the United States of America. No part of this book may be used or reproduced in any manner whatsoever without written permission except in the case of brief quotations embodied in critical articles and reviews. For information, address HarperCollins Publishers, 10 East 53rd Street, New York, NY 10022.

HarperCollins books may be purchased for educational, business, or sales promotional use. For information, please e-mail the Special Markets Department at SPsales@harpercollins.com.

FIRST EDITION

Designed by Renato Stanisic

Library of Congress Cataloging-in-Publication Data has been applied for.

ISBN: 978-0-06-226673-6

14  15  16  17  18   OV/RRD   10 9 8 7 6 5 4 3 2 1

*I dedicate this book to all the children and adults who have been misdiagnosed with ADHD and have had their treatment delayed or denied.*

"We are to admit no more causes of natural things than such as are both true and sufficient to explain their appearances. Therefore, to the same natural effects we must, so far as possible, assign the same causes."
—Isaac Newton


"Listen to the patient, and they will give you the diagnosis."
—Sir William Osler, cofounder of
Johns Hopkins Medical School

# Contents

*Author's Note  xi*
*Preface  xiii*
Introduction: The Nonexistent Disorder Called ADHD  1

**PART I: THE BIRTH OF A CRISIS**
1. Where We Are and How We Got Here  7
2. An Easy Answer: The Role of Cultural Bias  19
3. The Stimulant Epidemic and Side Effects  25
4. A Summary of the Conditions Behind
   ADHD Symptoms  33

**PART II: THE CONDITIONS AND DISORDERS RESPONSIBLE
FOR ADHD SYMPTOMS**
5. Vision Problems  39
6. Sleep Disorders  51
7. Substance Abuse  65
8. Mood Disorders (Bipolar and Major Depressive Disorder)  79
9. Hearing Problems  93
10. Learning Disabilities  105
11. Sensory Processing Disorder  117
12. Giftedness  129

13. Seizure Disorders 141

14. Obsessive-Compulsive Disorder 151

15. Tourette's Syndrome 161

16. Asperger Syndrome (An Autism Spectrum Disorder) 171

17. Neurochemical Distractibility/Impulsivity 185

18. Schizophrenia 197

19. Fetal Alcohol Syndrome 209

20. Fragile X Syndrome 223

21. Other Conditions 235


**PART III: TAKE ACTION**

22. When There's No Diagnosis 253

23. Evaluating and Managing Your Symptoms 259


*Acknowledgments 273*

*Notes 275*

*Index 297*

# Author's Note

Throughout this book, I will use the term "ADHD" as a form of shorthand for talking about the group of attention-deficit/hyperactivity symptoms that have gained that label through the American Psychiatric Association, the *DSM*, and the multiple parties that have embraced it. Moreover, in multiple places in the book I've noted how or where ADHD and other diagnoses overlap. In all cases, my intention is for you to read "ADHD" as "the set of symptoms associated with that diagnosis," rather than taking my use of the diagnostic term literally. If I meant the latter, *this book* wouldn't exist. Also, for the inquisitive reader, I encourage you to turn to the Notes section after reading each chapter for more details and resources.

# Preface

I wrote this book to be provocative. Not provocative for the sake of provocation, but because I have been concerned for years about the multifaceted problems caused by the misdiagnosis of attention-deficit hyperactivity disorder, or ADHD, in children and adults. Attention-related symptoms are all too real, with negative consequences for children, adults, and broader society; those affected face challenges in academic, professional, and social settings, often with lifelong repercussions. But the medical establishment's reliance on the ADHD diagnosis—and the medical community's embrace of it—has also had several negative consequences: the failure to diagnose underlying conditions that explain attention symptoms in whole or in part; the omission of much-needed treatment for those primary diagnoses; the health-related, economic, and emotional costs of undiagnosed and hence untreated conditions. I wrote this book to provoke deeper thinking about debilitating attention-deficit and hyperactivity symptoms for practitioners, patients, and others, with the hope that it will help more people get the help they need.

My route to gaining a complete picture of attention-deficit symptoms has had multiple turns. An early experience with attention symptoms arose through my faculty position as professor of clinical medicine with the University of Health Sciences in Chicago. Starting in the 1970s, I was responsible for establishing new programs that would engage and educate medical students and faculty about medical conditions that could interfere with learning. In this role I started a program to identify factors interfering with children's learning (kindergarten through eighth grade) in the Lake County, Illinois, school system. Our guiding question was "What's preventing them from learning?" From our first day in the schools, one observation stood out: A very high percentage of the children—more than one in five—faced attention challenges. These took the form of learning problems, disruptive behavior, even sadness and withdrawal. Over time, I developed a protocol for evaluating children with attention-related issues and others that interfered with learning. I still remember the stack of articles I went through to develop the protocol: It was taller than I was, more than six feet high!

At the time, I still held a conventional view of the attention deficit diagnosis. We called it attention-deficit disorder, or ADD (the "Hyperactivity" part would come later), which remains a very popular acronym for the condition. Among our research questions were "Do all children with learning disabilities have ADD?" (they didn't) and "Do all children with ADD have learning disabilities?" (most did, but they also had higher IQs than their average peer). I didn't realize it at the time, but one of the components I developed for the Lake County schools program laid the foundation for my eventual belief that attention deficit and hyperactivity were symptoms rather than a diagnosis. To help our medical students understand the challenges associated with attention deficits, we simulated the classroom experience for them, for example by having them wear "reverse binoculars" that made everything look farther away than it really was. Due to their compromised depth perception, students wearing the binoculars tended to knock items off their desks and accidentally bump into other students when moving around the room—both hallmark signs of ADHD. Similarly, we had the medical students wear headphones that transmitted lecture material, but with brief, frequent periods of silence (that is, gaps in the audio feed) that made comprehension difficult, another symptom of attention deficit or a learning disorder. In retrospect I realized that I was simulating not only attention deficits but many of their *underlying causes*. As we'll see in later chapters, vision and hearing problems, or even absence seizures, are responsible for a significant number of patients misdiagnosed with ADHD. Not surprisingly, once we had students take off the binoculars or headphones their "ADHD" symptoms disappeared.

Another influence on my thinking about attention deficit arose soon after my experience at Lake County schools, but from a very different source. The mother of a patient named "Bobby," a fourth grader, told me that Bobby's teacher had called her in for a meeting because he was disrupting the class. Bobby's mother said she was surprised, given his record of good classroom behavior up to that point. I asked her to find out if her son was engaging in the behavior all day or only during certain periods. On her next visit she reported that Bobby was only disruptive—including throwing spitballs, talking to classmates, and tapping his fingers on his desk—during the class's math section. Moreover, Bobby, who tested as gifted in most subjects, had already completed the entire fourth-grade math curriculum in the first month of school. Now my patient's behavior made more sense: He was probably bored. Bobby's mom confirmed that he was expected to "sit and be quiet" while the others did their exercises. It would have taken a rare fourth-grade boy to toe that line! I helped Bobby's mother arrange for him to attend a fifth-grade math class. His disruptive behavior disappeared overnight. Importantly, I saw again how a specific condition—giftedness, in this case—could manifest itself through attention-deficit symptoms. Bobby wasn't diagnosed with ADHD, but it was easy to see how a child like him in different circumstances might be. One of the chapters in the book is devoted to children like Bobby, whose talent can lead to boredom and a misdiagnosis of ADHD.

In the early 1980s I began to pursue my evolving hypothesis about attention deficit and hyperactivity more fully. I had won a multi-year federal grant to work with a director of special education to raise statewide awareness of children's learning and attention issues. But our work also raised my own awareness of institutionalized problems related to these issues. For example, it became clear that physicians weren't performing comprehensive examinations of children with attention/learning deficits, even though that was suggested by the American Academy of Pediatrics and other leading medical organizations. There were multiple reasons for this. Among them were knowledge gaps (doctors just didn't know how to examine these patients) and economics (securing full reimbursement for such evaluations was becoming increasingly difficult). These and related observations motivated me to open a referral office in 1983. A "referral office" is one that handles patients sent by other physicians, psychologists, and other patients, usually because the patients represent complicated cases or fail to respond to initial treatments. Many of the patients sent to me had already seen multiple doctors, with no relief.

Working with referred patients over the next decade confirmed what I'd suspected for years: The symptoms of ADHD are better explained by other conditions. In other words, ADHD, as we currently define it, does not exist. The majority of patients who came to my office with a primary diagnosis of ADHD qualified for other diagnoses that explained their symptoms. Many other patients had no condition at all. For many of those patients who did qualify for other diagnoses, their previous physicians had diagnosed the other conditions as comorbid (occurring simultaneously) with ADHD. Once I treated what I saw as the primary diagnosis (the non-ADHD diagnosis), the attention-deficit and hyperactivity symptoms usually disappeared, leading me to believe that "ADHD" was a product of other primary conditions, and not a condition on its own.

As you might imagine, my patients and their families were very relieved to have a diagnosis that made sense to them and treatment that actually worked. As I had more and more success with child patients, something interesting happened: Many of the parents said, "I've had attention challenges, too. Can you help me?" Using the same protocol of discovering a primary diagnosis other than ADHD, I treated these patients and reduced their attention symptoms significantly. So many adults started addressing their attention-related issues that over time my practice went from a 25 percent focus on adults to a 75 percent focus, though the ADHD diagnosis still tends to be more common in children. Diagnosing and treating both children and adults has helped confirm my view that attention deficit and hyperactivity are primarily symptoms of other conditions.

Helping those labeled with ADHD find the right diagnosis and treatment is an ongoing mission for me. In my clinical practice I continue to see many patients who have been diagnosed with ADHD or who believe they have the disorder. I also work with several medical associations that focus on ADHD and related conditions. These include the Society for Developmental and Behavioral Pediatrics and the American Academy of Neurology's section on Behavior and Development. In both groups I help my colleagues understand the dangers associated with misdiagnosing ADHD, along with issues related to the increasing levels of stimulant use and abuse. Our shared understanding will help shape the practice guidelines advocated by these groups and, hopefully, the broader medical establishment.

At the beginning of this preface I said I wrote this book to provoke. What I hope to provoke is deeper understanding of attention-deficit symptoms among patients, practitioners, and the public, with the goal of stopping the knee-jerk diagnosis of ADHD. As I discuss in this book, there are many reasons for the misdiagnosis of ADHD, driven by patients, physicians, pharmaceutical companies, and the media, among others. There are also many costs—medical, economic, and psychological—for the individuals and families affected by the diagnosis. By portraying attention-deficit and hyperactivity symptoms in a new context, I hope to help many more patients enjoy the outcomes my patients have: accurate diagnoses, the right treatments, and much more satisfying lives.

# ADHD DOES NOT EXIST

# Introduction: The Nonexistent Disorder Called ADHD

Over 4 percent of all adults and 11 percent of U.S. children are diagnosed with ADHD—more than a 40 percent jump in the last decade. Two-thirds of these children are prescribed stimulants such as Adderall or Ritalin. Think about that for a second . . . . That means many adults and teens are abusing these medications as well for better performance at school and work.

These are alarming findings. But perhaps even more startling is the central claim of this book: that *ADHD does not exist*. Okay, you might be saying, ADHD is probably overdiagnosed. And yes, some people who are on a stimulant probably shouldn't be, like the college student struggling to focus on a boring lecture or the kid who's fidgeting a bit too much for his teacher's liking. But how can it be that among the millions of people diagnosed, not one of them actually has ADHD? Because we've all encountered someone with severe attention or hyperactivity issues—the boy who is always daydreaming, the girl who gets out of her seat to run around the room while her classmates sit calmly, the woman who consistently asks questions that have just been answered, the man who talks a mile a minute. Surely at least some of these people have ADHD!

Actually, not one of them does. Let me be clear: The premise of this book is that not a single individual—not even the person who finds it close to impossible to pay attention or sit still—is afflicted by the disorder called ADHD as we define it today. Ever since 1937, when Dr. Charles Bradley reported that children who exhibited symptoms of distractibility responded well to stimulant medication, the core definition of ADHD has remained essentially unchanged. The earlier version of the disorder, as you may recall, was ADD, or attention deficit disorder, defined by the American Psychiatric Association's *Diagnostic and Statistical Manual* (or *DSM*, which we'll explore in more detail later). The definition was based on symptoms related to inattention, such as failure to pay attention to details or instructions, difficulty with organization, and distractibility. Later versions of the *DSM* added symptoms of hyperactivity-impulsivity, taking the disorder from ADD to AD*H*D, or attention-deficit *hyperactivity* disorder. These symptoms included things like fidgeting, excessive talking, interrupting, and difficulty staying seated or awaiting turns. (In the next chapter I'll go over all the symptoms of "ADHD" in detail.)

Nevertheless, there is something striking about the way we define this "illness"—that is, by its symptoms, rather than its *cause*. If we were to define a heart attack by the chest pain one feels while undergoing one, then the appropriate cure would be painkillers, rather than ways of actually reviving and repairing the heart. Other examples are easy to find: Nasal congestion can be a *symptom* of a cold, allergy, or many other conditions, but a runny nose is not a *diagnosis*; abdominal pain can be associated with appendicitis, gastroenteritis, cancer, and other illnesses, but the stomach pain itself is not a diagnosis. In the same way, I will argue here that the symptom complex associated with the ADHD diagnosis is related to more than twenty medical diagnoses that, when treated effectively, can result in the disappearance of the attention-deficit and hyperactivity symptoms.

The symptoms of distractibility and impulsivity are all too

real, but we're using an outdated, invalid definition of ADHD, one that has been kept in place for decades by physicians and other practitioners, pharmaceutical companies, the media, and even patients themselves. The millions of false diagnoses result in a cascade of consequences including delayed or denied treatment, spiraling health-care costs, and significant health risks and frustration for patients and their families. There is no need for patients and their families to continue suffering, and for us as a society to bear the large, mounting costs of the ADHD-stimulant epidemic. It's time to change our thinking about what really drives distractibility and impulsivity and help people get the right treatment.

My goal is to provide an unprecedented, honest look at the disorder called ADHD and give people the tools they need to get the right diagnosis and treatment for their ADHD-related symptoms. I wrote this book for you, whether you're the mother or father of a child with attention issues, a teacher with too many distracted and medicated students, a physician concerned about the escalating diagnoses of ADHD, or someone struggling with distractibility and impulsivity yourself. I want this book to be a guide for you, one that can help you gain a much better understanding of the many potential sources of ADHD symptoms and the correct treatment for these individual conditions. If you've been struggling with ADHD even after being diagnosed and medicating with stimulants, take heart: Once the underlying condition or disorder is found and treated, the symptoms almost always go away.

In Part I of this book I'll lay out the landscape of the ADHD problem, including the history of the disorder, how it's defined and treated today, the factors driving its misguided definition and treatment, and the large costs of the disorder for individuals and broader society. I'll also explore the idea that multiple other conditions can account fully for attention-deficit and hyperactivity symptoms, and how recent genetic evidence supports the overlap between ADHD and many of these conditions. I've devoted an entire chapter to the effects and consequences of stimulants, and why these are "Band-Aids" at best and have the potential to worsen symptoms and elicit dangerous side effects. In Part II of the book I'll provide an in-depth view of the sixteen most common disorders and conditions with underlying attention-deficit and hyperactivity symptoms (and an overview of the less common conditions), unearthing the clues pointing to these conditions and sharing their most effective treatments. I will also illustrate each condition with real case examples taken from my experience. Finally, in Part III, I'll provide tools for evaluating the conditions responsible for attention-deficit/hyperactivity symptoms, along with general tips for managing these conditions.

I hope you emerge from reading this book with an important insight I've gained over decades of working with patients with attention-deficit and hyperactivity symptoms: that treating ADHD as a real disorder is doing all of us a disservice, felt most by patients and their families. My goal is to eradicate the misguided definition of ADHD that drives a vast and damaging cycle of overprescription, one that the United States and the rest of the world is finding more and more difficult to escape.

PART I

# THE BIRTH OF A CRISIS

# CHAPTER 1

# Where We Are and How We Got Here

Imagine a person who is somewhat distracted or impulsive in nature. Someone close to them—a friend, parent, family member, or educator—recommends that they undergo a professional evaluation. They make an appointment with a family doctor or one they found within their health insurance network. If that doctor is like most physicians practicing today, he or she will ask the patient some general questions about their symptoms. More thorough physicians might ask the patient to fill out some forms—one possibly specific to ADHD (like the Vanderbilt Assessment Scale[1])—but even assessments like these are becoming increasingly rare in practice. The doctor would then compare the patient's responses to this list of symptoms, provided by the fifth edition of the *Diagnostic and Statistical Manual of Mental Disorders*:[2]

### Inattention
- Fails to pay close attention to details (for example, careless mistakes in schoolwork)
- Has difficulty sustaining attention in tasks
- Does not seem to listen when spoken to directly
- Does not follow through on instructions (for example, for schoolwork, chores)

- Has difficulty organizing tasks/activities
- Avoids, dislikes, or is reluctant to engage in tasks requiring sustained mental effort (for example, schoolwork)
- Loses things necessary for specific tasks (such as homework assignments)
- Easily distracted by external stimuli
- Forgetful in daily activities

**Hyperactivity-Impulsivity**
- Fidgets with hands/feet
- Leaves seat in situations where remaining seated is expected
- Runs about or climbs excessively in situations in which this is considered inappropriate (this often manifests as restlessness in adolescents/adults)
- Has difficulty engaging in leisure activities quietly
- Often on the go or acts as if driven by a motor
- Talks excessively
- Blurts out answers
- Has difficulty awaiting turns
- Interrupts or intrudes on others (for example, in conversations)

There are eighteen symptoms in total, but to meet criteria for the diagnosis, the patient would have only needed to display five symptoms from one or both of the categories. And, as easy as that, possibly in a matter of minutes, they went from being distracted or impulsive to having a classified "disorder."

If you (or your child) have been diagnosed with ADHD, it most likely happened under circumstances similar to those above. It may have been a surreal moment, or perhaps it was an expected one. It may have seemed too quick of a judgment to be true, or perhaps you were grateful for an explanation that answered all of your (or your child's) problems, but as we'll see later, there are no shortcuts to finding the source of ADHD symptoms. For an evaluation to be effective, it must be thorough.

You'll notice that the symptoms above are split into two categories: inattention and hyperactivity-impulsivity. Those diagnosed with ADHD fall into one of three subtypes:

predominantly inattentive type,
predominantly hyperactive-impulsive type,
or combined type.

According to the *DSM*, features associated with the symptoms include temper tantrums, stubbornness, volatile mood, rejection by peers, and poor self-esteem. I don't have to convince you that the checklist above is highly prone to subjectivity. What level of disorganization is considered "too disorganized"? How much talking is "excessive"? Indeed, one could easily argue that the loose criteria above have led to an overstatement of attention deficit and hyperactivity in the population, associated, in turn, with a low threshold for diagnosis. Quite alarmingly, with the recent introduction of the *DSM-V*, that threshold for diagnosis of ADHD has dropped even further.

The ease and carelessness with which ADHD is diagnosed is nothing short of jarring, but like so many wrongs, the ADHD diagnosis took time to reach its current state of prevalence, steadily sneaking up to the cliff we see today. This chapter is about where we are now with regard to the diagnosis of ADHD, and how we got here. We will discover how our understanding of ADHD has evolved over time and why this presents a problem for individuals and society today.

## A BRIEF HISTORY OF ADHD

THE STORY OF FIDGETY PHILIP
*Let me see if Philip can*
*Be a little gentleman*
*Let me see, if he is able*
*To sit still for once at the table...*
*But fidgety Phil,*
*He won't sit still;*
*He wriggles and giggles,*
*And then, I declare*
*Swings backwards and forwards*
*And tilts up his chair....*

THE STORY OF JOHNNY HEAD-IN-AIR
*As he trudg'd along to school,*
*It was always Johnny's rule*
*To be looking at the sky*
*And the clouds that floated by;*
*But what just before him lay,*
*In his way,*
*Johnny never thought about;*
*So that everyone cried out—*
*"Look at little Johnny there,*
*Little Johnny Head-in-Air!"*

—POEMS WRITTEN IN THE LATE 1800S OR EARLY 1900S[3]

Some see these poems, most likely written at the turn of the twentieth century, as the earliest accounts of what we know today as attention-deficit/hyperactivity disorder. After all, Philip and Johnny do display elements of the two main symptom categories associated with the disorder called ADHD: inattention and hyperactivity-impulsivity. Today, more than a century after those verses were penned, parents and teachers could easily point to at least one Fidgety Philip/Phyllis or Johnny/Joanna Head-in-Air they know. Nor do Philip or Joanna have to be children; the estimated rate of adults diagnosed with ADHD is 4.4 percent.[4] Everyone has a friend, colleague, or family member who has difficulty concentrating or staying on task; many adults self-identify as having "ADD" and make statements like, "Sorry I forgot to call; it's my ADD again."

But, as alluded to in the introduction, there's a big problem here: The diagnosis and treatment of ADHD as we know it today are wrong. The symptoms of attention deficit and hyperactivity can be explained fully by other conditions, from something as simple as poor sleep, to something as complex as bipolar disorder. Fidgety Philip's table manners could easily have been consequences of early-stage bipolar disorder or Tourette's syndrome. Vision problems, depression, or a seizure disorder could have explained why Johnny's head was always "in the air." Through the historical lens we see that our understanding of distractibility and impulsivity has changed shape over time, and is likely to continue changing.

Symptoms associated with ADHD have likely been part of the human experience since before recorded history. As far as documented accounts of the disorder, Edward Hallowell and John Ratey, in their book *Driven to Distraction*, point to the 1902 description of a group of twenty children (fifteen boys and five girls) with strong traits of defiance and disinhibition by a physician named George Still.[5] Dr. Still pointed out that the children had adequate parenting, and thus may have inherited a biological predisposition to the behavior—highly unconventional thinking at a time when most psychological and behavioral symptoms were attributed to the family environment. The physician-psychologist William James, too, saw a potential neurological basis for such behavior in children. Later, in 1934, Eugene Kahn and Louis Cohen published an article in the *New England Journal of Medicine* linking hyperactivity and impulsivity to encephalitis infections.

In 1937, Charles Bradley found additional evidence for the biological basis of attention-deficit hyperactivity when he treated children displaying such symptoms with Benzedrine, a stimulant. Soon after, child patients with attention-deficit symptoms were diagnosed with "minimal brain dysfunction," or MBD, and treated with the stimulants Ritalin and Cylert. The *DSM-II*, which came out in 1968, labeled the symptom set "hyperkinetic reaction of childhood."[6] Maurice Laufer hypothesized that the syndrome was related to an overactive thalamus (part of the midbrain), an early explanation in a series of similar ones involving excessive activity within the central nervous system.

By the 1970s, it was commonly accepted that hyperactivity, distractibility, and impulsivity tended to cluster together, and that genetic-biological explanations for the symptoms were most apt, though difficult to prove conclusively. The *DSM-III* (1980) introduced the concept of attention deficit disorder with and without hyperactivity (ADD-H and ADD, respectively). Seven years later, the revised version of the *DSM-III* (known as the *DSM-III-R*) changed the label to attention-deficit hyperactivity disorder (ADHD), which remains the current name for the condition.[7] The *DSM-III-R* and *DSM-IV* (released in 1994) had very similar criteria for ADHD. Studies conducted around the time of each manual's release were essentially in agreement.[8]

An additional source of evidence that ADHD should not be diagnosed as a separate disorder is that some mental conditions (many of which are discussed later in this book) share a common genetic link with "ADHD." Specifically, Harvard University research released in 2013 shows for the first time that some of the same genetic patterns underlie autism, depression, bipolar disorder, schizophrenia, and ADHD.[9] The study examined the genetic codes of more than sixty thousand people with and without those conditions—the largest study to date of the genetics of these conditions. The lead researcher calls the findings "just a tip of an iceberg," suggesting that deeper genetic linkages among multiple disorders are likely to be discovered. While these findings don't "prove" that ADHD symptoms can always be explained by other diagnoses, they suggest that there is much more overlap among what we call "ADHD" and other conditions than previously thought, lending further support to my argument.

Nevertheless, this long and varied history of ADHD highlights the persistent ambiguity and controversy around the symptoms and their sources, a pattern that has continued into the present day.

## THE LATEST CHANGES TO THE *DIAGNOSTIC AND STATISTICAL MANUAL OF MENTAL DISORDERS*

In May 2013, the American Psychiatric Association released the fifth edition of their "bible," the *Diagnostic and Statistical Manual of Mental Disorders*.[10] Despite the fact that we've seen tremendous growth in the number of people diagnosed with ADHD in the past decade, the *DSM-V* reflects even less strict criteria for ADHD than its predecessor, the *DSM-IV*. For example, where the *DSM-IV* required that symptoms should be "more frequent and severe than typically observed in individuals at a comparable level of development,"[11] the *DSM-V* merely suggests that symptoms should be "inconsistent with development level."[12] Similarly, while the *DSM-IV* stipulated that attention-deficit/hyperactivity symptoms should be present before age seven, the *DSM-V* raised this cutoff to age *twelve*, extending the window into an age when distractibility and impulsivity are likely to occur spontaneously. The *DSM-V* also reduces the number of symptoms adults need for diagnosis to five from the *DSM-IV*'s six. These subtle changes significantly broaden the pool of people who meet the criteria for an ADHD diagnosis.

But that's not all. To diagnose ADHD the *DSM-IV* also required "clear evidence of *clinically* significant impairment in social, academic or occupational functioning" (emphasis added).[13] The *DSM-V* loosens this criterion considerably, requiring only "clear evidence that the symptoms interfere with, or reduce the quality of, social, academic or occupational functioning."[14] Finally, unlike the *DSM-IV*, the *DSM-V* devotes a full section within its description of ADHD to comorbidity, or the likelihood that other disorders will co-occur with ADHD. The *DSM-V* says comorbid disorders are "frequent" in individuals with ADHD, naming several conditions likely to be observed—including anxiety disorders, depression, personality disorders, and autism.[15] This understanding of comorbidity will arguably make practitioners even more likely to diagnose ADHD, but as I intend to prove in this book, these "comorbid" conditions are in fact the *only* cause of distractibility and impulsivity symptoms.

## THE *DSM* IS FLAWED

The American Psychiatric Association and many other health-care practitioners rely heavily on the collection of diagnostic and epidemiological information provided by the *DSM-V*. Even insurance companies use the *DSM* to decide what treatments they'll pay for. We've already seen how ADHD is diagnosed, the inherent issues with the criteria, and the perpetual relaxing of that criteria, but it's also important to understand that while the *DSM-V* is used widely, it shouldn't be considered the "final authority" on all of the conditions it covers. More thoughtful practitioners consider it a work in progress, an idea supported by the fact that there have already been five main versions (and additional revisions) of the reference, starting with the *DSM-I* in 1952 and continuing through the 2013 release of the *DSM-V.* There is already significant controversy about how the *DSM-V* handles other conditions (for example, it has done away with the diagnosis of Asperger's syndrome, which we will discuss later in the chapter on that disorder).

The point is that while the *DSM* provides useful guidelines for assessing and diagnosing a range of conditions, it's always important for practitioners to use their own experience and judgment in making diagnoses. And as we'll discuss in detail in this book's last chapter, it's also extremely important for the general public to avoid self-diagnosing based on the manual (which sells very well to nonpractitioners as well). Often, we in the field are ahead of the APA in understanding diagnostic and treatment trends; my view on the misdiagnosis of ADHD fits this general pattern. In subsequent chapters we will look at *DSM-V* criteria for several specific conditions (including mood disorders like depression) with the same warning: The manual is good for understanding general guidelines, but not as a final authority. In other words, it's the best general guide we have for now, but you should never use it without consulting an experienced practitioner, and even physicians need to be careful in making *DSM*-based diagnoses. In the case of ADHD, I believe the APA, like most everyone else, has overlooked the fact that many other conditions (including those within and outside the *DSM-V*) are better explanations for attention-deficit/hyperactivity.

## PREVALENCE AND GROWTH OF ADHD

The rise of ADHD diagnoses is nothing short of staggering. According to the *DSM-V*, about 5 percent of children may be diagnosed with ADHD;[16] that's in contrast to the "3% to 5%"

suggested by the *DSM-IV*.[17] But the most recent study (including data for 2011 and 2012) by the U.S. Centers for Disease Control and Prevention (CDC) suggests a much higher rate, as mentioned earlier: As much as 11 percent of all school-age children in the United States are diagnosed with ADHD at some point, and about 20 percent of high-school-age boys receive the diagnosis; that represents a 41 percent rise in ten years. Two-thirds of the children diagnosed have been prescribed a stimulant. Early in the new millennium, rates of use for stimulants rose 11.8 percent annually. As noted earlier, an estimated 4.4 percent of adults qualify for the disorder. Though there are fewer large-scale studies of ADHD's growth in adults over time, I've observed a steady increase in the number of people diagnosed each year. Overall, the ratio I've observed for ADHD in the general population is about two children for every one adult diagnosed, which is more or less in line with these statistics. The case examples presented in later chapters reflect that proportion, as well.

I see this stunning growth rate for ADHD and stimulant use not as a true rise in the number of people deserving diagnosis, but a reflection of the multiple trends that make diagnosis and the use and abuse of stimulants more likely. In the next chapters, we will explore the machinations behind these trends more closely.

## THE COST OF ADHD

What does all this misunderstanding of ADHD mean for individuals and society? As we mentioned in the introduction, ADHD may not be a condition on its own, but its symptoms are all too real, and have drastic consequences for individuals, families, and greater society when left untreated. While there have been no direct studies of the social, economic, educational, and health-care burdens associated with what we call ADHD, the CDC used their own and other studies to estimate these costs in the middle of the 2000s.[18] Here are some of their findings:

- With an estimated prevalence rate of 5 percent of the population, the total costs of ADHD would have been $36 billion to $52 billion (in 2005 dollars), or up to $17,458 per person. (Note that currently estimated prevalence rates are much higher.)
- Of this total, only $1.6 billion (as low as 3 percent of the total) was for the treatment of patients; $12.1 billion was for other health-related costs of the patients and $14.2 billion was for ADHD-related health-care costs for their family members.
- ADHD was associated with 143.8 million lost days of productivity annually across ten countries; workers with ADHD were more likely to have missed at least one day due to sickness in the past month, compared to their peers without the diagnosis.

The National Education Association cited academic studies estimating the total "hidden" cost of ADHD (for example, parents' lost productivity because they have to pick up their ADHD-diagnosed child early from school) as up to $266 billion in the United States in 2010, or about $2,360 per household.[19] Smaller, more specific studies have also shown costs associated with an ADHD diagnosis in a variety of areas. For example, families of children diagnosed with ADHD are more likely to experience conflict and stress, including divorce.[20] Why exactly this happens is unclear, but it is an important finding nonetheless. As we'll see in later chapters, bipolar disorder and depression run in families, and are fairly common instigators of ADHD symptoms; both of these mood disorders may contribute to family conflict.

There's no doubt that symptoms associated with ADHD incur large costs for society on multiple levels. The idea, then, is that by targeting the true sources of these symptoms and by helping people get the right treatment, the costs associated with ADHD can be reduced significantly. That's the thrust of this book.

# CHAPTER 2

# An Easy Answer: The Role of Cultural Bias

We've already seen some ways in which ADHD evaluations can be subjective, but there are also many ways in which our culture reinforces false beliefs about the disorder. How often do we hear the excuse "Sorry, I forgot to call. It's my ADD again," or the terms "free-spirited" and "ADD" in the same description of someone? ADHD is an easy catch-all label for children and adults who have trouble with concentration and/ or impulsivity. Unlike other diagnoses that include attention-related and hyperactivity symptoms, ADHD has those signs right there in its name: *attention-deficit/hyperactivity* disorder. Human nature is to choose the simplest explanation for an observed pattern, and what could be simpler than a diagnosis that spells out its major symptoms so clearly? What's more, teachers and parents are busier than ever, and thus more likely to place a low-performing or disruptive child into the easiest category possible. Most teachers and parents aren't health professionals, so that makes their application of the ADHD label even easier. Unfortunately, these and other biases lead to a vast amount of ADHD misdiagnoses.

## INHERENT BIAS IN A DIAGNOSIS

According to the *DSM-V*, to diagnose someone with ADHD, the symptoms should be present before age twelve and cause impairment in at least two settings—social, academic, or occupational.[1] As children age, the symptom picture usually becomes more subtle, with excessive movement (like running) and fidgeting less common—pointing to the fact that many children "grow out of" their impulsive behavior. As evidence for this, consider a Canadian study that found that the youngest children in a given grade were more likely to be diagnosed with the disorder, suggesting that normal age-related immaturity was being mistaken for ADHD.[2] Yet we often worry that an impulsive child will grow up to be a poorly functioning adult unless treated at a young age. This anxiety leads to too many parents rushing their kids to psychiatrists, with predetermined notions about the source of their child's problem.

Adult cases of ADHD are believed to have started in childhood, even if the disorder wasn't formally diagnosed. Again we face the issues of subjectivity and bias, as it's easy for adults to "remember" childhood attention difficulties (before age twelve) and to exaggerate current ones, once they're convinced they have "ADD." Like children diagnosed with ADHD, adults labeled with the disorder suffer from poor concentration and distractibility. Adults with ADHD may fidget less than their child counterparts, but they tend to avoid sedentary activities, such as jobs that require long periods of sitting. Adults labeled with the disorder may also be more likely to change jobs—and spouses—more frequently than those without the diagnosis. Society holds many stereotypes of adults with ADHD, one of which is the "free spirit." Artists, actors, dancers, forest rangers, and a host of other creative professionals are often assumed to be drawn to these jobs because they lack the ability to "focus" their attention, but as any actor will tell you, their labor demands a substantial amount of focus. It is thought that people with ADHD have higher IQs, on average, than their peers (this is supported statistically), but given the concept of this book, it's hard to differentiate those diagnosed with ADHD from others on such dimensions, given that a different condition can usually explain the symptoms. These stereotypes exacerbate the potential for a self-diagnosis of ADHD, and because the evaluation process relies so heavily on the patient's testimony, the progress in these cases is often swayed.

Another area where we see cultural bias affecting diagnosis is in gender. ADHD is diagnosed in boys more frequently than girls, with the *DSM-V* placing the boy-to-girl ratio of diagnosis frequency at 2:1.[3] The CDC reports a 15 percent ADHD prevalence rate among boys, and a 7 percent rate for girls, or again about a 2:1 ratio. For adults, the split is much closer to even, with the *DSM-V* suggesting a 1.6:1 male-to-female ratio and other sources noting that about an equal number of men and women are diagnosed.[4] I think there's a ready explanation for this discrepancy in gender rates between childhood and adulthood: Specifically, boys, especially in the past, were more likely to "act out," causing disruptions such as rising from their seats or interrupting others, symptoms that are easy to observe; girls, on the other hand, were generally encouraged to be more quiet, leading to attention-related symptoms that might be harder to see, such as daydreaming. In adulthood, there is less pressure for men and women to adhere to these societal expectations, which may explain the nearly equal rates of ADHD diagnoses in men and women.[5] As these sociocultural pressures continue to transform, I anticipate that rates of ADHD diagnoses will become even more equal across boys and girls.

## MORE REASONS WHY ADHD IS MISDIAGNOSED

- *The media barrages people with information about ADHD.*
  It would be difficult to find someone in the developed world
  who hasn't heard of ADHD. It shows up in print publica-
  tions, in television shows, and everywhere online. At the
  time I was writing this book, a Google search for "ADHD"
  quickly returned more than *60.5 million* results, even more
  than a search for "depression." A search for the stimulant
  "Ritalin"—a popular ADHD medication—generated 18.6
  million hits; "Adderall" generated 19.6 million. Given how
  readily available information about ADHD has become, it's
  no surprise that rates of the diagnosis have risen so quickly.
- *Medical practitioners lack time and incentive for full evaluations, and sometimes knowingly misuse the ADHD diagnosis.* "I think I have ADHD." That's a common complaint
  in medical offices across the United States, including mine.
  Adults will come in having self-diagnosed themselves with
  the disorder. Parents will bring their child saying, "I think
  he has ADHD" or "Her teacher says she may have ADHD."
  As physicians, it is our responsibility to do a full evaluation before assigning a clinical diagnosis. But the reality is
  that many doctors, faced with fast-shrinking appointment
  times and the challenges associated with HMO and insurer
  guidelines, will take shortcuts to diagnoses. And we, like all
  humans, are subject to "confirmation bias," or the tendency
  to pay attention only to evidence that supports our first
  guess, while dismissing evidence for alternative explanations.
  So when someone comes into a doctor's office saying, "I
  think I have ADHD," and they have many of the symptoms
  associated with ADHD, they're very likely to walk out of
  the office with an ADHD diagnosis and a prescription for a

stimulant—with other possibilities left unexplored. I know physicians who brag about the "two-minute checklist" they use to confirm an ADHD diagnosis. Worse, in a growing number of cases, physicians have knowingly misapplied the ADHD diagnosis to justify prescribing a stimulant for people they think will benefit from them. It's a common problem related to students in highly competitive high schools, as discussed in the next chapter, on stimulants. Similarly, physicians in low-income communities have been using the diagnosis to secure stimulants to help children struggling in school.[6] Many of these physicians acknowledge that it's a far from optimal solution, but the only one they have in an increasingly underfunded system. Regardless of the reasons, the practice increases the number of erroneous ADHD diagnoses and unnecessary stimulant prescriptions.

- *ADHD makes a great excuse.* Among "useful" diagnoses to have, ADHD is better than most, especially for adults. Why? Because it can be a good excuse. "I lost my keys again. It's my ADHD." "Sorry, I forgot to pick up milk. It's my ADHD." "My ADHD is making it hard to perform on the job." The diagnosis can become a crutch that is easy to reach for. Moreover, there's an attractive element to an ADHD diagnosis, especially in adults—it can be exciting to think of oneself as involved in many things at once, rather than stuck in a boring rut. The usefulness and potentially positive dimension of ADHD make the diagnosis more likely to be embraced.

Taken together, these trends mean it's likely that there are many more explanations for attention-deficit and hyperactivity symptoms than an ADHD diagnosis. Further evidence includes the Centers for Disease Control and Prevention's highlighting "the limited effectiveness of current interventions to attend to all the impairments associated with ADHD, and the inability to demonstrate that intervention provides substantial benefits for long-term outcomes."[7] Current treatment for ADHD doesn't appear to cure all the symptoms associated with the disorder, and patients continue to suffer in the long term. As we will see, the real problem isn't ADHD at all, but a different disorder or condition.

# CHAPTER 3

# The Stimulant Epidemic and Side Effects

While misdiagnosis occurs for numerous reasons, perhaps the most disturbing cause is when a patient purposefully seeks a prescription for stimulants without a medical condition. In this chapter I will discuss the rising use and abuse of stimulants like Ritalin and Adderall, and the high price we pay as individuals and a society. I will also explore the effects of stimulants on the body, and how in the case of treating inattention and impulsivity, they were Band-Aids, at best.

When "Greg" came into my office last year, I could tell immediately that something was wrong. I didn't notice any symptoms of a medical condition, but I did notice the peculiar way in which he described his problem. "I just can't concentrate," the nineteen-year-old said. He noted that he had trouble focusing on his college classes and homework assignments, and that his grades were suffering. Greg said, "I think I have ADD," and told me that many of his friends had similar problems with attention and that "prescriptions" had helped them sharpen their focus. "I think a prescription would help me, too," he said. I didn't doubt what the student said about his lack of focus. But when I suggested that it would make sense to do thorough testing before coming to any conclusions about diagnosis and treatment, Greg was dismayed. "Can't you just ask me a few questions and write a prescription?" he said. Now I knew that he, like a rising number of people, was more interested in a prescription for a stimulant than in getting the right diagnosis and treatment for whatever symptoms he was experiencing. When I made clear to Greg that writing a prescription for any medication before confirming exactly what was going on was not a good idea for either of us, he mumbled something about "getting a second opinion" and left my office. Not surprisingly, I never heard from him again.

Patients like Greg have become increasingly common in doctors' offices across the country. They're seeking quick prescriptions for stimulants like Ritalin and Adderall, often for the wrong reasons. As mentioned earlier, rates of stimulant use have risen dramatically and show few signs of slowing. Misdiagnosis of ADHD is a big part of this trend, but equally guilty is the increase in stimulant-seeking behavior. Among those who typically abuse stimulants are teens and college-age individuals seeking to improve their test scores, and professionals pulling long hours at the office. This creates problems on multiple levels. Like all "uppers," Adderall, Ritalin, and other stimulants used to treat ADHD lead to the development of tolerance. Over time, stimulant users require higher dosages to achieve the same effects. Moreover, negative side effects emerge from stimulant use, such as loss of sleep and poor appetite, and, in extreme cases, highly self-destructive behaviors including potentially fatal ones (more on this later). Because ADHD and stimulants are so closely linked, it's important to understand what stimulants are, the positive and negative effects they have on the body, and the trends driving their increased use.

## WHAT IS A STIMULANT?

The term "stimulant" refers to a diverse group of substances that promote alertness and other physical and mental effects by acting on the nervous system in different ways. Stimulants include the caffeine in coffee and soft drinks, the nicotine in cigarettes (and electronic cigarettes) and other tobacco products, the pseudo-ephedrine in cold medicines, and illegal drugs like some amphet-amines (speed, crystal meth, cocaine) and ecstasy (which contains the stimulant MDMA), along with many others. Because of their effects on the body, stimulants have been used historically for medical purposes. For example, Dexedrine was prescribed for weight loss, while other stimulants have been used for narco-lepsy and mood disorders. They've also been used recreationally. Amphetamines like cocaine and ecstasy are frequently taken as "party drugs." In recent years, especially on college campuses, the readily available and prescribed drug Adderall is popular among partiers for its ability to combat alcohol-induced drowsiness. Sometimes, the oral pills are crushed into powder and snorted (like cocaine) for more immediate effects of the drug. Any combi-nation of alcohol and stimulants is extremely dangerous and may be life-threatening.

Of course, stimulants are commonly prescribed for ADHD, as well, which is why we're talking about them here. The stimu-lants most often prescribed for ADHD represent several different types of agents that help control attention and behavior. These include methylphenidate (like Ritalin and Concerta) and mixed-salts amphetamines (like Adderall and Vyvanse).  Each of these has a specific effect on the body's neurotransmitters, or the chem-ical compounds that help transmit signals within the nervous system. Examples of neurotransmitters include serotonin, epi-nephrine, norepinephrine and dopamine. The exact mechanisms by which these chemicals interact are very complex and beyond the scope of this book, but essentially, if levels of these chemicals are too low or their activity is blocked, the transmission of messages within the nervous system decreases, corresponding to a state of inattention or impulsivity. Specific medications aimed at targeting attention-deficit and hyperactivity symptoms help increase levels of neurotransmitters and their activity. For example, methylphenidate-based medications like Ritalin increase the activity of the neurotransmitters dopamine and noradrenaline in the parts of the brain that help to control attention and behavior. Adderall also increases dopamine's effects, but in a more gradual way than Ritalin and similar agents do.

So let's back up a moment. If stimulants can increase one's attention span and reduce impulsivity, why shouldn't we use them? Furthermore, even if we're masking another underlying condition, aren't we at least solving the problems of inattention and impulsivity in the patient? The answer to both of these questions is a resounding NO. While stimulants can help people with a variety of symptoms in the short term, they have multiple damaging effects in the short- and long-term. The most common short-term side effects associated with stimulants involve *over*stimulation, but perhaps more troubling are the longer-term effects of stimulant use, which include the development of tolerance. After a while, the body adjusts its natural production of these same chemicals in the brain, and the temporary improvements in attention and behavior begin to disappear. This is why we see doctors prescribing higher and higher doses of the stimulant to achieve the same effect in the patient as time wears on—a dangerous pattern.

## SHORT-TERM SIDE EFFECTS OF ADHD STIMULANT MEDICATION*:

1. Decreased appetite (especially during the daytime)

2. Sleep disturbance (including difficulty falling asleep and loss of quality of sleep, which can further exacerbate attention-deficit symptoms [see chapter on Sleep Disorders])
3. Increased anxiety (feeling jittery or on edge for no specific reason)
4. Irritability (feeling easily angered or annoyed)
5. Depressed mood
6. Dry Mouth
7. Headache
8. Sexual Problems (erectile dysfunction)
9. Trouble breathing and fast heartbeat (at high doses)

## LONG TERM EFFECTS OF ADHD STIMULANT MEDICATION*:

1. Increased tolerance and the need for more of the substance (hallmarks of addiction, which we will explore at length in the chapter on substance abuse)
2. Long-term consequences of decreased appetite, sleep disturbance, and anxiety, such as unhealthy weight loss, poor concentration and memory, impairment in occupational, academic, and social settings, and even reduced life expectancy
3. In extreme cases, long-term use of stimulants have been linked to self-destructive behaviors including suicide

*Note: These are some of the more common side effects of stimulant medication. This is by no means a list of all the possible symptoms that can be experienced by a patient taking stimulants—that list would occupy a dozen pages!

## A NOTE ON TIME-RELEASE STIMULANTS

Time-release or long-acting stimulants, (marketed under the brands Adderall XR, Vyvanse, and Ritalin SR, among others), are a relatively new variation for "ADHD" medication, in which the effects of the drug purport to last for a full 8-12 hours, compared with the approximate 3-6 hours of standard stimulants[1]. Many of my patients seem to think that these long-acting variants are a safe alternative to instant-acting stimulants, but that is far from the whole story. While it is true that the side-effects of long-acting stimulants can be felt to a lesser degree than in instant-acting stimulants, both medications come with the same risks, especially with potential for addiction in the long run. The reason why side-effects of long-acting stimulants appear to be less severe is because the drug is absorbed more slowly into the bloodstream and maintains a consistent level through its course. The "peak-and-crash" effect that is commonly experienced with instant-acting stimulants is not as prevalent. To help illustrate this point, if you're familiar with the effects of sugar on the body, the difference between time-release and standard stimulants is similar to the difference between complex carbohydrates and simple ones. The latter has more potential for severe highs and then a crash. However, unlike "good" and "bad" sugars, the potential for addiction is the same in time-release and instant-acting stimulants, and they should both be treated with equal caution and gravity.

So, while stimulants can help some people in very specific circumstances (as we'll see in Part II), they are too often used inappropriately and sought out by people like my patient Greg, resulting in negative short- and long-term consequences. But perhaps the greatest injustice is when these medications are prescribed to unknowing patients who are told they have ADHD, while their symptoms worsen and the underlying condition causing these symptoms remains untreated.

## FACTORS DRIVING THE STIMULANT PROBLEM

One contributor to the trend of stimulant overuse is the misdiagnosis of ADHD, which results in a large amount of unnecessary prescriptions. But for all those patients who are wrongly diagnosed, there are many more people abusing stimulants without prescriptions. If about one in ten high school students are prescribed Adderall or Ritalin, imagine how many of their friends are casually asking for a "boost" when final exams come around? Stimulants are everywhere and have never been more readily available.

There is a general perception that one can be more energetic and productive while taking a stimulant. Because we live in a "pill-focused" culture, reinforced by profit-hungry pharmaceutical firms, we've seen a large uptick in stimulant-seeking behavior by everyone from students looking for better grades to long-haul truck drivers hoping to drive all night. Greg was far from my only case of a young person pretending to have textbook ADHD symptoms just to secure a prescription for a stimulant. It's becoming a large-scale problem, with students routinely securing stimulants through their physicians by faking or exaggerating attention-deficit and hyperactivity symptoms, or through their friends, sometimes with the approval of their parents, to give them an edge in increasingly competitive college admissions and other academic efforts.[2] Students would be better off learning more effective study habits, like time management, and we would all be better off if truckers stayed off the road while drowsy! Stimulants are a Band-Aid solution to an underlying problem, but they are much worse than a bandage because they have the potential to create new problems for those who use them.

Perhaps the scariest part of the stimulant problem is that an increasing number of physicians and parents are willing participants in this potentially deadly game: One psychiatrist went so far as to promote stimulants as "safer than aspirin," which reassured parents seeking a pill-based academic boost for their children, and others.[3] I know of far too many colleagues who are willing to write a prescription for a stimulant with only a cursory examination of the patient, such as the "two-minute checklist" for ADHD. For Greg and others like him, such physicians aren't hard to find. To make matters worse, many practitioners prescribe stimulants to test for ADHD, then use the short-term benefits of stimulants (like improved attention and decreased hyperactivity) as confirmation of the diagnosis and to justify keeping patients on them longer term. That's a false premise and a big mistake, given the negative consequences discussed earlier.

Fortunately, some in the medical field are aware of the problem. In 2013 the American Academy of Neurology (of which I am a member) released a review of "neuroenhancement," or the use of prescription medications like stimulants to improve performance on mental tasks in healthy people; the authors point out the numerous "social, developmental, and professional integrity issues" associated with this practice, urging much more caution around it.[4] However, these cautionary statements are rarely heeded by a large portion of the medical community.

The worst part about the use of stimulants for those diagnosed with "ADHD" is that had they been diagnosed correctly in the first place, they wouldn't have wound up with the prescription and all the potentially negative consequences. Many of the case examples we will consider in later chapters include children and adults who've lost appetite, sleep, and general well-being to stimulants they didn't need. Practitioners and the general public alike must be much more cautious with stimulants and the potential for addiction when using these drugs, regardless of an ADHD diagnosis.

# CHAPTER 4

# A Summary of the Conditions Behind ADHD Symptoms

S o far, we've seen the many circumstances by which individuals are diagnosed with ADHD when they simply do not exhibit severe enough symptoms, or any at all. But sometimes the symptoms of attention-deficit and hyperactivity are very real and debilitating. The thesis of this book is that other conditions can explain these symptoms fully and ought to be treated individually. Over decades of clinical work I've observed the multiple disorders and conditions that explain attention-deficit and hyperactivity symptoms. These conditions can explain the symptoms typically considered part of ADHD, either because they officially include the symptoms as part of the diagnosis (for example, poor concentration is a symptom of mood disorders) or they have other symptoms that can result in the ADHD symptoms. Symptoms of inattention can point to certain conditions, while hyperactivity can point to others. However, the two often occur hand in hand.

- *Inattention (for example, difficulty sustaining attention, poor listening skills):* mood disorders (depression and bipolar disorder, seizure disorder), hearing and vision problems, sleep deprivation, among others

- *Hyperactivity-impulsivity (for example, fidgeting, excessive talking):* bipolar disorder, Tourette's syndrome, fragile X syndrome, endocrinological conditions (like hyperthyroidism), among others

While ADHD patients are sometimes diagnosed with conditions other than ADHD, practitioners usually consider these conditions "comorbid," a medical term meaning that they occur at the same time as ADHD, and the patient qualifies for *both* conditions. As we mentioned in chapter 1, new findings support that there are genetic links between these mood disorders and "ADHD," which from my experience indicates that the ADHD symptoms are simply being caused by these other mood disorders. Importantly, once the patient is treated for the non-ADHD condition, the attention-deficit and hyperactivity symptoms usually disappear. Part of the goal of this book, then, is to take the "co" out of "comorbidity," and get patients and their families the right treatment more quickly.

The next chapters dive deep into the medical conditions that can explain attention-deficit and hyperactivity symptoms, from simple hearing or vision problems to neurological conditions. Each chapter presents a different condition or set of related disorders, opening with an example of a diagnosed (or a soon-to-be-diagnosed) "ADHD" patient who had another disorder or condition. I have changed the names of the patients in these examples to protect their identities. Each chapter also presents information related to the epidemiology of the condition (for example, how frequently it occurs, gender patterns, etc.), along with general information about treatment. The chapters are arranged in order of the prevalence of the condition they cover; that is, the most commonly occurring disorders are presented earlier, such as vision problems and sleep disturbance, as these are more likely to explain attention-deficit and hyperactivity symptoms than the conditions that appear later in the book, such as fragile X syndrome. Here's a full list of the conditions we'll cover (one per chapter, except for the last chapter, which contains a composite of other medical conditions), in order:

- Vision problems
- Sleep disturbance
- Substance abuse
- Mood disorders (bipolar disorder, depression)
- Hearing problems
- Learning disabilities
- Sensory processing disorder
- Giftedness
- Seizure disorders
- Obsessive-compulsive disorder
- Tourette's syndrome
- Asperger's syndrome (an Autism Spectrum Disorder)
- Neurochemical Distractibility/Impulsivity
- Schizophrenia
- Fetal alcohol syndrome
- Fragile X syndrome
- Other medical conditions (diet, iron deficiency, allergies, hyperthyroidism, pituitary tumor, prematurity, metal poisoning)

The conditions presented range from harmless to potentially debilitating, but all conditions, no matter how severe, can be better treated with an accurate diagnosis. The material in the following chapters is intended to help readers gain a better understanding of their symptoms and to arm themselves with information when seeking a diagnosis. However, one should always consult with their medical provider before making a self-diagnosis. I also encourage other practitioners to employ this information so as to mitigate the vast overprescribing of ADHD medication in the United States and worldwide.

# PART II

# THE CONDITIONS AND DISORDERS RESPONSIBLE FOR ADHD SYMPTOMS

# CHAPTER 5

# Vision Problems

## The Big Point

Problems related to vision are among the most overlooked explanations for attention-deficit/hyperactivity symptoms. Children (and adults) who struggle to see normally are likely to demonstrate short attention span and distractibility that may be mistaken as symptoms of ADHD. Steps taken to address the vision problem should resolve the attention/hyperactivity symptoms.

Eyeglasses and contact lenses are something we often take for granted, with nearly the majority of the U.S. population requiring some kind of vision correction by adulthood. But what we may fail to realize is that undiagnosed vision problems can cause problems well beyond those related to eyesight. Specifically, individuals—especially children—with untreated vision problems are likely to develop cognitive and behavioral symptoms such as poor focus, distractibility, and impulsivity because they are unable to see the things they need to see, such as a classroom board. Those symptoms, in turn, are likely to be misdiagnosed as part of ADHD, leading to a misunderstanding of the problem and the wrong treatment. I experienced this issue firsthand when treating an active young patient who had recently moved to the United States.

## OUT-OF-HER-SEAT AVIVA

On her first visit to my office, seven-year-old Aviva spoke quickly in a combination of Spanish and English, gesticulating excitedly around the room and running to examine the paintings on the wall. "She is adjusting very well to this country overall," her father said. The family had moved from Argentina to the Chicago area several months earlier, when Aviva's father accepted a management position with a manufacturing company. The girl had never been outside South America before.

Aviva's parents confirmed that she was learning English very quickly in her first-grade class, and that she seemed happy at school and in her neighborhood; she had already made several friends. "The teacher is happy with her academic progress," her mother said, "but she told us Aviva is causing trouble for the other children." Both parents mentioned that several notes had been sent home discussing their daughter's "behavior problems." To get more information, the parents had met with the teacher, who told them that Aviva had been impulsive and distractible nearly from the start of her time at the school. For example, while other children were copying words and sentences from the board, Aviva fidgeted and talked loudly to the classmates at her table. Sometimes she even rose from her seat to walk to the bookshelf or arts area, prompting the teacher to send her back to the table. She also asked for frequent bathroom breaks. Believing that her table mates may have been part of the problem, the teacher moved her to a table near the back of the room. Not surprisingly, that only made her attention-related and behavioral problems worse. By contrast, when Aviva worked one-on-one with the teacher or with the English as a Second Language teacher, she was much better focused and able to complete assigned tasks.

Aviva's parents said they asked her why she was bothering her classmates and whether she could stop, but Aviva didn't have an answer for them. Because the disruptive behavior had persisted, they had taken her to see a pediatrician, who prescribed a low dose of a stimulant medication, under the hypothesis that the girl suffered from ADHD. On the medication, she quickly displayed overstimulation-related side effects, including loss of appetite and difficulty sleeping. She was also very irritable, especially in the morning. "It is like she's not herself anymore," her father said, noting how quickly she lost her temper at even the slightest provocation. Moreover, Aviva's disruptive behavior in school hadn't stopped after she'd started on the medication; in fact, she had even more trouble focusing, and sometimes acted irritably toward her teacher and classmates.

The girl's parents were very concerned about the ADHD diagnosis and were tempted to stop the medication, given the side effects their daughter had experienced, but were worried about making that decision prematurely. I told them they were probably right about taking her off the stimulant. And, after asking several more questions about Aviva's behavior at school and at home, I was confident we would pinpoint an explanation for her behavior soon.

## CLUES TO LOOK FOR

Given my hypothesis about Aviva's condition, I started with the simplest and least invasive tests: those related to hearing and vision. She tested normal on all hearing measures, but the vision test was positive for significant myopia (nearsightedness), which was likely the best explanation for her distractible and impulsive behavior in school—the result of being unable to see the board, rendering her unable to do the in-class work that it required. Rather than conducting a full battery of further tests (for example, physical, neurological, and educational) with Aviva, I suggested her parents explore the vision problem first, and that we could continue evaluating her if her symptoms persisted. They admitted that Aviva had never had her vision tested because it was not a requirement in her school in Argentina (most U.S. schools require regular vision tests, starting in kindergarten) and she had never complained about being unable to see, perhaps in part because her classroom back home was much smaller.

Vision problems are among the simplest (and most overlooked) explanations for attention-deficit/hyperactivity symptoms and mistaken ADHD diagnoses. The symptoms of ADHD related to poor eyesight can be corrected easily once the source is discovered.

> ### Main Clue
>
> Vision difficulties (for example, seeing the board at school) can be difficult to detect, especially in children, as they may not recognize or admit to these. Simple questions (for example, "Can you see everything your teacher writes on the board?"), careful observation, and an eye exam can confirm the problem and point to the best treatment.

## WHAT ARE VISION PROBLEMS?

Vision problems can have multiple sources and courses. Among the five human senses, vision is the most important and requires the largest part of our brains. A significant vision problem influences functioning deeply on multiple dimensions: academic, occupational, and social. Vision problems can take many forms including:[1]

- Myopia (nearsightedness, as was the case for Aviva)
- Hyperopia (farsightedness, or seeing distant objects more clearly than near ones)
- Astigmatism (blurred vision caused by a misshapen cornea or lens)
- Eye-teaming disorders (that is, convergence insufficiency and excess)
- Cataracts (blurred vision caused by clouded lenses within the eye)
- Glaucoma (blind spots and other problems caused by increased pressure within the eye)
- Presbyopia (trouble keeping nearby objects in focus)
- Night blindness
- Multiple visual disturbances related to diseases and conditions such as diabetes, stroke, brain tumors, migraine headaches, and multiple sclerosis

Errors of "refraction"—or the way our eyes focus light rays for transmission to the brain—result in the most common vision problems, including nearsightedness, farsightedness, presbyopia, and astigmatism. In many cases, the remainder of the eye's functioning is healthy. Most refraction errors arise when images are being focused in front of or behind the retina (the multiple tissue layers at the back of the eyeball), rather than directly onto it, resulting in blurred vision. This typically happens because of the shape of the lens within our eyes or the strength of the muscles that alter the lens shape when we try to focus on objects at greater or lesser distances. Astigmatism, as noted above, usually results when the cornea (clear outer layer of the eye) is misshapen, and results in the focusing of images at multiple points on the retina, rather than just one, again resulting in blurriness.

Many children suffer from "eye-teaming" disorders such as convergence insufficiency and convergence excess, which means they struggle to use their eyes together for close-distance tasks such as reading or writing.[2] These cases are much harder to identify than myopia, for example, because the difficulty only arises during certain tasks. Asking a child whether they can see the words clearly on a page may help uncover this diagnosis. Other types of vision problems can be related to specific eye diseases, including those mentioned above (for example, glaucoma, cataracts) and conditions like macular degeneration, or the progressive worsening of vision due to internal damage to the central part of the retina.

Of course, injuries to the eye can also result in vision problems. In children this is oftentimes sports-related trauma. Getting hit by a ball or kicked in the eye may cause retinal detachment. Retinal detachment and other eye problems can also occur without traumatic injury.

In my patient Aviva's case, the vision problem was simple: As my preliminary vision test confirmed, she was nearsighted, and struggled to see at longer distances, including reading the board at school. That problem likely explained her distractible and impulsive behavior at school, as discussed in the next section. A more complete vision test at an ophthalmologist's (a physician specializing in vision) office confirmed Aviva had moderate myopia that would worsen without treatment.

## PREVALENCE OF VISION PROBLEMS

How common are vision problems? Extremely. About 40 percent of all people are nearsighted, with the condition first appearing in childhood and peaking by early adulthood (for example, the twenties).[3] A 2012 study estimated that about 17 percent of all U.S. adults over age forty suffered from cataracts (much more common in older age segments), and 10 percent of all U.S. adults had diagnosable hyperopia (farsightedness).[4] The next most common specific vision conditions were diabetic retinopathy (that is, retinal damage resulting from diabetes; occurs in about 5 percent of all adults over forty) and glaucoma (2–3 percent of adults). Many vision problems are hereditary, partly because many types are based on genetically determined physiological structures (for example, the shape of the cornea and lens). Because vision problems (especially myopia) first arising in childhood are most likely to be undiagnosed and result in symptoms misdiagnosed as ADHD, these are most relevant to this book—though any type of vision impairment may cause attention-related and behavioral problems at any age. As such, it's important to consider vision problems in both children and adults when they have trouble with attention-deficit/hyperactivity symptoms.

As far as prognosis, some vision problems disappear naturally over time, such as farsightedness in children—as their eyeballs grow to full adult size, they may have less trouble seeing nearby objects. Others (for example, macular degeneration) may worsen progressively, or have no effective treatment. The effects of some treatments (for example, laser surgery) may fade over time, as well, as discussed later.

Not surprisingly, vision problems were common in Aviva's family. Both her parents had worn glasses (her mother also wore contact lenses) for myopia since childhood, though they admitted they had trouble seeing well before they were diagnosed. Aviva's father, who was in his early forties, was beginning to have trouble reading text up close, and was considering wearing bifocals or progressive lenses. These glasses correct for both nearsightedness and farsightedness. All of Aviva's aunts and uncles had also needed vision correction from childhood or early adulthood.

## RELATION TO ATTENTION-DEFICIT/HYPERACTIVITY SYMPTOMS

"Eyestrain can make classroom attention impossible," reads the subtitle of an online article published by the Children's Vision Information Network.[5] The article goes on to note that about 20 percent of schoolchildren suffer vision problems that make it difficult for them to sustain focus on academic tasks. As a result, many of these children are "highly distractible, have short attention spans, make careless errors, fail to complete assignments, and are often fidgety and off task"—in other words, many of the hallmark symptoms of the ADHD diagnosis. The article draws special attention to the eye-teaming disorders (for example, convergence insufficiency) discussed earlier. Children with these conditions struggle to read and write (not as the result of a learning disability) and tend to lose control of their eye movements due to excessive straining. Naturally, children dealing with such symptoms will seek relief by avoiding close-distance tasks through a combination of behaviors: fidgeting, taking bathroom or water breaks, looking out the window, or disrupting their nearby classmates, among others. Again, these "vision breaks," when part of a consistent pattern of attention-deficit/hyperactivity, are likely to be misdiagnosed as ADHD.

I tell my patients and their families that struggling with academic tasks due to vision problems is like reading a foreign language with which they are unfamiliar. It may be easy to concentrate on specific words and sentence construction briefly, but they will quickly tire of the task and seek a break, whether through daydreaming or abandoning the task altogether.

Academic studies have also examined the link between ADHD and vision problems. For example, research in 2001 found that children diagnosed with ADHD were significantly more likely to report vision difficulties than those without the diagnosis.[6] A subsequent study showed that vision therapy improved symptoms (related to ADHD and others) in diagnosed children.[7] Still another academic study confirmed the specific link noted earlier: that children with eye-teaming disorders are particularly likely to demonstrate attention-deficit/hyperactivity symptoms.[8] Finally, other research has confirmed that vision problems, attention-deficit/hyperactivity symptoms (diagnosed as ADHD), and other health issues result in decreased academic performance in children, making it even more important to provide the right diagnoses and treatment for them.[9] As for all the conditions discussed in this book, *treatment delayed is treatment denied*, with significant negative consequences for patients and their families.

## TREATMENT FOR VISION PROBLEMS

Treatments for vision problems range from very simple and inexpensive to highly complex and costly. Among the simplest approaches is the prescription of corrective lenses for refraction-related issues. For example, nearsighted children and adults diagnosed correctly typically wear eyeglasses or contact lenses to see distant items. Similar measures can be used for farsightedness. Reading glasses or bifocals are very common among adults over age forty, as many suffer from both nearsightedness and presbyopia (inability to focus on near objects, such as text). Corrective lens prescriptions are based on the results of eye tests usually administered by an ophthalmologist or an optometrist (a non-MD practitioner trained specifically to treat vision problems), including those employed at large U.S. retail chains. Specific vision-related prescriptions may change over time, especially in later adulthood, as vision deteriorates.

Another popular treatment approach is laser eye surgery. The most common form is Lasik, which uses lasers to alter the cornea's shape, thus correcting refraction problems that result in myopia, hyperopia, and astigmatism.[10] All laser surgeries are performed by ophthalmologists. While Lasik is considered a "permanent" cure for these conditions, it can result in complications including corneal damage and side effects, including seeing halos and starbursts, eye dryness, and difficulty with night-driving vision. Moreover, Lasik tends not to diminish presbyopia (difficulty focusing on near objects), meaning that many of those who have undergone the procedure still require reading glasses or bifocals in middle to later adulthood.[11]

Other eye diseases or conditions require more complex treatment. For example, cataract treatment involves surgical removal of the clouded eye lens, and correction of the resulting refraction issues using either a surgically inserted lens, corrective lenses, or a combination of these. Similarly, treating retinal detachment involves using lasers or other technology to seal all retinal breaks and, in some cases, replacing the eye's vitreous gel (that is, the liquid in the eye) with a gas bubble or silicon oil. Hard-to-treat conditions like macular degeneration (age-related deterioration of the retina's center) can be slowed with drugs or managed by teaching patients to rely on their remaining field of vision—peripheral vision, in the case of macular degeneration.

In Aviva's case, the treatment for her vision problem was straightforward and highly effective. The ophthalmologist gave Aviva a prescription for eyeglasses to correct her nearsightedness and, within a day, Aviva was wearing a pair of pink glasses she had picked out herself. "She actually likes wearing them more than not wearing them," her mother said. "She thinks she looks like a movie star, and of course they help her see much better." The glasses not only allowed Aviva to see distant objects better at school and at home—her father said, "She sits farther from the TV now!"—but they also improved her attention and focus dramatically. Aviva's teacher told her parents that her behavior in class had improved "one hundred percent" and that she was now one of the most attentive students in class. "The teacher says she sometimes tells her other students they should follow Aviva's example," the girl's mother said proudly. Both parents were deeply relieved to have a solution to their daughter's "ADHD."

Because Aviva's vision, focus, and behavior improved so well with the glasses, her parents and I decided that she needed no further evaluation or treatment, unless her behavioral symptoms returned or other types of problems arose. We also agreed to have her stop taking the stimulant medication immediately.

Her mother called me several months after I had seen the family, to inform me that Aviva had continued to do very well, making great progress on academic and social fronts. She added, "I've told all our relatives back in Argentina to get their children's vision checked early, to avoid these kinds of problems."

# CHAPTER 6

# Sleep Disorders

### The Big Point

Symptoms of sleep disturbance, including poor concentration and distractibility, may be mistaken for ADHD, especially when they are part of a long-standing pattern. Improved sleep hygiene should alleviate the symptoms.

According to a recent ABC News article online, the United States has become a "nation of walking zombies"—not truly the undead, but a country of sleep-deprived citizens.[1] As discussed later in this chapter, a very large percentage of every U.S. age group reports not securing enough sleep. The problem is widespread, with a range of serious consequences, including compromised health. Not surprisingly, one of the more common outcomes of poor sleep is distractibility and inattention, which may be mistaken, in turn, for ADHD. Many people are aware that they are failing to get sufficient sleep, and may even recognize the consequences of this condition for their ability to concentrate, but many also report feeling drowsy even after a full night's sleep—unaware that their "quality" of sleep is being compromised. Others, like my patient described below, may be surprised by the extent and effects of sleep disturbance.

## THE DISTRACTIBLE TEACHER

The first thing James said to me was, "I think I have ADD." The way the thirty-six-year-old behaved in my office was certainly typical of the diagnosis. He had trouble staying focused on our conversation, often asking me to repeat what I had said moments earlier. James's eyes darted around, taking in the items on my desk and the books on the shelf. He often stopped midsentence to comment on them: "I've heard of that book. Is it worth reading?"

James looked fatigued, his eyes rimmed red, with dark circles underneath. One of the things keeping him up at night was his job. A fifth-grade teacher at a public school, he admitted that he was having increasing trouble performing in the role. He said, "I feel like my concentration's just as bad as my students', if not worse." He described how he sometimes lost his place in the lesson plan, and lately had even begun to forget some of his students' names, though he'd been teaching them for months. "The principal called me in last week to ask if everything was okay," James said. "I'm worried about losing my job." This fear had motivated him to make an appointment with me.

James pointed out that his poor concentration and distractibility had become problems only in recent years. "I was a model student all the way through college," he said. He had also performed very well early in his career as a teacher's aide and then a full-time elementary school teacher, even winning an award about five years earlier and being selected to mentor his junior peers. As far as his social life, James had been in several long-term romantic relationships but was single at the moment. He said that he had several friends whom he saw occasionally. "It's easier to communicate online," James said, noting that he had become a big fan of online games, chat rooms, and forums. He said, "When I'm doing those things, my concentration's great." Unfortunately, in most other settings, he was much more distractible.

Our first session revealed no clear explanations for James's symptoms. I told him we would take a more in-depth look at his situation, including blood testing. But he was frustrated by the lack of answers. "The more I read," he said, "the more I think it's just ADD." James seemed resigned to his situation, and worried that the symptoms would worsen, jeopardizing his career and other important parts of his life. He was also anxious about the possibility of having to take a stimulant. "I've heard they can help," he said, "but I'm worried about what I hear about addiction."

## CLUES TO LOOK FOR

As for many of my patients, the source of James's symptoms wasn't immediately apparent, making it easy for him to fall back on the ADHD diagnosis. It's natural for people to seek a medical diagnosis for themselves, and ADHD is a readily available one. In fact, a more comprehensive history and physical assessment of James, including blood testing and family history, failed to reveal any medical basis for his symptoms.

In our second session, rather than continuing to seek medical explanations, I asked James a bit more about his life. "Tell me what you enjoy doing," I said. Now he seemed excited, sitting up in his chair, eyes wide. He talked about how much he enjoyed online games, especially social ones including Scramble (a word-finding game played against others through Facebook) and chess. He said he played against people from all over the world and was becoming a "minor celebrity" in Scramble, with a score consistently in the top 1 percent of all players.

"When do you play these games?" I asked. James said that when he first started playing, it was mostly in the evening, after dinner. He noted that he had been in the habit of working out at the gym, then coming home for dinner, followed by an hour or two of TV and social gaming. "But then I started skipping the gym and coming straight home to play," he said. "I was even eating in front of the computer." He confessed that he often played until well after midnight, taking breaks to chat with other players in online forums or to text his friends, many of whom also stayed up late. He also said that he had begun drinking more coffee, including in the evening, to stay awake. "How much sleep are you getting?" I asked. James estimated he got no more than four or five hours nightly, on average.

Now the likely source of his distractibility and other symptoms became clear: James was sleep-deprived. As we will see, sleep deprivation is becoming an epidemic in the United States, with multiple causes and consequences.

### Main Clue

Patients with disturbed sleep may not realize how much the condition is disrupting their lives—including by way of attention-deficit symptoms—and may not volunteer information about their sleep patterns unless asked directly. Careful questioning (for example, "About what time do you go to sleep and wake up?") and asking patients to monitor their sleep patterns carefully (for example, using a sleep diary) can reveal the sleep issues underlying attention symptoms.

## WHAT ARE SLEEP DISORDERS?

Sleep is a precious commodity in the United States and many other countries. The pervasiveness of sleep deprivation is due in part to our culture, and the stresses and demands of modern life, but legitimate medical issues may interfere with sleep as well. Entire books have been written about the causes and consequences of sleep disturbance, so we will focus on the highlights of the condition here, before considering how sleep issues are associated with ADHD-like symptoms. Seven hours is the well-documented minimum amount of sleep required for adults to avoid attention-related and other cognitive deficits.[2] However, this amount can vary by individual, and many doctors recommend eight hours of sleep for adults. Children require even more: ten to eleven hours on average. (See the tables on the following pages for a distribution of recommended sleep times.) A study quoted in a recent *New York Times* article found that nearly 40 percent of adults polled were not securing at least seven hours of sleep; in fact, the average amount of sleep enjoyed by Americans is a mere 6.9 hours.[3]

Sleep disturbance can have multiple causes, with categories including physical (for example, pain), medical (for example, respiratory disorders), psychological (for example, depression), and environmental (for example, urban noise).[4] Shift work, stress, genetics, and aging are all related to sleep problems. The American Psychiatric Association's most recent *Diagnostic and Statistical Manual* presents multiple categories of "sleep-wake" disorders, including:[5]

- Insomnia/hypersomnolence (sleeping too little or too much)
- Narcolepsy (lapsing into sleep unexpectedly)
- Breathing-related sleep disorders (such as sleep apnea)
- Circadian rhythm sleep-wake disorders (disturbance due to sleep-wake schedule issues such as shift work)
- Parasomnias (abnormal behavioral or physiological events during sleep, such as nightmares and restless-legs syndrome)

While many practitioners rely on the *DSM* to make diagnoses, it's important to remember that this remains a work in progress, with criteria for specific conditions shifting considerably over time, as discussed earlier in the book. The best use of the *DSM* is as a set of guidelines rather than as final word.

According to the *DSM*, insomnia is characterized by at least a month of difficulty falling asleep or staying asleep, with the disturbance causing significant distress or problems in occupational, social, and other functioning. Insomnia may be caused by a specific event or issue (for example, work or relationship stress) but persists long after that factor has been resolved. Hypersomnolence includes multiple periods of sleep in the same day (at least three times per week for at least three months), with a main period lasting at least nine hours but failing to reinvigorate the patient. Narcolepsy is a condition characterized by frequent instances (at least three times per week for at least three months) in which affected individuals fall asleep without warning. An increasingly diagnosed category of sleep disturbance is breathing-related sleep disorders such as sleep apnea. "Apnea" means "without breath," and such an individual's breathing may stop hundreds of times during the night, sometimes for as long as a minute.[6] Sleep apnea can be caused by obstruction of breathing or faulty nervous-system signals during sleep and is associated with health consequences including high blood pressure, heart disease, and depression. According to the *DSM-V*, circadian rhythm sleep disorder can result from "a misalignment between the endogenous circadian rhythm and the sleep-wake schedule required by an individual's physical environment or social or professional schedule."[7] In others words, the condition is associated with job-related (for example, shift work) or other schedules that prevent sleeping at "normal" times, resulting in disturbed sleep. Finally, parasomnias include what the *DSM-V* calls "non-rapid eye movement sleep arousal" disorders, such as:

- Sleepwalking or sleep terrors (intense fear episodes the patient doesn't remember upon awakening)
- Nightmares (distressing dreams that are remembered well)
- Restless-legs syndrome (uncontrollable urges to move one's legs)
- Substance/medication-induced sleep disorder (disturbance caused by agents including caffeine, tobacco, stimulant medications or drugs, or alcohol)

One of the largest nonmedical sources of disturbed sleep in modern society is technology. The ability to be "connected" 24/7, whether through home computers, cell phones, or tablets (for example, the iPad), has motivated many of us to trade sleep for time surfing, chatting, gaming, or any other online activity, as was the case for my patient James.[8] While most people in a given person's country of residence may be asleep after midnight, they have many alert peers online in far-flung time zones, meaning one can always find someone to engage with, at least virtually. In fact, James may have qualified for a *DSM-V* condition under further study: Internet gaming disorder. The *DSM* says that this is not yet a formal diagnosis, but that it is marked by "persistent and recurrent use of the Internet to engage in games, often with other players, leading to clinically significant impairment or distress." Symptoms are similar to those of substance abuse and include withdrawal (irritability when unable to play), increased tolerance (needing to play more to feel satisfied), and an inability to quit. Polls show that people from every age group are losing sleep to technology, and researchers suggest that beyond people's willingness to stay up late, part of the problem is that the light emitted by computer and other screens can disrupt the biological rhythms related to sleep.[9]

Of course, general stress is a large contributor and often a primary cause of sleep disturbance. People in cultures worldwide are facing a surge in levels of responsibility and worry, whether related to work (having to be always available, thanks to improved connectivity through the Internet and other means), school (increased competition for admission to and performance within schools at all levels), or family (increasing number of single-parent and blended families). Proof of the rise in stress goes well beyond anecdotal. For example, a U.S. study of thousands of people showed that perceptions of stress increased 18 percent for women and 24 percent for men from 1983 to 2009.[10] Stress has been linked to many health issues—including to most of those discussed in this book, and certainly to sleep disturbance.

The consequences of sleep disturbance are multiple and serious, with sleep problems linked to heart disease, diabetes, and obesity.[11] According to the director of the National Center on Sleep Disorders Research, "Sleep is just as important for general health as diet and exercise."[12] Of course, sleep problems are linked to poor work performance, mood issues including anger and depression, and driving-related accidents. The attention-related consequences of sleep disturbance are discussed in the section below.

James was clearly sleep-deprived, securing far less than seven hours of sleep nightly. His sleeplessness was rooted not in physical, medical, or environmental conditions, but in his willingness to sacrifice sleep for activities including gaming and chatting. Over time, his nighttime activities had become habitual, and he had failed to realize how much his schedule was affecting his functioning, especially at work, where he struggled increasingly to concentrate.


## PREVALENCE OF SLEEP DISORDERS

James is not alone. As noted earlier, nearly 40 percent of Americans enjoy less than the recommended seven hours of sleep nightly.

The *DSM-V* notes that about one-third of all adults complain of problems with insomnia, the most commonly reported sleep disturbance.[13] Because sleep disturbance has multiple causes, the demographics associated with it vary. For example, while insomnia is reported more commonly in women,[14] sleep apnea is more common in men than women, and more likely to occur among African-American and Hispanic men.[15] In my observation, while older adults tend to have more difficulty sustaining sleep (but may be able to fall asleep easily), their younger counterparts report more challenges falling asleep, compounded today by the technology-related issues discussed above. Unfortunately, sleep problems are becoming more common at every age, especially with the growing tendency for everyone to use electronics (for example, wireless phones, tablets) late into the evening. With such a high prevalence of sleep disorders, sleep patterns should be considered for anyone suffering from attention-deficit/hyperactivity.

## RELATION TO ATTENTION-DEFICIT/HYPERACTIVITY SYMPTOMS

Not surprisingly, disturbed sleep is associated with attention-related symptoms. Nearly 100 percent of my patients with sleep issues—regardless of the cause—suffer from distractibility, inattention, and impulsivity, often in debilitating ways. Beyond what I've observed, in a study conducted at the University of Pennsylvania researchers tested differences in people's ability to sustain attention based on how much sleep they had gotten: four, six, or eight hours (the researchers controlled the amount of sleep for each group).[16] As expected, the eight-hour group performed the best, with few declines in attention over the course of a day and over a two-week period. The four-hour group performed the worst, again as expected, but even the six-hour group had major difficulty sustaining attention: By day six, a quarter of the people in that group were falling asleep during computer-based tasks, and these lapses got worse over time. The four- and six-hour groups also performed poorly on memory and simple addition and subtraction tests. After two weeks the six-hour group's performance was as poor as that of subjects from a different study who had been deprived of sleep for twenty-four hours! A Stanford University study in the late 1990s even showed that sleep-disturbed individuals (those with sleep apnea, in this case) performed as badly or worse than *legally drunk* peers on reaction-time tests.[17]

As for most of the conditions discussed in this book, other practitioners and researchers have observed the association between sleep issues and ADHD. For example, one study found a high rate of sleep-related complaints in youths with ADHD.[18] The researchers performing that study saw sleep disturbance as comorbid with ADHD, rather than as a full explanation for the diagnosis. More in line with my view, the National Institutes of Health (NIH) notes: "Sleep deprivation can cause daytime hyperactivity and decreased focused attention. This can be mistaken for Attention Deficit Hyperactivity Disorder (ADHD) or other behavior disorders" in children.[19] A separate study confirmed that parents of children diagnosed with ADHD reported more sleep problems among their children than did parents of children without the diagnosis.[20]

The link between sleep problems and ADHD symptoms is global. For example, a researcher at National Taiwan University suggests that based on academic research, "In some patients with ADHD, symptoms are caused or exaggerated by primary sleep disorders, and therefore treatment of the sleep disorder will improve ADHD symptoms."[21] As for all the conditions discussed in this book, the misdiagnosis of sleep disturbance as ADHD results in delayed treatment, and *treatment delayed is treatment denied.*

## TREATMENT FOR SLEEP DISORDERS

The simplest treatment for sleep disturbance is improved "sleep hygiene," or an individual's practices related to sleep.[22] The goal, of course, is for the person to sustain a healthier sleep pattern. Getting an adequate number of sleeping hours is the first step. But how much sleep is enough? It depends on one's age. According to the Mayo Clinic, the right amount of sleep for a given age group may be found in the table below:[23]

| AGE GROUP | RECOMMENDED AMOUNT OF SLEEP |
| --- | --- |
| Infants | 14–15 hours |
| Toddlers | 12–14 hours |
| School-age children | 10–11 hours |
| College students and adults | 7–9 hours |

Of course, as mentioned earlier, a given individual may require a different number of hours than the guidelines above suggest, but most Americans with sleep issues are securing less sleep than they should. Moreover, it is difficult to make up for lost sleep, or what researchers have labeled "sleep debt"—the difference between the sleep one gets and the rest one actually needs, a gap that grows over time. While many of the sleep-deprived, especially those skimping on sleep to put in more work hours, believe they can catch up on sleep by increasing their sleep time on weekends or vacations, that's generally not the case: True payment of the sleep debt is best achieved by increasing the nightly rate by at least an hour or two.[24]

While nighttime is likely the best period in which to secure adequate sleep, daytime naps are another possibility for those who work long shifts or who have significant control over their schedules. A Stanford University research team studied the effects

of mandated forty-minute, midshift naps for health-care professionals who worked twelve-hour shifts, finding that the napping
group fared much better on cognitive tests than their sleepy peers;
for example, the latter group consistently "crashed" on a simulated drive![25]

Regardless of the time period in which individuals try to sleep,
several practices can help them sleep better and longer:

- Going to bed when one feels tired and waking up naturally,
  rather than to an alarm, can improve the quality and amount
  of sleep.[26]
- Window blinds that block light and, possibly, a "white-noise"
  machine to reduce external sounds from intruding into the
  bedroom are other helpful measures.
- Reducing daily caffeine intake, especially during later hours
  of the day, is an important step.
- Some people benefit from breathing exercises and meditative
  techniques. This reduces general stress and improves sleep
  hygiene.
- As discussed earlier, one of the largest new impediments to
  sleep is technology—we simply can't "turn everything off"
  the way we used to, one of the many contributors to our
  increased stress levels and sleep disturbance. Taking steps
  to address this issue is crucial for many of those with sleep
  disturbance.

Once James understood that sleep issues were at the core of
his attention-deficit symptoms, we developed a non-medication-
based plan to improve his sleep, including several of the ideas
above. James pledged to drink no coffee after noon, and was
pleased that this would save him some of the money he had begun
to spend on caffeinated drinks. He also purchased blackout

blinds and an inexpensive white-noise machine for his bedroom.

As expected, the more challenging task for James was to reduce his online activities. As a first step he said he would try to turn off his computer and all other Internet devices (for example, cell phone) at midnight. He also agreed to aim to set up one social get-together (for example, meeting up with a friend or going on a date) per week, understanding that he had unwittingly traded his in-person social life for an online one.

The next month James reported that the reduced caffeine intake, the blinds, and the white noise helped him secure more restful sleep, but he confessed that he hadn't stuck to his plan of going offline at midnight. "I missed the games too much," he said, "and I worried that I would lose my ranks." We discussed the consequences of continued sleep disturbance, how it had the potential to cost him his job, and James said he would "try harder."

At the next session James told me that while simply trying harder to stay offline hadn't worked, he'd found a simple solution: a low-cost application that turned off his computer and phone-based Internet connection at a preset time (midnight, in his case). "It comes back on automatically in the morning," James said, "and if I want to turn it on before then I have to call a number and punch in a code." He said that he'd turned it back on once or twice, but had been able to resist since then. James smiled, telling me that he'd already seen his concentration at work improve, and that he'd "forgotten" how much he enjoyed socializing offline. He was also pleased to report that his fear of losing his standing in the gaming community had been unfounded: In fact, feeling better rested had actually helped him improve his performance on several games he enjoyed. Without using medication or psychotherapy, James had found a way to improve his attention—and his life.

# CHAPTER 7

# Substance Abuse

## The Big Point

Chronic substance abuse, or the recurrent overuse of legal or illicit drugs or alcohol, is likely to result in distractibility, impulsivity, and attention deficits that can be mistaken for ADHD. Intervention for the underlying substance-related problem can often eliminate the attention-deficit and impulsivity issues.

Substance abuse is a very common problem in the United States and other countries. A large percentage of the population consumes alcohol, marijuana, prescription medications, and other substances that may affect attention. For many of these individuals, their patterns of substance abuse result in attention problems, distractibility, and impulsivity that can interfere with multiple areas of functioning, including work, school, and social situations. These symptoms can also be mistaken for signs of ADHD, leading to the delay or denial of the most effective treatment. Substance-related problems are especially common in younger age groups, including teenagers like my patient Ralph.

## RALPH'S ROUGH SENIOR YEAR

"I've been a wreck," Ralph said the first time he came to my office. The athletic-looking eighteen-year-old was a senior at a large local high school, where he had been an honor student and a star member of the lacrosse team—until recently. "I can't concentrate at all anymore," he said, admitting that he had been missing school more frequently because he "just didn't feel good," and that when he did attend school he struggled to maintain his attention level. "I used to have no problem with homework and tests," he said. "But now everything's a lot harder." Further questioning revealed that Ralph was also having frequent headaches and difficulty sleeping, sometimes in the form of insomnia and sometimes as a problem with oversleeping, including on school days. He nervously chewed on breath mints for the duration of our session.

Ralph seemed troubled by his symptoms but resigned to them. He also said that he had been feeling "sadder" and "really depressed" at times, and that he wasn't sure if his down mood was because of the lack of concentration and related problems or vice versa. Ralph said, "My parents think I have ADHD," but he seemed skeptical. When I asked him what *he* thought he had, he said he wasn't sure. A phone call with his parents confirmed what Ralph said—they thought he might have ADHD—and also just how concerned they were about their son. "He doesn't seem like the same person anymore," his father said. Both parents were mystified by how Ralph had gone so quickly from being a well-adjusted, high-achieving student to one struggling to keep up on multiple fronts.

Ralph said that he'd always had a good social life, including multiple friends from the lacrosse team and several past romantic relationships. "But lately I haven't been feeling like hanging out with people as much," he said. Again he wasn't sure why his feelings had changed, and he seemed resigned to his change in fortunes. He said his performance on the lacrosse field had also declined, and he'd gone from being one of the team's starting members to playing less than half of each game, on average. Ralph was especially concerned that his symptoms would affect his college applications, which were due imminently. He said, "But I'm not sure how I could even handle college if I can't concentrate."

His parents were also deeply worried about his future, of course. "Things have changed so much in the last year," his mother said. "I don't know what happened." I assured them we would do a full evaluation of their son to get to the bottom of his symptoms.

## CLUES TO LOOK FOR

Over the next sessions I had Ralph complete a full battery of physical, neurological, educational, and hearing and vision tests. Everything came back negative (that is, he didn't test positive for any specific condition or problem). With one exception: Ralph's urine tested positive for marijuana and alcohol.

At the next session I shared the test results with Ralph and asked him for any information he was willing to provide. "I guess I've been keeping a pretty big secret," he admitted. He went on to explain that he had been very careful about using drugs and alcohol until late in his junior year of high school. That spring and the following summer, he had attended many lacrosse team parties, where the alcohol had been free-flowing. "A lot of my friends' parents go out of town a lot," Ralph said, "so it's easy to have drinking parties at their houses." He said another common party venue was the riverbank just outside his town; again it was easy for the students to secure alcohol, whether by using fake identification or asking older friends to purchase it for them.

Ralph said he hadn't enjoyed his first few experiences with alcohol but gradually came to look forward to the "buzz" he felt when consuming it. During summer break he had begun drinking more and more, including beer, wine, mixed drinks, and shots of spirits like vodka and tequila. He said, "Now it takes more and more for me to get the same effect." Ralph said that after weekends involving heavy drinking it was hard for him to concentrate and, while he'd been able to maintain his attention and grades in school through the end of his junior year, he had been struggling throughout his senior year.

I assured Ralph that drinking is a common issue with individuals his age, and he became more open to discussing the problem in depth. For example, he told me that for the last two months he had been drinking while alone, often consuming alcohol in his room, including before and after school, then using breath mints to cover the odor. "I don't go to school drunk," Ralph said, "but I definitely feel the effects of it in my first few classes." He said it was harder and harder for him to understand the teachers' presentations, and that several of his teachers were concerned about his declining performance, even though none of them seemed to suspect the source of it.

Ralph said, "When I feel sad I drink more, but that only helps for a little while." He also admitted that he had begun using marijuana in addition to alcohol. "A friend who's really into pot told me it would give me a different kind of high," Ralph said. He had been smoking marijuana with friends for the past few months and, as with alcohol, had begun using the drug on his own, as well. "I feel a little better when I smoke it," he said, "but my concentration gets a lot worse." Ralph was visibly distressed as he spoke about his substance use, and he admitted that he had tried to stop using alcohol and marijuana several times—or at least to use less of the substances—but had not been able to. He also made clear that he recognized the damage his drug-related patterns had caused to several aspects of his life, and that his substance-related habits had resulted in risky behavior such as driving while intoxicated.

After Ralph revealed the extent of his substance use, the source of his attention-deficit symptoms became clear. As we will see, substance abuse is a frequently occurring problem that can be treated by multiple means.

> **Main Clue**
>
> Many people abusing alcohol, marijuana, or other substances fail to make the connection between their attention-deficit symptoms and their substance-related behavior. They may also be unwilling to admit the extent of their substance use, motivated by poor self-awareness or the stigma associated with such behavior. Thorough evaluation and testing (including blood tests), in the context of a trust-based relationship, can reveal individuals' substance-related issues.

## WHAT IS SUBSTANCE ABUSE?

Substance abuse is a highly common behavior that often goes undetected—even by those suffering from its effects. According to the fourth edition of the *Diagnostic and Statistical Manual of Mental Disorders*, "substance-related disorders" involve ten classes of substances, including alcohol, amphetamines, caffeine, cannabis (marijuana), cocaine, sedatives, tobacco, inhalants (for example, paint), and hallucinogens (for example, LSD), with the recognition that "all drugs that are taken in excess have in common direct activation of the brain reward system."[1] All of these substances can diminish attention or cause hyperactivity, but we will focus here on those that are most likely to be abused among the general population—namely alcohol and marijuana.

The *DSM-V*—which, as we noted in chapter 1, should be seen as a work in progress, but one that provides a good overview of the universe of dysfunctional mental conditions—distinguishes among the categories of "substance use disorder," "substance intoxication," and "withdrawal."[2] According to the *DSM*, a diagnosis of substance use involves criteria including:

- Overuse of the substance
- An interest in stopping use of the substance, and/or multiple unsuccessful attempts to quit use
- Craving the substance
- Social/occupational impairment, including failure to fulfill major role obligations
- Risky use of the substance, including use of the substance in hazardous situations (such as drinking and driving) and continued use of the substance despite its damaging physical and psychological effects
- Tolerance, or the development over time of the need for more and more of the substance to achieve the desired effect
- Withdrawal, which involves unpleasant symptoms (for example, trembling) that arise when the individual stops using a substance after a long period of use, often prompting them to begin using the substance again to relieve the symptoms

To qualify for the *DSM-V* diagnosis of substance use, individuals should show at least two of the specified symptoms over the preceding twelve months. The degree of severity of the diagnosis depends on the number of symptoms present: two to three symptoms is considered mild; four to five is moderate; six or more is considered severe.

The *DSM-V* also discusses the "substance-induced disorders" of intoxication, withdrawal, and substance-induced mental disorder. Criteria for substance-induced disorders include substance-specific symptoms caused by ingestion of the substance. Intoxication, for example, can involve problems in perception, attention, judgment, and social behavior. Substance-induced mental disorder involves the presentation of symptoms of a mental disorder (such as depression) during or soon after substance use and not better explained by an independent mental disorder—meaning the substance use is the best explanation for the symptoms.

As noted above, substance-related conditions can result in attention problems. In fact, because all substance-related conditions and diagnoses can include disruptions in attention and other symptoms that can be mistaken for signs of ADHD, for the purposes of this book determining the exact substance-related diagnosis a given person qualifies for is less important than developing the general understanding that substance abuse of any form will likely lead to attention-related challenges.

That was certainly the case for my patient Ralph, who showed symptoms of the *DSM-V* substance use and intoxication diagnoses. Among these were an increased tolerance for the substances (that is, the need for more alcohol to achieve the same effect), unsuccessful efforts to reduce his use of alcohol and marijuana, negative academic and social consequences (for example, lower grades, fewer friends) of using the substances, impaired judgment (for example, driving while intoxicated), and continued use of the substances despite recognition of these consequences and risks. Not surprisingly, Ralph's substance use was affecting his concentration significantly at school and elsewhere. His attention problems were particularly acute after heavier periods of substance use.

Another important feature of Ralph's condition was *self-medication*, or the tendency to use alcohol and drugs to "treat" underlying symptoms of sadness or anxiety. In Ralph's case, it appeared that symptoms of depression were likely the *result* of his substance use (as suggested by the *DSM-V* criteria for substance-induced mental disorders) rather than the target of it, but over time he began using more of the substances to combat feelings of sadness, further exacerbating his pattern of abuse and attention-related symptoms (that is, depression is associated with significant concentration problems and fatigue, as discussed in another chapter in this book). Again, the exact diagnosis or diagnoses are less important than the recognition that conditions like Ralph's will likely result in the erroneous assumption of ADHD, and that treating the underlying problem should resolve the attention-deficit/hyperactivity symptoms.

## PREVALENCE OF SUBSTANCE ABUSE

Estimates of the prevalence of substance use and abuse vary. The U.S. Centers for Disease Control and Prevention found that just over 50 percent of the population reports drinking regularly—defined as at least one drink per month over the past year.[3] A 2010 survey by the National Institute on Drug Abuse (NIDA) found that 8.9 percent of the United States (more than 22 million Americans) had used an illicit drug or abused a medication, up from 8.3 percent in 2002.[4] The NIDA survey also showed that 17.9 million Americans (7 percent of the population) felt that they were dependent on alcohol or had problems related to their alcohol use; 4.5 million U.S. respondents said they had problems related to dependence on or abuse of marijuana. Note that self-reported rates of substance use tend to be lower than actual rates.

While substance-related problems can occur even as early as the preteen years, patterns of abuse and dependence are most likely to emerge for people in their twenties, thirties, and forties, leading to associated attention-deficit symptoms. The *DSM-V* notes that alcohol use disorder is especially common among individuals between the ages of eighteen and twenty-nine, with 16.2 percent of people in this age range showing diagnosable levels of symptoms.[5] Moreover, the substance use tends to be chronic, often lasting years and including brief or longer periods of reduced use. Not surprisingly, alcohol use disorder is also linked to accidents (especially those involving motor vehicles), violence, and suicide; the *DSM-V* notes that alcohol may account for up to 55 percent of all fatal driving accidents.[6]

Substance-related issues tend to run in families, with the best evidence for such patterns among users of alcohol. There are some gender differences related to substance abuse. For example, the NIDA survey found that alcohol abuse was more common among men than women, with an approximate 2:1 ratio of males to females. Importantly, patterns of substance use can be related to culture, as some cultures and religions strictly forbid some substances (for example, strict Mormons avoid alcohol) while others encourage their use in certain circumstances. Again, for our purposes the individual's pattern of substance use (that is, whether or not it is excessive) is more important than that of his or her broader culture or community.

Ralph's family history suggested some risk for addictive behavior, as his maternal grandfather and a paternal uncle had undergone treatment for alcoholism and drug addiction, respectively. Both of Ralph's parents were social drinkers. Moreover, as a late teen Ralph was in the high-risk period for substance abuse, as many high school and college students struggle with binge drinking and frequent use of marijuana. Some keep their substance use under control, with no noticeable negative consequences, while others develop problematic addictive behaviors. Based on his symptom pattern and consequences in several areas, Ralph was heading steadily toward the latter group.

## RELATION TO ATTENTION-DEFICIT/HYPERACTIVITY SYMPTOMS

Substance abuse is clearly linked to attention-deficit/hyperactivity problems, ranging from concentration problems to risky social behavior. By some estimates, as much as 25 percent of adults with substance-use disorders meet criteria for an ADHD diagnosis.[7] As mentioned earlier, the *DSM-V* points out that substance abuse, including as related to alcohol, will often result in problems with perception, concentration, and judgment, all of which can contribute to attention-deficit/hyperactivity symptoms. This claim has been supported by multiple research studies. For example, a 2000 study found that moderate and high doses of alcohol resulted in significant declines in attention (as measured by the ability to identify specific symbols accurately) and elevations on measures of impulsivity.[8] An earlier study used a similar method to conclude that intake of alcohol affects attention mainly by influencing how attention is directed, rather than reducing overall attention capacity.[9] A Spanish study found that even low doses of alcohol reduced individuals' ability to shift and divide attention, capabilities especially important for activities like driving.[10] Similarly, use of alcohol has been associated with increased "disinhibition," or a tendency to behave in risky or less appropriate ways, including increased aggression and sexual behavior;[11] at moderate levels, these may be viewed as evidence of hyperactivity and mistakenly linked to the symptoms of ADHD.

Marijuana use has also been linked to attention problems. Several studies have found that attention, memory, and learning are impaired among heavy marijuana users, even a full twenty-four hours after they've used the drug.[12] The American Council for Drug Education cites similar research that found that adult marijuana users showed reduced memory, math, and verbal skills compared to their non-using peers, and points out that marijuana, like alcohol, can result in disinhibition and impaired perception. The council notes, "Although it has yet to be proven conclusively that heavy marijuana use can cause irreversible loss of intellectual capacity, animal studies have shown marijuana-induced structural damage to portions of the brain essential to memory and learning."[13] In other words, long-term marijuana use can cause long-term memory and learning problems, including those that may be mistaken for ADHD. Any time substance abuse is misdiagnosed as ADHD, it results in delayed treatment, and *treatment delayed is treatment denied.*

## TREATMENT FOR SUBSTANCE ABUSE

There are multiple treatments for substance abuse, some of which may be used together. Unfortunately, a large percentage of those who could benefit from substance-disorder treatment never receive it. According to the National Institute on Drug Abuse, approximately 90 percent of substance abusers fail to seek treatment.[14] A subset of this group may be those mistakenly diagnosed with ADHD and treated only for that diagnosis, resulting in the delay or denial of treatment for their true underlying condition. NIDA also points out several important ideas related to treatment for substance abuse, including:[15]

- There is no universal treatment that works for everyone.
- Effective treatment deals with multiple aspects of functioning (for example, family relationships), not just the substance abuse.

- Treatment needn't be voluntary to be effective; some substance-abuse treatment may be court-mandated, for example.
- Treatment plans should be assessed regularly and refined as needed.
- Substance use during treatment should be monitored carefully, as lapses during treatment are common with any addiction.

The two main forms of substance-abuse treatment are medication and counseling (individual or group). Medications are often used to manage withdrawal symptoms during an initial detoxification period. In some cases, pharmaceuticals can also be used to disrupt substance dependence longer term. Specific medications can be prescribed for specific addictions. For example, drugs including naltrexone and disulfiram have been approved for treatment of alcohol dependence.

Counseling-based therapy for substance abuse takes several forms, depending on the setting (inpatient versus outpatient), format (group, one-on-one, or couples/family), and school of thought underlying the approach (for example, cognitive-behavioral, or treatment focused on thoughts and actions, are among the most common).[16] Inpatient or residential treatment is recommended for especially severe cases of substance abuse, and typically involves both medication (especially in early phases) and counseling, both in one-on-one and group formats. Cognitive-behavioral treatment may help the patient identify and avoid the cues related to their substance abuse (for example, avoiding certain people or places associated with drugs). Family therapy is often used—with or without individual counseling—for younger patients, to identify systems and patterns within the family that may contribute to the substance abuse behavior and to help each member play a role in the patient's recovery. Most counseling- and medication-based treatments include a strong education component, to help patients understand the biology and psychology related to substance use and dependence.

Among the best-known treatments for alcoholism and other substance-abuse disorders are group therapies based on twelve-step self-help programs, such as Alcoholics Anonymous. Such programs typically involve features including group sharing, in which patients are encouraged to tell their story to fellow members; sponsorship, where experienced group members serve as mentors and guides for new members; and forgiveness for relapses. Many, but not all, twelve-step programs include a religious component. Some members find it helpful to place their trust in a higher power.

To treat my patient Ralph I used several of the interventions noted above. As a first step, we discussed in detail the addictive nature of alcohol and marijuana, including how such chemicals compete with neurotransmitters that aid in nervous-system functioning, resulting in poor attention, distractibility, and impulsivity. We also agreed that Ralph would share his "secret" with his parents, to help them understand why he had changed so much over the past year and to recruit them to help in his recovery. Because Ralph's substance abuse was relatively moderate and he was still functioning at a reasonably high level, we opted not to use medication, but agreed that this might be an option if his symptoms didn't improve. Similarly, there was no need to use inpatient or residential treatment as an early step, but this was viewed as a future possibility, if required. I also encouraged Ralph to attend group therapy sessions (whether based on the twelve-step model or not) and helped him locate possible groups in his area.

Ralph committed to addressing his substance abuse, and made early progress. "I think I can do it on my own," he said in response to my suggestion to consider attending group sessions. Initially, he successfully weaned himself off the marijuana completely—it helped that he had been using the substance for only a few months—and reduced his drinking to "a few beers" at parties. As a result of his efforts, his attention improved considerably, as did his performance in school and on the lacrosse field, to his and his parents' delight. I praised Ralph's progress but also warned him and his family that relapse is very common with substance issues.

Within two months, Ralph had gone back to drinking heavily most weekends. "I thought I had it under control," Ralph said. We agreed that he should attend group therapy, to add to his available tools and support system. Within a month of attending, Ralph had made further progress, with the help of a sponsor and a "buddy," or a fellow new member. He had made the difficult decision of cutting ties with some of his best friends, who were heavy users of alcohol and marijuana.

Importantly, he recognized the long-term nature of his challenge. "I see now that it's a marathon, not a sprint," he said. Armed with better understanding of his substance abuse and some of the resources for combating it, Ralph felt much better about his present situation and his future, and was working hard on his college applications while continuing to see me and attend group sessions.

# CHAPTER 8

# Mood Disorders (Bipolar and Major Depressive Disorder)

## The Big Point

Early symptoms of impulsivity, short attention span, and distractibility often evolve into a mood disorder such as bipolar disorder or depression. These mood disorders are often accompanied by symptoms of attention deficit and impulsivity, and are in turn mistaken for ADHD.

Mental illnesses, including mood disorders, are among the most common conditions affecting the general population. World-wide estimates of mental disorders suggest that about *one in three* people will meet criteria for at least one such diagnosis over their lifetimes.[1] U.S. lifetime rates of mental disease among adults have been estimated at 46 percent.[2]

Mental disorders are also linked closely to attention deficit symptoms, given their effects on concentration and mood. When a child or adult patient comes to my office with a long list of other doctors they have seen and medications they have tried without success, I know to assess them carefully for non-ADHD mental symptoms, especially those related to mood disorders. I also take a look at their family history, as mood disorders tend to have a genetic component. Such was the case for William, whose parents brought him to my clinic when he was twelve years old.

## THE BOY WHO THREW TANTRUMS

A blond boy with a big smile, William was the third of four siblings, and a student in sixth grade. His parents were deeply concerned about his behavior and had already been to four other doctors; the physicians' consensus was ADHD, possibly accompanied by depression. Over the past year, William had been placed on six medications, including several stimulants and an antidepressant. The treatments had done little to improve the boy's symptoms, which included significant learning challenges. His parents said that he generally performed well on standardized tests—above the 80th percentile for both math and verbal skills—but struggled to complete even the most basic homework assignments. His mother said, "Sometimes he forgets to bring his homework home from school, or he'll bring it home but forget to take it out of his backpack until it's too late." She added, "Unless I sit with him until he's done, he'll often stop when he's halfway through his assignment, then never come back to it." It was clear that William's poor organization skills and concentration were affecting his schoolwork; his grades were slipping fast. At home, he often failed to listen to his parents or siblings. "I'll ask him to do a chore or come to dinner and he doesn't even respond," his father said. "Sometimes he just stares out the window for a long time." Both parents reported that they and their other children were frustrated by William's short attention span and distractibility.

Even more troubling for the boy's family, teachers, and friends were his other symptoms. He had become increasingly moody and irritable, especially when he had to do schoolwork. "Last week he threw his book across the room and ripped up his assignment," his mother said. "He said he hated his homework and he was no good at it." Many mornings, William had trouble getting out of bed for school. His parents said he had been asking to stay home because he felt sick or tired, but he had no specific symptoms (such as fever) other than appearing fatigued. When they forced him to go to school, he would often throw tantrums, crying for long periods. During these times, the boy also lost interest in activities he usually enjoyed, including soccer and guitar lessons. His parents reported that he asked to skip practices, games, or lessons, again because he felt tired or ill.

At other times, William acted "way too happy and goofy," as described by his parents and teachers. The boy behaved impulsively, blurting out answers in school and poking his siblings at the dinner table. "Sometimes he just talks and talks," his mother said, "like his mouth can't keep up with his brain." William had gotten in minor trouble at school for distracting classmates by talking and clowning around, sometimes sticking pencils in his nose for laughs or throwing paper clips across the room while the teacher was presenting a lesson. The boy said his friends had initially been entertained by his behavior, but even they had grown tired of it, showing less interest in talking to him or coming to his house. "Sometimes I say mean things to them because I'm mad about it," he said, admitting that such behavior isolated him even further.

The medications recommended by William's previous doctors had exacerbated some of his symptoms, including his fidgeting and poor concentration. His mother said, "They made him worse, not better." His parents had even noticed that he was losing weight and not sleeping well. A generally gaunt appearance and dark circles under the boy's eyes confirmed their concerns. "It seems like he's mad, sad, or both—all the time," his mother said.

Both parents were deeply worried about their son, and frustrated that past treatments hadn't helped at all.

## CLUES TO LOOK FOR

In William's case, we were quickly able to rule out several potentially contributing factors to his symptoms using a thorough history and medical tests. His hearing and vision were fine. He was normal on all physical tests and blood work, including screenings related to thyroid hormones, iron, and lead; abnormal amounts of those neurochemicals can result in attention-deficit symptoms, as we will see in later chapters. The much more relevant features in William's case were his cognitive (thought-related) and behavioral (in other words, how he was acting) symptoms: poor concentration, low energy, feelings of worthlessness, sleeplessness, difficulty getting out of bed, irritability, tantrums, impulsivity, pressured speech, and others. Together these form a picture of a likely mood disorder. But which one? The *DSM-V* includes diagnostic criteria for depressive disorders—or what's known as "unipolar" depression—and bipolar disorders, or what's popularly known as "manic depression."

When I suspect a mood disorder, I usually have patients (and their parents, in the case of children) chart their moods, keeping track of their level of happiness or sadness on a daily basis from a scale of 1 to 10, with 1 being "really sad" and 10 being "really happy." I ask my patients to mark their moods separately in the morning, afternoon, and evening. When William's parents kept track of his moods, they saw a general pattern: He was typically most sad early in the day after getting up, with his mood improving over the course of the day and often going to the other extreme by displaying impulsivity and goofiness in the afternoon and evening. Sometimes the sad period lasted for as much as a few weeks, until it was again broken by a period of elevated mood, which tended to have a shorter duration. But more often William's periods of happiness and sadness tended to be short, shifting multiple times within the course of a day. Overall, William's symptom cycle fit criteria for a bipolar disorder diagnosis, and further inquiry confirmed this hypothesis.

The preliminary diagnosis was confirmed strongly by William's family history. Five relatives had been diagnosed with some form of mood disorder: his maternal grandmother and grandfather, paternal grandmother, and two aunts. Four of the diagnoses had been bipolar disorder. When I suggested the diagnosis to William's parents, his mother said, "I knew this ran in our family, but I didn't think it could show up so early." Moreover, the boy's doctors and family had focused on ADHD as the most likely explanation for his symptoms, even when the medications hadn't worked. Though at least one previous doctor had viewed the mood symptoms as severe enough to try an antidepressant (which hadn't worked), no practitioner had thought to chart William's mood or to consider the strong family history of bipolar disorder. They simply hadn't asked, and the family hadn't volunteered the information, given their focus on the attention symptoms and ADHD diagnosis.

### Main Clue

The main clue to a possible bipolar disorder diagnosis is the presence of alternating periods of energetic, "up" moods and depression. In children, these can be very short periods, with moods changing multiple times over a day. The main clue to a depressive disorder is the presence of multiple symptoms including sad mood, lack of interest in most activities, sleep or appetite disturbance, poor concentration, and feelings of guilt or worthlessness.

## WHAT ARE BIPOLAR AND MAJOR DEPRESSIVE DISORDERS?

Bipolar and major depressive disorder are mood disorders with multiple symptoms related to attention and hyperactivity. Effective treatment of a mood disorder can reduce attention-related symptoms dramatically.

While it is my view that the *DSM* is seriously wrong about ADHD, I am more confident in the *DSM*'s handling of mood disorders. That's partly because I've seen more scientific evidence for the multiple factors that contribute to depression and bipolar disorders, from chemical imbalances (especially in neurotransmitters like serotonin) to difficult life circumstances; some researchers even argue that depression is potentially an adaptive human response.[3] My confidence about mood disorders is also based on the evidence I've seen for the effectiveness of treatment. My patients and others whom I've observed with depression and bipolar disorder respond much better overall to approaches involving medication and psychotherapy than do their peers diagnosed with "ADHD." Again, that's largely because the ADHD diagnosis is wrong. Some who are diagnosed with ADHD actually have a mood disorder that explains their symptoms. For these reasons and others, I use the *DSM* as a general guideline, rather than as the final word on a diagnosis.

According to the *DSM-V*, depressive episodes include a combination of at least five of the symptoms outlined below. By contrast, bipolar disorder is marked by the occurrence of manic or "hypomanic" episodes in addition to depressive episodes.

### DSM-V Criteria for Major Depressive Disorder:[4]

At least five of the symptoms below must be present during the same two-week period:

- Sad or irritable mood (irritability is especially common in children and adolescents)
- Loss of interest or pleasure in most activities (one of these first two symptoms must be present)
- Weight loss or gain (for example, more than 5 percent of body weight in a month, not due to dieting); in children, failure to make expected weight gains
- Sleep issues (insomnia or excessive sleep)
- Psychomotor agitation (for example, fidgeting, restlessness) or retardation (for example, slowness observable by others)
- Fatigue
- Feelings of worthlessness or guilt
- Poor concentration
- Suicidal thoughts

These symptoms, when accompanied by manic or hypomanic episodes, indicate a diagnosis of bipolar disorder. Manic symptoms are associated with what the *DSM* calls Bipolar I disorder, and are what people imagine when they think of the "highs" associated with manic depression: inflated self-esteem (or what's called "grandiosity"), little need for sleep, racing thoughts, distractibility, and especially an involvement in risky activities. In adults, risky activities often take the form of shopping sprees, gambling binges, or promiscuous behavior. In children, risk-seeking may show up as efforts to jump off rooftops, attempts to cross busy streets, or petty crimes like shoplifting. The symptoms should cause significant impairment in functioning. Hypomanic episodes, part of what's called Bipolar II disorder, are similar to manic episodes, except in degree; hypomania involves less severe symptoms than mania and, consequently, less impaired functioning.

**DSM-V Criteria for Bipolar I Disorder:**[5]
Diagnosis of Bipolar I requires the presence of three or more of the following symptoms for at least a week:

- Inflated sense of self-esteem
- Decreased need for sleep
- Excessive talkativeness (or "pressured" need to keep talking)
- Racing thoughts
- Distractibility
- Increased goal-directed activity (for example, related to work or school) or psychomotor agitation (for example, moving around for no specific reason)
- Involvement in risky activities (for example, shopping sprees, foolish investments)

For diagnosis, these symptoms should cause impairment in social or occupational functioning or require hospitalization to prevent harm to oneself or others. The symptoms should also not be the result of substance use (which would qualify them for a substance-induced mental disorder). Most people diagnosed with Bipolar I disorder also experience at least one major depressive episode in their lifetimes, but this is not a requirement for diagnosis.

**DSM-V Criteria for Bipolar II Disorder:**[6]
Diagnosis of Bipolar II requires three or more of the same symptoms noted for Bipolar I above, but the symptoms need only last at least four days, rather than a week. Unlike Bipolar I, the symptoms *can't* be severe enough to cause significant impairment or require hospitalization. Also unlike Bipolar I, the diagnosis of Bipolar II requires at least one hypomanic episode and one episode of major depression. Like Bipolar I, however, the symptoms can't be attributed to the effects of a substance.

So, based on the *DSM-V* definition of major depressive disorder (or what most people refer to as "depression"), we can think of the disorder as bipolar disorder without the manic or hypomanic symptoms. The two disorders are so closely related that they accompanied each other in the *DSM-IV*. In the *DSM-V*, they have been split into two chapters—a matter of organization—but their definitions have remained essentially unchanged. The key to differentiating depression from bipolar disorder is to keep close track of symptoms. For example, an early depressive episode might be seen as evidence of major depressive disorder; but if a subsequent manic or hypomanic episode is observed, then the bipolar diagnosis may be more accurate. It's hard to say how long of an observation period is best. But symptom patterns are usually well established by early adulthood.

William displayed many of the symptoms of depressive episodes, including sadness and irritability; lack of interest in activities, including those he normally enjoyed; sleep disturbance; fatigue; and poor concentration. Meeting the requirement of the *DSM-V* for diagnosis of a depressive episode, he had experienced depressive symptoms that had lasted two weeks in the past, but he usually experienced shorter depressive periods, often lasting less than a day, which were interrupted by brief manic and hypomanic episodes. Note that in my observation of both depression and bipolar disorders, the average duration of depressive/manic/hypomanic episodes tends to be shorter, often much shorter, than what the *DSM* specifies. Also, according to the *DSM*, to qualify for a depressive disorder the symptoms must cause significant distress and/or impairment in functioning to be considered part of a true depressive episode. William's symptoms were disrupting his performance in school and his relationships with friends.

Without the presence of hypomanic symptoms, William would have qualified only for a diagnosis of depression. William's symptom picture fit the criteria for hypomania over mania, as they caused less impairment in functioning, though they were observable by others, including his parents, teachers, and friends. In general, whether the episodes are manic or hypomanic, the change in mood and functioning should be clear to others. According to the *DSM-V*, hypomanic episodes can evolve into full manic episodes, but this hadn't happened in William's case. Because the boy was experiencing depressive and hypomanic episodes (rather than full manic episodes), he met criteria for the diagnosis of Bipolar II. Had he exhibited full manic episodes, he would have qualified for Bipolar I.

## PREVALENCE OF MOOD DISORDERS

Depression is a common condition. A mid-1990s study suggested a U.S. lifetime prevalence rate of depression of 17.1 percent— meaning that about one in five people will develop diagnosable depression in their lifetime.[7] According to the *DSM-V*, about 7 percent of the U.S. population qualifies for depression in a given year.[8] Prevalence in the 18–29 age range is higher than in older age groups, and females experience up to three times the rate of depression as males.

However, there is controversy about the prevalence of depression and bipolar disorder. Like ADHD, many jump to a conclusion of clinical depression when a patient is experiencing normal depressive episodes. The validity of the diagnostic criteria is also questioned. Are symptoms of major depression too common in the general population to be considered part of a disorder? The motivations of the *DSM-V* authors, like with ADHD, are also questionable. Some have argued that the medical practitioners behind the *DSM-IV* depression criteria had financial ties to pharmaceutical companies, which motivated them to ensure a high rate of diagnosis for the disorder (ensuring, in turn, a larger number of customers for antidepressants).[9] Notwithstanding these issues, both bipolar disorder and depression can be extremely debilitating. The disorders run strongly in families; depression is particularly likely to be passed among female family members.

According to the *DSM-V*, bipolar disorder of both types typically begins in adolescence or the twenties (though it can start earlier, as was the case with William), with Bipolar I tending to start earlier than Bipolar II. The odds of a given individual experiencing some form of bipolar disorder in a given year in the United States is about 0.6 percent (Bipolar I) to 0.8 percent (Bipolar II). Bipolar I is equally common in men and women, whereas women may be more likely to be diagnosed with Bipolar II.

## RELATION TO ATTENTION-DEFICIT/HYPERACTIVITY SYMPTOMS

Not surprisingly, attention-deficit symptoms will be likely in patients who meet criteria for depression, given the poor concentration and distractibility that depression involves. Researchers have pointed out the strong overlap between ADHD and depression, but these are usually seen as comorbid conditions (conditions that occur together).[10] In my experience, the depression often explains the ADHD symptoms fully, and successful treatment of the depression eliminates the attention-deficit/hyperactivity symptoms.

Both core elements of bipolar disorder drive attention deficits: depression and mania (or hypomania, which William displayed). Indeed, a common symptom of depression is poor concentration. Similarly, depression is characterized by irritability. Impulsivity is a hallmark symptom of mania; in children, this symptom can look like distractibility, or an inability to stay on task, whether homework or home chores. The impulsivity was also related to

William's disruptive behavior in class and invasion of his siblings' personal space at home.

Many others have pointed out a strong link between attention symptoms and bipolar disorder. For example, researchers have found overlap in diagnoses of bipolar disorder and the disorder known as ADHD based on symptom patterns. One group found that irritability, hyperactivity, accelerated speech, and distractibility were commonly observed in adolescent and pre-adolescent patients diagnosed with bipolar disorder or ADHD.[11] A different research group showed that adult bipolar patients, including those treated with medication, displayed significant attention deficits compared to individuals without a bipolar diagnosis.[12] It's not surprising that others have linked bipolar disorder with attention symptoms, given how much bipolar symptoms—related to both depression and mania—can interfere with concentration and be expressed as distractibility and impulsivity. Importantly, as we discussed in chapter 1, researchers have recently uncovered significant overlap in the genetics underlying mood disorders (both bipolar disorder and depression) and ADHD, further evidence that diagnosing these conditions separately is misguided.[13] *And misdiagnoses result in delay or denial of treatment, with significant costs for patients, their families, and broader society.*

## TREATMENT FOR MOOD DISORDERS

Bipolar disorder is usually treated with a combination of medication and psychotherapy. Medications that have been used for successful treatment of bipolar symptoms include lithium, anticonvulsants, antipsychotics (some cases of bipolar disorder include psychotic symptoms such as hallucinations and delusions), and antidepressants. As far as psychotherapy, bipolar patients have benefited from individual and group cognitive-behavioral therapy (which emphasizes thoughts and behaviors) and family therapy. Severe cases of bipolar disorder, in which patients display extreme symptoms of depression (for example, suicidality) or mania (for example, risky behaviors), often require hospitalization until the symptoms improve. According to the *DSM-V*, prognosis for bipolar disorder is poorer when the patient meets criteria for rapid cycling, or the occurrence of four or more mood episodes in one year (in children, rapid cycling is more common).

Similarly, the best treatment for depression is typically a combination of medication and psychotherapy. Pharmaceuticals that have been documented to work for depression include selective serotonin reuptake inhibitors and serotonin-norepinephrine reuptake inhibitors. Some of the best-known psychotherapeutic approaches to depression include individual and group therapy based on cognitive-behavioral (that is, changing patients' thought and behavior patterns) and psychodynamic (that is, understanding the effects of early experiences on mood and personality) principles. Severe cases of depression often involve extreme fatigue (for example, inability to get out of bed) and/or suicidal thoughts, and may require hospitalization. Though controversial, electroconvulsive treatment can also be effective for chronic cases of depression.

In William's case, the family agreed to try medication first without psychotherapy, to see what kind of impact the pharmaceutical treatment could have. The first medication we tried, an antiseizure drug commonly prescribed for bipolar disorder, reduced the boy's mood and behavioral symptoms dramatically but resulted in side effects including upset stomach and dizziness. A second drug of the same type elicited no side effects, but the symptoms returned to moderate levels. Finally we started William on lithium, which requires careful monitoring of its blood levels as the dosage is raised. Within two months we found a dosage that worked well for him, reducing his symptoms to very mild levels, with no significant side effects.

With regular use of the lithium, William's functioning improved on every level. Instances of forgetting his homework at school or in his backpack became rare. Schoolwork-related tantrums subsided and his grades rose. His teachers noted a marked improvement in his classroom behavior, and his parents found him much more attentive at home. "It's like a switch was flipped," William's father said. Though everyone was pleased with the outcome, I emphasized to William and his family that bipolar disorder is a chronic illness that for the vast majority of patients requires lifelong medication. Fortunately, the family already understood this, having seen their relatives manage the condition over time.

The bottom line is that many patients diagnosed with or treated for ADHD may have undiagnosed mood disorders—depression or bipolar disorder—that explain their attention-deficit/hyperactivity symptoms. Getting the right diagnosis and treatment eliminates or reduces the symptoms in most cases.

# CHAPTER 9

# Hearing Problems

## The Big Point

Difficulty with hearing is a surprisingly common source of attention-deficit/hyperactivity symptoms, especially in children. Similar to those with vision problems, individuals with hearing problems often display short attention spans and impulsivity, which may be mistaken as symptoms of ADHD. Steps taken to treat the hearing issue typically improve the attention and impulsivity symptoms.

Hearing has become a harder task than ever in today's world, with background noise at unprecedented levels, with everything from cell phones to subway cars competing for our auditory space. While most of us face this challenge with unimpaired hearing, a significant minority has the additional difficulty of fighting through hearing loss to connect with the world. Just as for vision problems, hearing issues can cause problems related to attention and distractibility. Children with hearing loss are especially likely to remain undiagnosed, because, unlike most adults, they may fail to recognize they have a hearing issue. The hearing loss makes them more likely to display attention-deficit/hyperactivity, not only falling behind in school but being mistakenly diagnosed with ADHD based on their symptoms. This was the case for my patient Thom.

## THE TWO THOMS

Nine-year-old Thom's parents brought him to my office because they were deeply puzzled about his behavior. At home Thom, the middle child of three (he had an older sister and younger brother), was "very well behaved," according to his mother. She said that he got along with his siblings nearly all the time, and often took on a "peacemaker" role when his sister and brother got into arguments. Thom enjoyed building model cars and drawing elaborate pictures of cars, trains, airplanes, and rocket ships. In fact, he spent most of the first visit to my office working on a picture of a race car. "He already says he wants to be an engineer, like his father," his mother said. "Right, Thom?" She looked at her son but he didn't respond, engrossed in his pictures. His mother shrugged and said, "He just loses himself in those drawings."

Thom's behavior at school, however, offered a stark contrast to what his parents observed at home. From the start of third grade his teacher reported that he was fidgety and poorly focused, with a short attention span for many subjects. "His teacher says he pokes at the kids sitting near him and often interrupts her when she's reading to them or going over new vocabulary words," Thom's mother said. Thom seemed to enjoy doing math problems and other individual work, though, and during those exercises he rarely disrupted his classmates. His mother said, "His father and I think the problem is that Thom really prefers math and science to reading and writing, so he only pays attention to certain parts of class." As an example she talked about how much the boy enjoyed taking part in science experiments like rolling dice to see how many times certain numbers came up. Thom's academic performance (for example, as reflected on his report cards) was also stronger in math than in classes involving more verbal skills. But his mother admitted that Thom had displayed few behavioral problems in earlier grades, regardless of the subject being studied. When I asked Thom what his favorite subjects were, he said (after his mother helped shift his attention from his drawing) he liked "all of them, most of the time." Thom had also become more withdrawn at school, according to his teacher. His mother confirmed that he had less interest in socializing over the past year or so.

Because Thom's problems at school had persisted and even worsened over the past year, his teacher had suggested the family consult a physician. Their family practitioner had evaluated Thom and sent behavioral questionnaires for the parents and teacher to fill out. As Thom's mother had explained, the reports suggested his behavior at school was much worse than at home. "It's like there are two of him," his mother said. "The one we see at home and the troublemaker they see at school." She said she'd asked Thom why he was disrupting the classroom, and he had no explanation.

To address the boy's attention and behavioral symptoms, the family's doctor had placed him on a stimulant medication, telling the parents he had given Thom a "preliminary" diagnosis of ADHD. The drug seemed to decrease Thom's impulsive behavior (for example, he interrupted the teacher less frequently) but it failed to improve his focus. Moreover, the boy's appetite diminished and he had trouble sleeping, as suggested by the dark circles I observed under his eyes. "We're worried he's losing weight," his mother said. Understandably, Thom's parents were deeply concerned about keeping him on the medication, given its mixed results.

## CLUES TO LOOK FOR

To assess most of my child patients I start with basic tests including preliminary assessments of hearing and vision; these are simple and highly noninvasive tests. Thom's vision tested perfectly (confirming the results of earlier tests given by his school) but he had significant hearing loss in both ears, due to underdevelopment of the inner ear. That result gave us a likely explanation for his poor focus and impulsivity in school. That is, his hearing loss was preventing him from focusing on tasks involving auditory material, such as the teacher's vocabulary lessons; while he could offset his hearing problem by using what he could see (for example, the writing on the board), this often wasn't enough, and his attention would wander, sometimes leading him to disrupt classmates or interrupt the teacher.

Rather than conducting extensive additional testing of other areas of functioning with Thom, I suggested to his parents that we address the hearing issue, to see whether it resulted in improvement on all symptoms, including those related less directly to hearing (for example, disrupting the class). They agreed, and we arranged to have Thom's hearing tested more thoroughly.

In general, hearing issues can be easily overlooked as explanations for attention-deficit/hyperactivity symptoms (which are often mistaken, in turn, for signs of ADHD). The hearing issues can usually be treated successfully, which often addresses the attention and behavioral symptoms.

### Main Clue

When a child displays attention-deficit/hyperactivity symptoms in some settings but not in others (for example, at school versus at home) or complains of failure to understand what they hear, it's worth checking their hearing as a possible source of the problem. Hearing problems may be difficult to detect, since children may not recognize or admit to them. Careful questioning of the child and their family (for example, "Do you hear your teacher well all the time?"), along with simple hearing tests, can help diagnose the problem.

## WHAT ARE HEARING PROBLEMS?

Hearing problems can result from multiple causes; identifying the specific nature of the problem is crucial for deciding the best treatment. Most of us take our hearing for granted—until there's a problem with it. Even then some adults have trouble recognizing and acknowledging hearing disturbance, and it's even more challenging for children to do so. To understand ear-related problems better, let me discuss how hearing works at a basic level. The ear includes the outer ear, middle ear, and inner ear. Sound waves vibrate our ear drums, and the vibrations are amplified by three tiny bones located in the middle ear: the hammer, anvil, and stirrup. From there the vibrations travel to the cochlea, a spiral-shaped inner-ear structure that includes thousands of tiny hairs (called cilia) that react to the vibrations in different ways, sending patterns of signals through the auditory nerve to the brain, which interprets these as specific sounds.

Hearing problems result from one of two main causes: 1) underdevelopment of or damage to the inner ear or auditory nerve, which usually means permanent hearing loss; 2) prevention of sound waves from reaching the inner ear, which can result from anything from a punctured eardrum to excessive earwax, and can usually be overcome.[1] Hearing-related issues can take the form of full or partial hearing loss, or the perception of sound that isn't actually present; for example, people with tinnitus hear high-pitched ringing, buzzing, or other sounds.

Root causes of hearing problems include:

- Heredity
- Congenital diseases (such as Usher syndrome, a rare genetic disease causing progressive hearing loss)
- Noncongenital diseases (for example, meningitis and other illnesses causing high fevers)
- Ear infections
- Ear-based tumors
- Injuries; for example, a ruptured eardrum can result from changes in air pressure, sudden loud noises, or puncturing by an object
- Side effects of medications (for example, from some antibiotics)
- Long-term exposure to loud noise (for example, jet engines)
- Aging
- Earwax-based blockage

Of course, combinations of these factors can also result in hearing loss. For example, damage to the inner ear can be caused by both aging and prolonged exposure to loud noise (for example, from a farming job requiring regular operation of heavy machinery).

Symptoms of hearing loss or other disturbance include difficulty understanding words (especially when there's significant background noise, like music or a crowd) and the perception of sounds as being muffled. Phone and Internet-based (for example, Skype) conversations can be particularly difficult for those with hearing loss. Coping mechanisms used by people with hearing problems include moving closer to sound sources, asking people to speak more loudly or repeat themselves, and withdrawal from social and other situations that involve spoken or other auditory content.

The results of my patient Thom's full hearing test (conducted by an audiologist) showed that he had more than 50 percent hearing loss in both ears, across a wide range of sound frequencies. The cause was hereditary: genetically based underdevelopment of some parts of the inner ear. While Thom's condition was rare, hearing loss among children is not, and it can have myriad sources, as noted above. The problem had worsened since Thom's birth, which helped explain why his behavioral symptoms had increased as he progressed through elementary school. Being unable to hear significant portions of the classroom experience had made Thom more likely to disrupt his classmates and the teacher's lessons. Moreover, Thom's hearing issue helped explain why he didn't respond to his mother's prompts (or mine) when he first visited my office, and why he had become more withdrawn socially (because he was having trouble hearing other children). Thom's parents were concerned to see the extent of his hearing loss but relieved to have an explanation for his puzzling behavior. There weren't "two" Thoms, after all—just one, whose hearing issue made it difficult for him to focus fully on school.

## PREVALENCE OF HEARING PROBLEMS

The National Institute on Deafness and Other Communication Disorders presents some patterns and statistics related to the prevalence of hearing problems:[2]

- About 17 percent of all U.S. adults report at least some degree of hearing loss.
- Men are more likely to have hearing problems than women.
- Reported hearing loss increases steadily with age: 18 percent

of adults ages forty-five to sixty-four have hearing problems, compared to 47 percent of those over seventy-five years.

- About 2–3 of every 1,000 U.S. children are born deaf or with partial hearing loss.
- About 15 percent of Americans have high-frequency hearing loss due to prolonged exposure to loud noise.

In addition to these statistics, a late 1990s study found hearing impairment in about 11 percent of all school-age children sampled.[3] Hearing problems are most likely to be mistaken for the disorder called ADHD in children, due to the demands of school-based settings; but given the large percentage of adults who suffer from hearing disturbance, it's important to consider this factor in adults with attention-deficit symptoms. While hearing disturbance can run in families due to the hereditary factor mentioned earlier, it's not nearly as common an inherited problem as vision impairment (as discussed in the chapter on vision problems) and other conditions (for example, high blood pressure). Similarly, about nine out of ten deaf children are born to parents without hearing problems.[4] As noted earlier, some hearing problems (such as earwax buildup) can be treated easily, while others (such as deafness from birth) may be irreversible.

Though Thom's hearing problem had a genetic basis, his family had no history of hearing loss other than that associated with aging.

## RELATION TO ATTENTION-DEFICIT/HYPERACTIVITY SYMPTOMS

The link between hearing problems and ADHD has been documented elsewhere, as well. A recent academic study found that even children with minimal hearing loss showed significantly more behavioral problems than their peers.[5] An earlier study examined hearing-impaired and normal children from six to fourteen years of age and found that the hearing-impaired group showed significant attention problems (understandably) and were more likely to be rated as having significant behavioral problems by their parents and teachers—symptoms that could easily be mistaken for ADHD.[6] Another research article points out the difficulty of diagnosing ADHD in children with hearing challenges, due to the attention-related and other symptoms that hearing problems can cause.[7]

Beyond the results of academic studies, it's easy to see how hearing problems can result in a mistaken diagnosis of ADHD. Children and adults who can't hear well may be misperceived as having poor attention spans, when in reality they have to work harder than unimpaired peers to understand auditory material. Similarly, they're more likely to be distracted by other stimuli (especially visual) in their environments because of the effort that hearing accurately requires. In children, this distractibility can transition quickly to disruptiveness in school and other settings, with the impulsivity again mistaken for a symptom of ADHD.

Securing accurate, timely diagnosis of hearing problems is particularly important because undetected hearing impairment in children can lead to crucial delays in their development, especially that related to social and verbal skills. For example, the American Speech-Language-Hearing Association highlights the fact that hearing issues can impede development of skills related to vocabulary, sentence structure, speaking, general academic achievement, and social capabilities.[8]

As for all the conditions discussed in this book, misdiagnosis results in delayed treatment, and *treatment delayed is treatment denied*, with damaging consequences for patients and their families.

## TREATMENT FOR HEARING PROBLEMS

Treatment approaches to hearing issues will of course depend on the specific type of problem. One of the most treatable hearing issues is loss related to earwax blockage. Excess earwax may be removed by procedures including loosening the wax with oil and scooping, flushing, or suctioning it out. The process can result in immediate improvement in hearing. Inner-ear problems are often approached with hearing aids, from inexpensive over-the-ear devices available in retail stores to costly custom-made devices that fit within the ear. Audiologists can perform careful testing of hearing and recommend the best hearing aid to address them. Newer hearing-aid-related technologies include aids that can communicate wirelessly (that is, from the hearing aid in one ear to the one in the other) and audio induction loops that allow hearing aids to connect directly with audio sources (for example, public address systems at train stations and other public places). While hearing aids can't reverse hearing loss, they can improve hearing significantly. Still, only an estimated one of five people who could benefit from hearing aids wears one.[9]

More severe cases of hearing loss can be treated with a cochlear implant, a device placed surgically within the skin behind the ear. Children who have lost most of their hearing before or after they've acquired language skills are among the more targeted candidates for cochlear implants. The implant works by sending specific signals to the auditory nerve, based on the sounds it picks up in the environment, thus mimicking the cochlea's activity. By 2011, about 220,000 people worldwide had cochlear implants.[10] While cochlear implants help many people hear better, they are associated with some risk of loss of residual hearing, due to the implantation procedure.[11]

The most effective treatment for my patient Thom was a hearing aid. The audiologist who conducted his full hearing test helped determine the best kind of aid for him: a custom-made device that fit snugly in each ear. Thom's interest in technology helped him adapt quickly to the aids. "He calls them his robot ears," his mother said. "He's not the least bit embarrassed about wearing them." Thom's parents and I also agreed to take him off the stimulant medication, which hadn't helped much in the first place and had caused side effects including disturbed sleep and appetite.

As hoped, Thom's behavior at school improved quickly, now that he could hear everything better. He no longer lost focus as easily, and rarely disrupted his classmates. The boy's performance in reading and writing improved dramatically as well. His mother said, "His teacher says he really likes story time now, and he asks really good questions." When Thom came to my office for follow-up visits, he attended to my questions much better, even when I interrupted his drawing to ask him something. Thom also expressed more interest in socializing at home and in his neighborhood once his hearing had improved.

On one of his last visits to my office, I asked Thom if he still liked the idea of becoming an engineer someday. "I do," he said with a smile. "But I also might want to be a writer!"

# CHAPTER 10

# Learning Disabilities

**The Big Point**

Patients who struggle with a learning disability such as dyslexia may exhibit context-specific poor focus, distractibility, and fidgeting that can be mistaken for ADHD. Careful observation, combined with a full psychoeducational evaluation, can uncover a symptom picture pointing to the learning disability, which can take one of several well-established forms.

Reading *b*'s as *d*'s and inverting the order of words. That's how most people still think about dyslexia, a common learning disability involving trouble processing written words. But dyslexia comes in multiple forms—one related to reading speed and accuracy, and the other linked to comprehension—and it's just one of several diagnosable learning disabilities that typically first appear in childhood. Students struggling with a learning disability are likely to display attention-deficit and hyperactivity symptoms due to their processing challenges and related frustration. Those symptoms, in turn, may be mistaken for ADHD, as was fast becoming the case for one of my young patients.

## ELLEN'S SECRET STRUGGLE

"We don't know what the problem is," Ellen's mother said to me the first time she brought her seven-year-old daughter to my office. The bright-eyed second grader was highly attentive during the visit, responding to my questions quickly and appropriately. While Ellen played with a small set of plastic animals she had brought, her mother explained more.

Ellen's teachers said that the girl was a "model student" in class most of the time. She participated in classroom activities, and her hand was often the first to rise in response to questions—especially those related to arithmetic or other math concepts. "Her teacher says she excels at math," her mother said. But at other times, the girl lost focus and fidgeted. Sometimes she disrupted the class by whispering to nearby classmates or nudging them. This behavior was observed more often during class periods devoted to reading, including silent reading times.

"But she reads so well," her mother said. Indeed, when I asked Ellen to read from a picture book in my office, she performed beautifully, reading aloud in a strong, clear voice. Ellen said, "I like reading a lot," before turning back to her plastic animals. Her mother said that Ellen's distractibility and fidgeting were most evident at school; they rarely appeared when she was at home or in other settings, including family outings or playdates with friends. In general, Ellen had a healthy social life, with several friends in her neighborhood and school. "She really gets along with everyone," her mother said.

There was no evidence of the girl's attention-related or behavioral symptoms during our initial session. But the troublesome behavior in school had increased over past months, to the point that Ellen's mother had asked a pediatrician friend about the symptoms. The doctor had suggested the girl might have ADHD and could possibly benefit from stimulant medication. But Ellen's parents decided to seek my opinion before starting down that path.

While the first session revealed no immediate explanations for Ellen's symptoms, it was likely the girl would be diagnosed with ADHD and given stimulant medication if her symptoms worsened. "We really don't want that for her," her mother said at our session's end.

## CLUES TO LOOK FOR

When Ellen and her mother first came to see me, it wasn't clear that the girl's distractibility and fidgeting were beyond what might be expected for a healthy child her age. At the same time, it was important to rule out medical explanations for what her parents and teacher had observed. Her vision and hearing tested as normal; comprehensive physical and neurological exams turned up no explanations, either. A full history revealed no evidence of mood disorder symptoms, obsessive-compulsive disorder, or other conditions with strong attention-deficit/hyperactivity components.

However, based on the pattern Ellen's mother and teacher had mentioned—that her symptoms were more likely to appear during reading periods—I had a hunch. In a follow-up session I asked Ellen to read a passage from a children's book to me again. As expected, she read it flawlessly, pronouncing each word correctly and showing clear understanding of punctuation. But this time I asked her specific questions about what she had read. When Ellen was unable to answer any of my questions well, I knew I was on to something.

To be sure, I referred the girl to a psychologist colleague for full psychological and educational testing. The results confirmed my suspicions: Ellen had early signs of a learning disability—specifically, dyslexia of understanding. While she could recognize and read words perfectly (that is, she demonstrated good "fluency," as discussed in the next section), she struggled to comprehend what she was reading at the sentence and paragraph level. That poor comprehension, in turn, was leading to Ellen's poor focus, distractibility, and minor behavioral problems during reading periods at school.

Dyslexia of understanding is a common learning disability that may improve with customized treatment, as discussed in the next sections.

> **Main Clue**
>
> Learning disabilities, especially those related to comprehension, can be difficult to diagnose without careful observation and testing. Attention-deficit symptoms related to specific settings (for example, school), subjects (for example, math), or activities (for example, reading) may point to a learning disability that may be confirmed by comprehensive psycho-educational evaluation.

## WHAT ARE LEARNING DISABILITIES?

"Learning disability" has become a household term in the United States. But many people remain unfamiliar with the specific categories that learning disorders fall into, along with what symptoms these involve and how they may be treated. According to the fifth edition of the *Diagnostic and Statistical Manual of Mental Disorders*, learning disabilities (or "specific learning disorders," as the *DSM-V* refers to them, or "LD" as they are referred to by many educators and much of the public) are part of a category of conditions usually first diagnosed in childhood or adolescence. As mentioned in earlier chapters, the *DSM-V* should be considered a work in progress, and one best viewed as providing a good set of general diagnostic guidelines, rather than final word on mental disorders. According to the *DSM-V*, learning disabilities are diagnosed "when there are specific deficits in an individual's ability to perceive or process information efficiently and accurately."[1] *DSM-V* criteria for diagnosis of a specific learning disorder include the presence of at least one of the following symptoms for six months or more:[2]

- Inaccurate or slow and effortful reading
- Difficulty understanding the meaning of written text (even if the individual can read the text accurately)
- Spelling difficulties
- Difficulty with written expression
- Significant challenges mastering "number sense," number facts, or calculation
- Problems with mathematical reasoning

The *DSM* states that the academic skills in question must be significantly below those expected for the individual's age on quantifiable measures and must interfere with academic or occupational functioning. There should be a clear deficit that's not explained easily by any other condition. Moreover, LDs should be distinguished from achievement deficits based on poor teaching, cultural factors (for example, poor test performance due to unfamiliarity with the culture the test is based on), and poor vision and hearing; if vision or hearing is an issue, the learning-related symptoms should be worse than those would suggest.

The *DSM-V* describes three specific learning disorders:

- *Specific Learning Disorder with Impairment in Reading*: Problems with reading accuracy, comprehension, or speed.
- *Specific Learning Disorder with Impairment in Written*

*Expression*: Difficulties with spelling and punctuation, sentence construction, paragraph organization, and general clarity of written expression.

- *Specific Learning Disorder with Impairment in Mathematics*: Deficits in calculation (for example, arithmetic, percentages), recognition, naming of mathematical terms and symbols, and math-related reasoning.

Other categorizations of LDs use somewhat different labels to describe the disabilities above.[3] Dyslexia, similar to the *DSM-V*'s reading-related specific learning disorder and recognized as an alternate term by that book, is a language-processing disorder that disrupts reading, writing, and, potentially, speaking. As noted earlier, though many think of dyslexia only as seeing letters backward or out of place—due in part to widespread media coverage of the condition—it can involve multiple symptoms including difficulty recognizing written words (including seeing letters backward), challenges understanding the meaning of written words, and even difficulty with rhyming. Dyslexia of *fluency* means difficulty with the accuracy and speed of reading. Those suffering from dyslexia of *understanding* can read at a normal pace, with accuracy, but they fail to comprehend what they read sufficiently.

Dysgraphia (like the *DSM*'s writing-related learning disorder) has to do with the *production* of written words, and involves problems with spelling, handwriting, and expression of oneself through writing. Dyscalculia (like the *DSM*'s math-related learning disorder and acknowledged as an alternative term by that source) involves *math-related* challenges.

However they are labeled, LDs tend to be accompanied by lower academic performance (for example, grades, standardized test scores) in the specific areas they affect (not surprisingly, as that's part of the definition), *frustration* related to the learning challenges, *boredom* and *distractibility* when confronted with a difficult task, and the behavioral symptoms (for example, classroom disruption) that tend to go with those latter symptoms. So it's no surprise that LDs often result in attention-deficit/hyperactivity symptoms that may be mistaken for ADHD.

As I had suspected, Ellen met early criteria for the *DSM*'s specific learning disorder with impairment in reading (specifically reading comprehension), or dyslexia of understanding. Her reading fluency (that is, speed and accuracy) was at or even above her age and grade level, but she struggled to comprehend what she read. As noted earlier, it was difficult to find evidence for the girl's disability, even for her parents and teacher. Because she was intelligent overall, Ellen had learned to compensate for her learning difficulty, including by asking her parents to help her understand what she was reading (for example, picture books) and by using cues from how her classmates reacted or spoke about what the class was reading to comprehend it or at least pretend to. Moreover, Ellen hadn't yet completed standardized testing at her school (it started in third grade), but the results of the psychological-educational evaluation she received showed that her reading comprehension lagged her other capabilities and overall IQ significantly.

## PREVALENCE OF LEARNING DISABILITIES

Many children and adults suffer from LDs. According to the *DSM-V*, overall estimates of the prevalence of learning disorders range from 5 percent to 15 percent among school-age children across cultures and about 4 percent for adults.[4] According to the National Center for Learning Disabilities, about three million U.S. children qualify for a learning disability, a figure toward the lower end of the range suggested by the *DSM-V*.[5] The *DSM* says that the ratio of LD diagnosis in males to females ranges from about 2:1 to 3:1, meaning that males may represent as much as 75 percent of those diagnosed. While growing awareness of LDs has helped promote earlier diagnosis and treatment (as discussed here later), many people with an LD will face lifelong issues related to it (but most will still be able to function well across settings).[6]

There are several risk factors for LDs, including genetic, physiological, and environmental types. Among these are family history (as suggested by the *DSM-V*), a long childhood illness (for example, rheumatic fever), significant prenatal drug or alcohol use by mothers, exposure to lead or other toxic elements, and abuse or neglect. One academic study linked low birth weight, low level of mother's education, and tobacco use by the mother to increased rates of LD in children.[7] In Ellen's case, there were no significant risk factors uncovered, but it is possible that others in her extended family had an undetected LD of some type; many people function very well in school, work, and social settings despite having a diagnosable LD.

## RELATION TO ATTENTION-DEFICIT/HYPERACTIVITY SYMPTOMS

LDs and the disorder called ADHD tend to be diagnosed together. A 2008 study by the Centers for Disease Control and Prevention involving twenty-three thousand U.S. children between the ages of six and seventeen found that 4 percent of the sample met criteria for both disorders.[8] According to the Learning Disabilities Association of America, up to 30 percent of children diagnosed with ADHD may also be diagnosed with a specific LD.[9] This association is one I've observed frequently in my own practice, and it's not a surprising link. As was the case for Ellen, when activated, LD symptoms can lead quite naturally to those considered part of ADHD. In her case, she was able to pay attention and avoid disrupting the classroom when engaged in subjects (for example, math, writing) in which she had no trouble or was even ahead of her peers. Yet when she had to read for comprehension, she struggled and often gave up. Her boredom and frustration appeared to the teacher as poor attention and concentration, rather than specific difficulty with reading. Moreover, when Ellen disturbed her classmates during reading exercises (it's difficult for many healthy seven-year-olds to sit still, even when they don't suffer LD symptoms), her teacher saw the behavior as distractibility and hyperactivity, again consistent with ADHD. So it's no surprise that many cases of LD are misdiagnosed as ADHD, especially when no one has taken the time to note specific symptoms patterns (for example, the attention-deficit/hyperactivity symptoms are only present in certain settings or in relation to specific activities).

It is possible that learning-related symptoms and those typically associated with ADHD are based in similar biological processes. For example, one study argues that learning and attention-deficit symptoms can result from neurologically based "encoding processes," including working memory.[10] In some sense, what matters more than the specific biological foundations of disorders or symptoms is how they may be treated and managed best.

## TREATMENT FOR LEARNING DISABILITIES

Learning disabilities are best treated early, often, and with care. Psychologist and education expert Robert Sternberg argues that early intervention can even reduce the number of children who may be diagnosed with an LD.[11] So what kinds of interventions may be effective for LDs?

Not surprisingly, most treatments of LD in children involve some form of specialized teaching or tutoring, often as part of a school-based individualized education plan (IEP).[12] After thorough testing to determine the child's specific needs, teachers, tutors, and teacher's aides can provide customized education focused on improving subject-specific skills through both content and teaching technique. Given the specificity of symptoms to learning, there is less emphasis on using medication and psychotherapy for LDs, but these may be considered if other conditions (for example, mood symptoms) are present, as those may exacerbate the LD.

Specific LDs benefit from tailored treatments. For example, dyslexia of fluency may be approached with methods that include teaching phonics and guided oral reading (students read out loud while receiving frequent feedback and guidance). Treatment for dyslexia of understanding may involve exercises to help children monitor and process their comprehension of written text more carefully, along with training them to create mental images, question the content, forge connections, and determine importance.[13] Individuals with writing-related learning disorder may benefit from hand-strengthening exercises, step-by-step instructions for letter writing (for example, sequence of lines and strokes), and practice with spelling and sentence and paragraph planning.[14] For math-related learning disorder, multisensory treatments (for example, "touch math," where students tap a pencil against numbers while making calculations), math games, and practice with visualization may improve their math skills. Software-based approaches have also been created for all three forms of LD.

No matter the form of LD, it is important for parents, teachers, and tutors to focus on strengths as well as weaknesses, along with providing as much encouragement as possible. Students with LDs tend to lose confidence in their abilities—in both the diagnosed area and others—so helping them maintain a positive, capable attitude is as important as any specific educational intervention.

More specifically, focusing on enhancing a particular strength makes working on weaknesses easier for the child and family.

After Ellen's parents and I discussed the results of her testing, her parents shared evidence for the diagnosis with the school and secured an IEP for their daughter. For one hour daily, Ellen worked with a teacher's aide who had specialized training in dyslexia interventions. The aide used many of the techniques described earlier, including helping Ellen monitor comprehension, use mental images to increase her understanding, and test learning by asking herself questions after every few pages of reading. At home, Ellen's parents used similar techniques, along with encouraging the girl to explore a wide range of books. "We want to help you find books you'll really like to read," they told her.

As Ellen's comprehension and confidence improved, she became more interested in reading, and more willing to try to answer reading-related questions in class. She found a series of early-reading books about fairies, which became her favorite, and her parents bought her one book a week if she practiced reading daily. "She concentrates really well during reading now," Ellen's teacher told her mother two months into the IEP; the teacher also pointed out that the girl's comprehension was improving, and that she no longer disrupted her classmates during reading.

While reading comprehension may never have become as easy as math or other subjects for Ellen, it was clear that she was quickly gaining mastery over an area that just a few months earlier no one even knew she was struggling with.

# CHAPTER 11

# Sensory Processing Disorder

## The Big Point

Sensory processing disorder (also known as sensory integration disorder), most commonly found in children, occurs when individuals have trouble integrating and responding to information from different senses, resulting in discomfort with multiple stimuli (like loud noises), attention deficits, poor coordination, and general difficulty with daily activities. Several of these symptoms can be misperceived as signs of ADHD, resulting in the wrong diagnosis and treatment.

Most of us take our five senses for granted, using them daily to interact with the world. But for a small minority of people, handling sensory input represents a constant challenge, one marked by extreme discomfort with certain stimuli (for example, loud noises), poor muscle coordination, and difficulty with social interactions, among others. These symptoms, which usually start in childhood, are part of a diagnosis of sensory processing disorder, in which the nervous system struggles to integrate input from the senses, creating chronic problems for patients, including secondary symptoms like depression and anxiety. By its very nature, sensory processing disorder results in attention deficits, and patients with the diagnosis sometimes show a tendency toward seeking excessive stimulation, resulting in hyperactivity. Attention deficits and hyperactivity can lead to a diagnosis of ADHD, along with the wrong treatment approach. My patient Julianne and her family were facing this problem when they came to my office.

## UNCOMFORTABLE IN HER OWN SKIN

Julianne literally couldn't sit still from her first moment in my office. The twelve-year-old had arrived with her mother; both of them looked exhausted. As Julianne, a blond girl with darting green eyes, wriggled in her chair and complained about the temperature in the room, her mother told me more. "I've lost count of all the doctors she's seen," she said. "The consensus seems to be that she has ADD." In line with that diagnosis, Julianne had been placed on multiple stimulant medications, but none had improved her symptoms, only disrupting her sleep and appetite.

The girl had no shortage of symptoms. Her mother said, "She can't seem to pay attention or focus herself—it happens at school and at home." By now Julianne had risen from her chair and was looking out the window. "I bet it's more comfortable out there," she said. "Can I go outside while you talk?" Her mother reported that she showed significant hyperactivity, sometimes going into "overdrive," pacing around the house and asking lots of questions. Her seventh-grade teachers reported that she did this at school occasionally as well, and that the behavior was disruptive for other students. When I asked Julianne if she enjoyed school, she shrugged.

Later, when I talked to her mother alone, she said that Julianne was "miserable" at school because she didn't feel like she fit in with anyone else: "She's not part of any specific group." Her mother mentioned that when she saw Julianne interact with peers, she seemed very uncomfortable, either standing quietly while others talked or saying things that failed to engage them. Moreover, Julianne's academic performance, which had never been strong, was declining. Her mother also felt that Julianne was "depressed," and that she sometimes showed this by withdrawing from her family (including her younger brother); at other times she acted irritably or lashed out at them for no reason.

Julianne's troubles had begun very early in life. "She was always a 'floppy' baby, and we had to be very careful holding her or she would slip out and fall," her mother said. As a toddler, the girl had cried much more than average, and reacted to moderately loud noises (such as TV commercials) by screaming and holding her ears, something that still happened sometimes. Starting in childhood, Julianne hadn't been able to tolerate the feel of certain fabrics (for example, nylon) on her skin, and had asked to have all labels removed from her clothes because they itched. She was similarly particular about what she ate. "About the only foods she eats now are apples, but only the green ones, and mild cheddar cheese, and peanut butter," her mother said. "I have to plead with her to try anything else, and we've pretty much stopped going out to restaurants." She added that the girl complained about "everything."

Julianne had also struggled with physical coordination for most of her life. Unlike her peers, she had never learned to ride a bike or a push scooter, despite repeated efforts, and still had trouble tying her shoes tightly. The girl had played soccer when she was younger—"She tried at first but got really frustrated," her mother said—and stopped playing sports altogether when she was nine. Her mother said, "It's like she doesn't understand how to move her body."

Near the end of the session Julianne's mother said, "She's just never been comfortable in her own skin, and I'm beginning to wonder if she ever will be." I told her I'd do my best to understand Julianne's condition and suggest the most promising treatment for it.

## CLUES TO LOOK FOR

I ran multiple tests with Julianne to examine potential explanations for her symptoms, including a full history and physical, vision and hearing tests, neurological exams, and tests for academic aptitude. Her physical and vision and hearing tests came back as normal. Her neurological exams revealed trouble with both gross-motor (for example, riding a bike) and fine-motor (for example, picking up small objects) skills, placing her at the low end of normal functioning for her age. Julianne's academic aptitude was lower than normal, but she did not meet criteria for any learning disorders. Similarly, while the girl came close to meeting criteria for clinical depression based on symptoms including low energy and a poor sense of self-worth, it seemed likely that her mood symptoms resulted mainly from her difficulties in other areas, rather than representing a separate disorder.

Because none of the standard tests revealed a specific condition that could explain Julianne's symptoms, I considered the "big picture" of her case more closely, with a good hypothesis in mind. The theme of the girl's symptoms was a difficulty integrating sensory information—whether about academics, body movements, emotions, or even the way her clothes felt—in a way that prevented her from functioning in multiple areas. Based on this observation I referred Julianne for deeper neurological testing that could explore her symptoms through more formal tests, including those related to sensory integration.

The neurological testing was consistent with a diagnosis of

sensory processing disorder, a condition in which one's nervous system fails to integrate signals adequately, yielding the types of symptoms that my patient was experiencing.

## Main Clue

Sensory processing disorder can be diagnosed when an individual has symptoms in multiple areas that involve challenges integrating sensory information and responding to it appropriately, whether in school, at home, in social situations, or at work. One clue to sensory processing disorder—other than the absence of other conditions that can explain the symptoms—is the wide number of settings in which the person has trouble: school, home, social interactions, and others. The primary symptoms can result in secondary symptoms including depression and anxiety. The sensory processing disorder diagnosis may be confirmed through a combination of the patient's history, observation of the patient, and formal neurological testing.

## WHAT IS SENSORY PROCESSING DISORDER?

Sensory processing disorder (SPD), formerly known as sensory integration disorder, involves difficulty integrating and organizing multiple types of signals (for example, environmental, physical, emotional, social) to develop the most appropriate response in a range of everyday situations—from eating, to playing a sport, to reading a book.[1] The Sensory Processing Disorder Foundation notes how SPD can be thought of as a "neurological traffic jam" that prevents the proper interpretation of and reaction to sensory information.[2] That problem results in clumsiness, academic struggles, and behavioral (for example, disruptiveness in school) and social difficulties. It can also drive discomfort and overreactions associated with any number of sensations: light, sound, physical contact, temperature, certain foods, and clothing, among others.

Not surprisingly, this wide range of challenges has the potential to bring on other conditions such as anxiety and depression, which may further exacerbate the symptoms of distractibility and impulsivity.

While most people experience occasional problems with sensory processing (for example, sensitivity to bright light), those with SPD have chronic and often more severe symptoms of this type. Some people diagnosable with SPD may have difficulties related to just one of the five senses, such as challenges related to touch (for example, overreacting to clothing and physical contact, having trouble with games that involve handling a ball). Others will experience problems related to multiple senses. Some cases of SPD involve a tendency to *seek* stimulation, rather than avoid it, as we will see.

Problems related to SPD tend to appear early in life. Many children diagnosed with SPD were floppy babies with poor muscle tone. The clumsiness associated with the disorder is usually easy to see, and can result in children being teased for dropping things repeatedly, bumping into others, or displaying poor athletic skills (for example, trying to kick a ball and missing it).

Diagnosis of SPD is usually carried out by understanding the patient's symptom history, along with observation and formal tests. As mentioned earlier, Julianne's mother described a long history of sensory problems. I observed several of these in my office, as well. Formal tests of SPD include the Sensory Integration and Praxis Tests (a battery of motor, visual, tactile, and other assessments for children four to eight years). Formal (for example, Short Sensory Profile) and informal assessments completed by parents and teachers can also be useful for diagnosis.

Julianne was a "textbook" case of SPD, displaying many of the symptoms described above, with problems in multiple sensory domains. She had been a floppy baby who overreacted to sounds.

Later she developed strong sensitivity to the feel of her clothing and to temperature (as demonstrated in my office), along with becoming an extremely picky eater unwilling to try anything new. She had always struggled with sports, and even as a twelve-year-old had difficulty riding a bike and tying her shoes. Julianne also faced increasing challenges with academic tasks, and couldn't find her place in middle school social circles. Not surprisingly, the girl's combination of problems had resulted in multiple symptoms of depression, including low energy and feelings of worthlessness.

## PREVALENCE OF SENSORY PROCESSING DISORDER

SPD is most commonly diagnosed in children. However, it can also be diagnosed in adults, especially those who had only specific or mild symptoms and thus failed to receive treatment as children or were misdiagnosed; for such individuals, SPD could be the underlying cause of attention-deficit/hyperactivity. A 2004 study based on parental reports of sensory symptoms estimated that SPD occurs in 5.3 percent of kindergarten-age children.[3] But other studies have shown much higher rates of "sensory over-responsivity" (that is, overreacting to specific sensory stimuli such as light or the feel of clothing) among school-age children, with these symptoms significant enough to affect their daily lives.[4]

As far as the disorder's course, children with SPD tend to have trouble in multiple sensory, cognitive, and behavioral areas (see the list presented earlier), along with secondary symptoms such as depression and anxiety. Adults who never received treatment for SPD continue to struggle with a wide range of symptoms, leading to a general picture of underachievement at school and work, dissatisfaction, loneliness, and related problems. While there is no "cure" for SPD, different intervention approaches can result in significant improvement of symptoms and, in turn, quality of life.

## RELATION TO ATTENTION-DEFICIT/HYPERACTIVITY SYMPTOMS

By definition, SPD will be associated with attention-deficit challenges, given that those diagnosed with SPD have trouble integrating and reacting to multiple types of information. For example, a child faced with difficulty integrating her teacher's words with related visual information (for example, figures on a chalkboard or digital screen) presented will likely appear unfocused and inattentive. The same would be true for an adult SPD patient trying to integrate multiple types of information (for example, meeting notes and follow-up conversations) related to their job. Moreover, according to the SPD Foundation, some children with SPD can "exhibit an appetite for sensation that is in perpetual overdrive," meaning that they appear impulsive and hyperactive, as my patient Julianne sometimes did.[5]

Given their tendency to display attention-deficit/hyperactivity symptoms, then, people with SPD are often misdiagnosed with the disorder ADHD—and mistakenly treated for it. This has been pointed out by multiple SPD advocacy groups.[6] The potential to confuse SPD with ADHD is so great that a 2007 *Time* magazine article about SPD was titled "The Next Attention Deficit Disorder?"[7] Another article refers to SPD and ADHD as "lookalikes," while cautioning that they are not the same, and require very different treatments.[8] While it is difficult to gauge the exact overlap (or percentage of those with SPD also diagnosed with ADHD), the link between the two is well documented in academic studies as well.[9]

There are, not surprisingly, multiple problems related to misdiagnosing SPD as ADHD. Chief among these is the delay of proper treatment. *Treatment delayed is treatment denied.* What's more, a mistaken diagnosis results in significant stress for the patient and their families, as they may come to believe they have an "incurable" case of ADHD. Accurate diagnosis should lead to the development of an appropriate treatment plan.

## TREATMENT FOR SENSORY PROCESSING DISORDER

While there is no specific cure for SPD, multiple interventions can improve patients' symptoms and quality of life. The primary form of treatment is part of the general approach known as occupational therapy, or helping patients improve their ability to carry out activities of daily living—allowing them to "engage in occupations of life."[10] A specific form of occupational therapy, called sensory integration therapy, has been designed to help children experience and respond to sensory input more effectively. Therapists work closely with children—often in special rooms designed for this kind of therapy—to help them develop strategies for specific challenges (for example, schoolwork, social interactions). The treatment places emphasis on developing "adaptive responses" within a fun setting (including the use of rewards) that makes children more willing to engage. Over time, the approach can help children develop higher tolerance for physical sensations and better responses to multiple kinds of environmental inputs.

As part of or in addition to sensory integration therapy, parents and teachers can learn strategies for dealing with SPD symptoms in children. For example, parents may be asked to participate in some of the sensory integration therapy sessions, and information may be sent to teachers regarding SPD. The goals include raising awareness of the types of environmental stimuli that result in overreactions (for example, loud noises, fluorescent lighting) and helping adults develop strategies for anticipating and managing the child's symptoms (for example, avoiding having them attend events with loud noises, such as loud school assemblies or fireworks shows).

Support groups can also be useful for managing SPD. These include in-person and online groups. Their value is manifold: Participants feel they are not alone in dealing with the disorder, while learning new strategies for handling the symptoms and receiving deep support from others who understand their situation firsthand.

Taking my advice, Julianne and her family explored multiple treatment options, starting with sensory integration therapy. Working with an occupational therapist, the girl learned to react more appropriately to a range of sensory stimuli, from uncomfortable clothes to stuffy rooms. The therapist helped Julianne and her parents understand that her discomfort was often temporary, and that she would "have more choices" if she learned to tolerate some things that she'd been reluctant to. "She doesn't make me cut the tags off her clothes anymore," Julianne's mother reported happily after several months. The girl also made progress in other areas, including eating. With a homework assignment of trying at least one new food a week, Julianne discovered that she liked pears and cottage cheese, and became more willing to try new foods in restaurants. Her parents attended some of the therapy sessions, where they learned more about Julianne's condition and strategies for addressing it at home and elsewhere.

With greater ability to handle sensory stimulation, Julianne also started doing better in school, with her academic performance rising to an average level within one year of starting the therapy. Her improved focus also helped her stop disrupting her classes by pacing and asking too many questions. "It's like her motor has switched from fast to normal," her mother said. Importantly, Julianne had stopped taking stimulant medication. According to her mother, the girl was sleeping "better than ever" and seemed much happier than before.

In other areas it was more difficult for Julianne to make

progress. She was still sensitive to loud sounds, though she was willing to be exposed to them as part of her therapy. The most challenging area was social interactions. Though Julianne's functioning had improved in general, she was still very reluctant to approach other children, given her historical difficulty with social situations (on top of the general social challenges most middle school students face). After a few failed attempts, she had given up. I helped the girl and her family place their disappointment about this in the context of all the progress she had made in other areas, and encouraged them to keep trying. I also suggested they look into local SPD support groups.

Two months later, Julianne and her mother came to my office to report significant improvements. They had started attending a local support group, meeting several families dealing with SPD. Among the other patients there was a girl Julianne's age who attended another school in the area. The two hit it off soon after meeting, and had already spent significant time outside the group together, including going to movies (but none with loud special effects!) and the mall. "It's like she understands everything I'm going through," Julianne said. I was pleased to see how comfortable the girl appeared in my office, sitting peacefully in her chair, never complaining about the temperature.

"She's finally comfortable in her own skin," her mother said. I couldn't have agreed more.

# CHAPTER 12

# Giftedness

## The Big Point

Gifted individuals are those with exceptional aptitude in one or more areas. Their levels of talent sometimes make it easy for them to become bored and inattentive, which may in turn lead to disruptive behavior, especially in children. These attention-deficit/hyperactivity symptoms may be misdiagnosed as ADHD, which prevents the individual in question from receiving what they really need: more engaging and challenging activities.

The word "gifted" may evoke images of pocket protectors and complicated molecular models. In reality, gifted individuals may excel in any number of areas, from math to ballet to fencing. In academic and other settings, gifted people sometimes find themselves bored with their experience, having mastered the material quickly or because they have little interest in it in the first place. Observers may see that boredom as a sign of poor attention. Moreover, gifted individuals sometimes act impulsively, whether blurting out "too easy" answers, sharing their opinions without waiting their turn, or whispering to classmates because they are bored. These behaviors may be viewed as consistent with a diagnosis of the disorder called ADHD, which too often leads to the wrong approach. My patient Bhavik faced this situation at an early age.

## ALWAYS-BORED BHAVIK

Third grader Bhavik's parents had come from India to the United States as visiting science professors at a large, prestigious Chicago-area university. When they brought their son in to see me, they had been in the United States for a year, and had another year to go before returning to their home country. "We're wondering if we made a mistake by coming to America," Bhavik's mother told me. She explained that Bhavik, an active nine-year-old, had been causing trouble at school, including not paying attention to the teacher and talking to his classmates during quiet times. Increasingly, he had been rising from his seat to get a book or to examine something (for example, a spelling word list) in the classroom more closely, often disrupting the class. (Bhavik also asked multiple questions about the charts in my office.) In a parent-teacher conference, his teacher suggested he should be tested for ADHD, which had prompted his mother to bring him in.

When I asked Bhavik about school, he said he "always felt bored," even though he liked his classmates and had fun at lunch and recess. He added, "I don't like just sitting all the time." Regarding his academic performance, his mother told me, "He is very smart, and his teacher says this too." She said that Bhavik was already doing math above a sixth-grade level, and that he was among the top performers in reading and writing, too; the boy had been learning English at his school in India since kindergarten, so the language part of the transition to the United States had been easy for him. When I asked about Bhavik's schooling in India, his mother said that the education system there was much more "rigorous," with even kindergartners taking full exams regularly. "They are at least two years ahead of the U.S. for what they learn in math," she said. Even within this system, Bhavik was one of the best students in his large class. I asked him several challenging multiplication problems (for example, 30 times 25) and he answered quickly and correctly. Moreover, his mother explained that Indian classrooms were much more structured and discipline-oriented than what she had observed in the United States: Students were punished harshly for misbehaving. Not surprisingly, Bhavik had rarely caused disruptions in his Indian school. "We think we should move him to fourth or even fifth grade," his mother said.

Outside of school, Bhavik's behavior was not a problem. "He asks a lot of questions," his mother said, "but he's very nice and even helps his younger sister with her homework." She had noted no significant attention problems at home, beyond those in the normal range for a boy his age. Bhavik had made several neighborhood friends who also attended his school, and he played with them regularly after school and on weekends, getting along with them well. His parents had also enrolled him in local private math classes, where he was already excelling at basic algebra. "I've talked to him about behaving better in school," his mother said, "and he says he understands, but then I get more notes about his disruptions from the teacher." She added that she had heard of ADHD even in India, but still didn't understand whether it applied to her son. I assured her I would help them figure out the best next steps.

## CLUES TO LOOK FOR

The explanation for Bhavik's behavior was clear even from his initial visit to my office: As a talented student from a more rigorous educational system, he was bored in his new school, and his disruptive behavior resulted directly from his boredom. To be safe, I ran basic tests with the boy and secured a full medical history, but, as I suspected, there were no other explanations for his symptoms. Further discussion with his parents helped me link his academic aptitude to his attention-deficit/hyperactivity symptoms. For example, I asked them to talk to his teacher about any patterns she'd noticed with his disruptive behavior, and she reported that the behavior was related closely to how bored he was by the subject matter, due to his advanced aptitude: He was most likely to act out during math classwork, a bit less so in reading and writing, and rarely in music and art. Other clues included Bhavik's good attention levels in his Indian school (based on a combination of more challenging material and stricter discipline) and at home.

Around the same time they came to see me, Bhavik's parents had taken him for intelligence testing. Not surprisingly, he tested in the "Very Superior" range, a category occupied only by about 2 percent of all children assessed (see the next section for more details on intelligence testing). He was considered "gifted." But what may have been a gift in terms of aptitude was counteracted by his behavior in school, as suggested by the boy's teacher.

### Main Clue

Academically gifted children often react to understimulation with attention-deficit/hyperactivity symptoms. Beyond their high observed or measured intelligence, a major clue to giftedness is that the child becomes bored and acts out only in specific classes (that is, for which he or she has greater aptitude). Similarly, behavioral difficulties for gifted children are often observed only in school, and not at home or in other settings. Giftedness can be confirmed by formal aptitude testing.

## WHAT IS GIFTEDNESS?

Generally speaking, a gifted person is one who displays superior intelligence and/or capabilities in one or more areas. Although, defining giftedness is not as easy as you may think. One of the challenges is that a given child or adult can have exceptional talent in any number of areas. Consider this definition from the National Association for Gifted Children (NAGC):

> Gifted individuals are those who demonstrate outstanding levels of aptitude (defined as an exceptional ability to reason and learn) or competence (documented performance or achievement in top 10% or rarer) in one or more domains. Domains include any structured area of activity with its own symbol system (e.g., mathematics, music, language) and/or set of sensorimotor skills (e.g., painting, dance, sports).[1]

By that definition, giftedness includes abilities within and outside the classroom. The NAGC presents other definitions of giftedness, including the idea that the condition is based on "asynchronous development in which advanced cognitive abilities and heightened intensity combine to create inner experiences and awareness that are qualitatively different from the norm," and the concept that giftedness stems from an "interaction among three basic clusters of human traits: above-average general and/or specific abilities, high levels of task commitment (motivation), and high levels of creativity."[2] The general definition of giftedness, then, emphasizes aptitude in at least one domain that is at a higher level or develops more quickly than that of one's peers; while the last definition presented above emphasizes commitment and motivation, my belief is that one need not be motivated to be considered gifted—that's where the term "underachiever" often applies.

For our purposes, we can consider giftedness mainly in terms of *academic* abilities (for example, math, reading, science), since that form is the easiest to measure through standardized tests and very likely to result in attention-deficit/hyperactivity symptoms in the classroom. But you can see how any type of giftedness may result in challenges related to attention and impulsivity. For example, a highly gifted teenage dancer may be unwilling to pay attention to academic subjects like math and find it hard to keep from moving in situations that require long periods of sitting in the classroom, due to his overwhelming passion for and focus on dance.

Beyond the definition of giftedness, there is disagreement about what percentage of the population falls into this category in a given area, along with how to measure giftedness in the first place. As noted earlier, the NGAC requires performance or achievement in at least the top 10 percent. Mensa, the international organization for individuals with a high IQ, requires performance in the top 2 percent on a standardized intelligence test (for example, SAT, LSAT, MCAT, GMAT).[3] Well-known IQ tests include the Stanford-Binet and Wechsler scales, but each test may result in a different score for the same individual. Perhaps most importantly, there is significant controversy about how to measure giftedness, as pointed out by an intelligence researcher who uses two examples as illustration: 1) a ten-year-old boy with an IQ of 140 (top 1–2 percent) with few friends or extracurricular activities and only average academic performance; 2) a ten-year-old boy with an IQ of 120 (top 10 percent) who is one of the most popular students in class, consistently displays high academic performance, and excels in activities including soccer and trombone-playing.[4] Which of these is a "gifted" child—the boy with the IQ of 140, the boy with the IQ of 120, or both? While these are very interesting questions, for our purposes we can consider giftedness as an explanation for misdiagnosis of ADHD when there are no other conditions driving the attention-deficit/hyperactivity symptoms and the person in question has displayed significant talent in one or more areas.

As the examples above suggest, even individuals who test in the gifted range may never display extraordinary performance in the area or areas in question. They may go their entire lives performing at an average or even below-average level, depending on their motivation and multiple other factors (for example, economic resources, social support). Again, for our purposes what matters most is whether their giftedness results in attention-deficit/hyperactivity symptoms that may be misdiagnosed as ADHD. Giftedness tends to run in families, and it is generally a lifelong trait, though whether and how it is expressed will differ by context and over time. Moreover, gifted adults may display similar traits as gifted children, which is of course what they once were. A gifted professional may be impatient with his or her peers or take on too many responsibilities, resulting in poor attention and concentration, distractibility, and other traits that may be misdiagnosed as ADHD.

Bhavik's giftedness was clearly expressed in his performance in multiple areas, especially mathematics, where he was several grade levels ahead of his peers. As a result, he was perpetually bored in the classroom (viewed mistakenly as an attention deficit) and sometimes acted disruptively. Bhavik's intelligence and academic prowess were no surprise, given that his parents were both high-performing academic professionals who had earned visiting professorships at a prominent U.S. university. The combination of genetic predisposition, economic resources, and parental support contributed to Bhavik's giftedness, which in turn resulted in attention-deficit/hyperactivity symptoms in the classroom.

## RELATION TO ATTENTION-DEFICIT/HYPERACTIVITY SYMPTOMS

It may seem counterintuitive that "giftedness" could result in hindering symptoms. So how does this happen? There are a few explanations. As discussed, a higher level of capability in a given area, especially in school, can make a child bored and more likely to appear inattentive, distractible, or impulsive, as was the case with Bhavik. Alternatively, a gifted child might tend to blurt out answers or disrupt peers to see if they are reaching the right answers on an in-class assignment. Again, this can be mistaken for the impulsivity associated with what we know as ADHD.

Several researchers and observers have pointed out the ease with which behavioral consequences of giftedness may be misdiagnosed as ADHD.[5] One group draws links between giftedness-related traits and how these may be viewed as behavioral symptoms or problems (including those consistent with ADHD diagnostic criteria), as suggested by the table below:[6]

| TRAIT | POSSIBLE PROBLEM |
|---|---|
| Learns quickly | Impatient with slowness of others; dislikes drills and other routine academic exercises |
| Inquisitive, curious | Appears strong-willed and resists direction |
| Creative, inventive | May reject conventional plans or ideas |
| Highly energetic, dynamic | Dislikes periods of inactivity |

It's easy to see how the traits on the left could lead to the behaviors on the right, which could be viewed as attention-deficit/hyperactivity symptoms. Other researchers have pointed out the similarity between ADHD symptoms and creativity, which again indicates a strong link between the two.[7] My view is that giftedness, creativity, and generally increased capability in one or more domains can explain *fully* the ADHD symptoms observed, with important implications for "treatment." As with all the conditions described in this book, a misdiagnosis of ADHD can result in multiple costs for patients and their families.

## "TREATMENT" FOR GIFTEDNESS

Rather than "treatment," we need to think of the best way to approach a situation where an individual's giftedness interferes with his or her functioning in a given area or disrupts others. In my approach, the theme of intervention is to engage the gifted child or adult more fully by challenging them at an appropriate level, while keeping in mind that their giftedness may only apply to particular areas. Even before looking for ways to engage gifted individuals more fully comes the important step of *recognizing* giftedness. Parents, for example, can compare their child's performance even before they are school age to that of others, and attend carefully to teachers' and others' observations about the child's abilities. Even a stranger's compliments on the child's abilities can be an important clue. Of course, more formal testing can also serve as evidence of giftedness. It's important to bear in mind that many parents see their children as gifted, when they may not actually qualify for this status; objectivity is important in determining the best for your child.

Once a child has been identified as gifted, the challenge for parents, educators, and others dealing with them is to balance offering more stimulating experiences with not expecting too much of them across areas. For example, I almost never recommend having a child "skip" one or more grade levels, because while they may be able to handle the academic challenges of this move, they can rarely deal with the social issues associated with it. On average, they're just not mature enough to interact successfully with older peers, often resulting in their feeling frustrated and isolated. This is the problem of "asynchronous development," where the individual's cognitive development has outpaced their physical and social development, leaving them poorly equipped to handle issues beyond the classroom. The further challenge is that observers—including parents and educators—sometimes develop unrealistic expectations of gifted children: If the child can discuss complex political issues at age ten, why wouldn't they be able to interact successfully with thirteen-year-olds? The answer is that they're just not emotionally mature enough to do so. It involves a set of skills they haven't yet developed.

Based on this thinking, I recommend a targeted approach to better engage gifted individuals. In children, this usually means increasing the level of challenge for them in the specific areas where they display more talent. That may involve a combination of moving them into higher-level classes at school (but not allowing them to jump to a higher grade) and finding supplementary educational programs that provide an appropriate level of challenge. In extreme cases (for example, where the child's range or level of talent far exceeds available learning opportunities), it may be best to consider a special school (for example, music academy, math/science school), depending on the child's interests.

In Bhavik's case, I suggested to his parents that allowing him to move to a higher grade level wasn't a good idea: While he could have handled most of the academic tasks, he would have struggled to fit in socially and emotionally. Instead, we agreed to have him join the fifth-grade math class at his school, which took him out of his third-grade classroom for only an hour a day. Because his performance in other subjects (for example, reading), while strong, was still within his grade level, we opted not to make any changes in those areas. I also suggested that Bhavik's parents work with his teacher to develop a simple, short-term rating system she could use to let them know how well he was behaving in class; they could then chart his progress (or failure to progress) over time. We figured Bhavik would be interested in this approach, given his passion for numbers.

Within just weeks of making the changes, Bhavik's family reported dramatic improvement. "He really likes being in the fifth-grade math class," his mother said. She mentioned that while some of the fifth graders had teased Bhavik initially, they had quickly grown accustomed to having him in class and many of them complimented his intelligence and were friendly toward him. "He feels special because he knows more older schoolmates than his friends do," his mother said. The combination of greater academic challenge and sitting in a class of older peers had helped Bhavik attend more carefully to the material and avoid rising from his seat, though he admitted that he still occasionally felt bored, especially when the teacher covered concepts he already understood well. Moreover, he had been asked to join a math quiz team made up of fourth and fifth graders who competed against teams from area schools. He was already one of the team's star players, which made him and his parents proud. Bhavik was also continuing to make progress with his private math class, mastering more and more algebra concepts.

His behavior in class had also improved. The teacher's ratings showed that Bhavik was disrupting the class much less frequently—the behavior had been most challenging during the math period, and the boy was no longer present during that time. Bhavik continued to behave well at home and with his friends, as well. "I was hoping he did not have ADHD," his mother said, "and now I know he does not." It was clear that with their support Bhavik would continue to be an exceptional student, one who challenged himself in math and other subjects without disrupting those around him.

# CHAPTER 13

# Seizure Disorders

## The Big Point

Patients who suffer from specific types of hard-to-detect seizure disorders often exhibit short attention spans and distractibility (due to momentary losses of sensory input) that may be mistaken for ADHD symptoms. Comprehensive questioning can reveal the underlying seizure disorder, allowing for appropriate treatment.

The word "seizure" usually provokes images of someone writhing uncontrollably on the ground, gnashing their teeth, eyes rolled back in their head. In reality, seizure disorders take multiple forms, including those with much less obvious symptoms. In fact, one type of seizure condition involves no observable symptoms—except for those experienced by the person with the disorder. Individuals, especially children, with this condition are very likely to appear distractible, with short attention spans. These consequent symptoms may be mistaken as signs of ADHD, leading to inevitably off-target treatment with stimulants. I encountered this firsthand when I met Sara, a new child patient in my practice.

## WHEN THE TV GOES BLANK

Nine-year-old Sara had been on ever-increasing doses of stimulant medications for several months when her father brought her to my office. "I've seen no improvement with the drugs," her father said. "In fact, it seems like she's doing worse." On that first visit Sara looked and behaved like a normal child her age. She answered my questions appropriately—sometimes pausing before speaking, or asking me to repeat them—and, understandably, became bored near the session's end.

Her father had brought her in because her teacher had reported increasing distractibility, poor attention span, and some behavioral problems (for example, talking during in-class exercises). Her father said, "At home she behaves pretty well. Her mom and I do sometimes feel like she's not paying as much attention to us as she could, but that's probably true of most kids her age." He told me that he and Sara's mother were going through a divorce—including maintaining separate residences—and that he thought that might explain some of her behavior.

Sara said she liked school, in general, and her father said she was performing at an average to above-average level academically, despite her increasingly poor attention span. She also appeared to have a healthy social life, with friends at school and in her neighborhood. Sara's behavior in school had first become a problem several months earlier, prompting her mother to take her to their pediatrician. The doctor had suggested she was in "early stages of ADHD," and suggested trying stimulant medication. When Sara had shown no improvement, the doctor had increased her dosage, twice since she'd begun the medication. Still Sara showed no improvement—in fact her attention-deficit symptoms worsened, as her father pointed out—and she complained of increasingly severe headaches and an upset stomach, common side effects of stimulant treatment. "I want her to stop taking the drug," her father said, "but maybe there's still a chance it could work."

I told him we had to do more testing to rule out several possible conditions. While the first session revealed few clues, we were far from having a complete medical picture of Sara.

## CLUES TO LOOK FOR

Early testing—including the results of physical, neurological, and hearing and vision tests—revealed no clear explanations for Sara's symptoms.

A psychological exam also uncovered no evidence of a mood disorder or obsessive-compulsive disorder underlying the attention deficit and distractibility. Since Sara's academic performance was appropriate for her age and grade level, we were able to rule out a learning disability.

I finally made real progress in understanding Sara's symptoms during her third visit, when I asked her more about school, something she'd always described as "good." "Tell me more about your favorite subject," I said. Sara said she enjoyed arithmetic—and her father confirmed she enjoyed doing addition and subtraction at home—but that she sometimes had trouble "understanding" the teacher. When I asked what she meant by that, she said that occasionally she couldn't really "see or hear" the teacher, even if she felt like she was paying attention. That was a big clue, and I asked Sara if it seemed like she was watching real life (for example, at home or at school) on a TV screen that suddenly turned off for a little bit— "Like your whole world goes blank," I said. She nodded vigorously and said, "Yes, it's just like that. And I really don't like it." Further, when I asked Sara why she hadn't complained about her symptoms earlier, she said, "I thought everyone had the same thing."

Now I knew the best next step: I ordered an electroencephalogram (EEG) test for Sara, to identify any abnormalities in her brain's electrical activity. As expected, the EEG showed a clear pattern consistent with "absence" seizures, or brief (typically less than twenty seconds and often only one or two seconds in duration) periods of impaired consciousness, or the loss of sensory input. These "blank" periods seemed to account for Sara's attention-deficit and distractibility symptoms, and likely explained her behavioral problems as well.

Absence seizures represent a subset of seizure disorders. Most such conditions may be treated successfully with medication.

### Main Clue

While many seizure disorders have obvious external symptoms, absence seizures are harder to identify, especially in children, who may think that frequent, brief loss of sensory input is normal. Close questioning about patients' sensory experience across settings, along with EEG testing, can help confirm the presence of a seizure disorder that may underlie attention-deficit/hyperactivity symptoms.

## WHAT ARE SEIZURE DISORDERS?

Seizure disorders can take more forms than most people realize, ranging from those involving violent physical movements (for example, thrashing) to conditions marked by brief loss of sensory input without fainting, as Sara had experienced.

Seizure disorders vary widely with regard to symptoms and causes. The most commonly cited categorization of seizures was provided by the International League Against Epilepsy in 1981, with an update in 2010.[1] The main categories of seizures have to do with where the seizure originates in the brain: general (or those involving a larger portion of the brain—for example, both hemispheres) or focal (those originating in a more localized brain region—for example, one hemisphere). One-time seizures may be caused by factors including:

- High fever
- Low blood sugar (for example, in diabetes)
- Stroke
- Infection
- Withdrawal from drugs or alcohol
- Head injury

Epilepsy is the name given to a varying set of neurological disorders or patterns that result in recurrent seizures.

A description by the University of Southern California's medical center summarizes well the physiological process underlying seizures:

A seizure is sometimes described as an electrical storm in the brain leading to abnormal movements, sensations, and states of consciousness. In reality, however, it is more orderly than a storm. During a seizure, nerves function in an abnormally synchronized manner, a kind of lockstep that can continue for seconds or minutes.[2]

Thus all forms of seizures involve the presence of abnormal brain signals, which disrupt the body's functioning. Exactly how that disruption takes place varies by type of seizure and person. For example, one person's seizure may involve only very mild shakiness in one hand, with no loss of consciousness, while another's might include violent shaking of the whole body, and loss of consciousness.[3] A temporal-lobe-based seizure can result in sudden violence (for example, punching someone) or emotion (for example, rage). Moreover, some people suffering from recurrent seizures experience "auras," or symptoms that precede the seizure, such as seeing spots or smelling strange odors.[4] Our main focus here will be seizure disorders—versus one-time seizures—with limited external symptoms, as these are most likely to go undiagnosed and result in further symptoms that may be mistaken for ADHD.

Absence seizures (formerly known as petit mal seizures), for example, represent a general form of seizure, based on the classification system described above. They typically involve loss of sensory function without fainting, such that the person suffering the seizure may appear to be staring into space or deep in thought. They appear awake but will fail to respond when someone calls their name or even taps them on the shoulder. They typically won't remember the period of blankness.

Sara's symptoms and EEG results were consistent with absence seizures. She was frequently losing her sensory functions—seeing and hearing, most notably—for several seconds at a time. That meant that while she looked as if she were conscious, she was unable to process anything she was seeing or hearing, including what her teacher or parents were saying. Moreover, once she lost track of what was happening around her, it was easy for Sara to become distractible—through no fault of her own—and even to disrupt her classmates, for example by talking to them because she was having trouble concentrating on the task at hand. However, because everyone (including Sara herself) thought she was seeing and hearing normally, Sara's poor attention, distractibility, and impulsivity were viewed as potential signs of the disorder called ADHD, and she was started on increasing doses of a stimulant. That's a big problem because such medication can actually increase the frequency of seizures, as it appeared to have in

Sara's case. As discussed throughout this book, for Sara and many others diagnosed erroneously with ADHD, *treatment delayed is treatment denied.* A correct diagnosis is important for securing the most effective intervention.

## PREVALENCE OF SEIZURES

How common are seizures and seizure disorders? According to one academic review, about 4 percent of the population will experience an unprovoked seizure (or those that aren't caused by fever, head injury, or one of the other factors mentioned earlier) at some point in their lives.[5] Of that group, about 30–40 percent overall will have a second unprovoked seizure. The risk of recurrence goes up to 60–70 percent for adult patients with a previous neurological injury, abnormal EEG or evidence of a brain lesion (a damaged area), or family history of seizures. Absence seizures, which are particularly likely to result in misdiagnosis of ADHD, are rare in adults.

Sara had no risk factors—no head injury or family history of seizures—but it is possible that others in her extended family had an undetected seizure disorder that either did not disrupt their functioning significantly enough to be noticed, or had been misdiagnosed or approached with an inadequate treatment.

## RELATION TO ATTENTION–DEFICIT/HYPERACTIVITY SYMPTOMS

Seizure disorders are related to symptoms associated with what we know as ADHD on multiple levels. As far as epidemiology, ADHD is more likely to be diagnosed in those with a history of seizures. For example, a 2003 research study found that 40 percent of children aged nine to fourteen who had been diagnosed with epilepsy also met criteria for an ADHD diagnosis.[6] Others have pointed out the challenge of differentiating the effects of absence seizures from symptoms typically associated with ADHD.[7] It's not surprising that an individual suffering from frequent absence seizures would display significant attention-deficit symptoms. After all, they are briefly losing sensory contact with the outside world, sometimes several times daily.

Nonetheless, there are subtle ways to differentiate absence seizures from attention-deficit symptoms better explained by other causes. For example, calling out their name may not provoke a response from someone undergoing an absence seizure *or* a person who's inattentive for some other reason, but a tap on the shoulder will likely yield a response from the latter individual only, as the absence seizure patient won't be able to sense it.[8] Researchers found that among children, two specific items on health-care assessment questionnaires differentiated children with absence seizures from those with attention-deficit symptoms unrelated to seizures: "Does not complete homework" and "Does not remain on task."[9] For children with absence seizures, parents overwhelmingly disagreed with those statements; parents of children with other attention-deficit issues (that is, those diagnosed as symptoms of ADHD) tended to agree with them. Thus absence seizures in children are less likely to disrupt their ability to complete homework and stay on task than are other attention-deficit/hyperactivity conditions. This was true in Sara's case, as her academic performance was appropriate to her age and grade level.

## TREATMENT FOR SEIZURE DISORDERS

Given their link to the brain's electrical activity, seizures are most often treated with pharmaceutical drugs. As of this writing, there were approximately twenty drugs approved for treatment of epilepsy in the United States. Most fell into a category known as "anticonvulsants." While there is good evidence for the effectiveness of anticonvulsants, they can also cause side effects, including rashes, mood changes, and drowsiness. A European study showed that a large number of epileptic patients on medication still experienced seizures with some frequency, along with side effects that diminished their quality of life.[10]

In severe cases of seizure disorders that fail to respond to medication, specific surgeries may be used to reduce the frequency of seizures or stop them altogether. Other nonmedication treatments include electrical stimulation of the nervous system (often the vagus nerve) and avoidance therapy, which seeks to reduce exposure to potential seizure triggers (for example, flashing lights, fluorescent lights, TV screens).

In Sara's case, the logical first step was to try standard anticonvulsant treatment and to have her keep track of her seizures carefully. I gave her a special "Blank TV Log" and told her to draw an X every time she experienced an absence seizure (or every time the "TV went blank," as I said), whether at school, home, or elsewhere. A low dose of the first medication we tried reduced her absence seizures: She went from having several per day to fewer than one, on average. Not surprisingly, her attention span improved, as well. After we increased the dose of the medication slightly, she went weeks without a single seizure. Her ability to pay attention soared—in school and at home—and her teacher reported that she no longer disrupted her classmates. Importantly, before Sara started the anticonvulsant, we had her stop taking the stimulant. After she did that, her headaches and stomach symptoms quickly improved.

I told Sara's parents she would likely have to take the anticonvulsant at least into her teens.[11] "That's okay," her father said. "We're just glad we know what was causing it, and that there's a safe treatment for it." Sara's take on her treatment was even simpler: "I'm just glad my TV doesn't go blank anymore," she said with a smile.

# CHAPTER 14

# Obsessive-Compulsive Disorder

## The Big Point

The mental obsessions (like a preoccupation with germs) and behavioral rituals (like excessive hand-washing) associated with obsessive-compulsive disorder can cause anxiety, distractibility, and other symptoms that may result in a mistaken diagnosis of ADHD.

In the chapter on mood disorders we saw that mental illnesses are among the most common conditions affecting the general population, with an estimated 46 percent of U.S. residents expected to experience a mental disease at some point in their lifetime.[1] Beyond mood-related symptoms, the anxiety and thought patterns associated with multiple mental disorders—from specific phobias (like irrational fear of heights or animals) to generalized anxiety disorder (excessive worrying)—can interfere with concentration and cause distractibility. The intense obsessions and compulsions that occur with obsessive-compulsive disorder (OCD) are particularly likely to have that effect. The distractibility and other symptoms caused by OCD, in turn, may be mistaken for signs of ADHD, resulting in erroneous diagnosis and treatment. Sometimes it can take many years before an accurate diagnosis is made. Such was the case for my patient Jeremy.

## GOING IN CIRCLES

The first time forty-two-year-old Jeremy came to my office, he was nearly an hour late. "I'm sorry, Doctor," he said, acknowledging his lateness, "but this is part of the problem." Jeremy, a salesman with a food-and-beverage company, looked miserable and fatigued, with dark circles under his eyes and deep lines in his forehead. He explained that his tardiness was becoming a problem in every aspect of his life: with his work, his girlfriend, his friends, and even his hobbies like playing softball. "I'm close to getting fired for it," Jeremy said, pointing out that he was often late for important meetings, including sales calls. He also acknowledged that his marriage had ended many years before because of his tendency to "worry" about things. He said, "It's like I can't concentrate on anything. I don't know what to do." He noted that his symptoms had gotten considerably worse in recent years, partly because he was worried about losing his job and his relationship. It was clear Jeremy was stuck in a dangerous cycle where his symptoms were interfering with his occupational and social functioning, and the stress related to these consequences was exacerbating his symptoms.

What was less clear was the source of Jeremy's symptoms: Why was he late for everything? What was he worried about in the first place? Our first session didn't reveal much in this regard. In our second session, Jeremy reluctantly explained his lateness: "While driving I'm always worried that I've hit a pedestrian, so I have to go back and check." This wasn't an occasional occurrence, but something that happened every time he drove any significant distance, whether to the store, to his girlfriend's house, or to a softball game. In each instance, Jeremy typically circled the block multiple times, convinced that he would see the body of a pedestrian his car had hit, along with emergency vehicles and personnel. When he had others—his girlfriend or friends—in the car, he was typically able to avoid circling back, but his anxiety was severe. He said that his checking behavior had started some years before, but had worsened significantly over time. Though his fears had remained unfounded, Jeremy was convinced he was already a hit-and-run driver, or soon to be one.

Jeremy's ritualistic behavior had some precedent in his child-hood. "I was kind of a nervous kid," he said. "Unlike a lot of boys I used to hate dirt and actually liked washing my hands." He said that he was able to keep his thinking about dirt and germs under control by washing his hands more frequently, but that it became more difficult in his adolescent years. When I asked if he had told his parents about his fears, he said, "They thought I was just ex-aggerating and told me it would probably get better with time." It didn't. So Jeremy learned not to talk about his obsessions (which grew to include a fear that he had hit someone while riding his bike), and had occasional success reducing them by distracting himself or engaging in compulsive behavior (for example, washing hands, checking for injured pedestrians).

As a teen, the mental effort Jeremy required to manage his symptoms began to show in his schoolwork and other domains. He said, "I had several teachers tell me I was smarter than my homework and test scores suggested." Based on his poor concen-tration and distractibility, his high school counselor suggested Jeremy's parents have him evaluated by a physician. Due partly to his reluctance to share information about his obsessions and compulsions, Jeremy was diagnosed with ADHD—then called "attention deficit disorder" (ADD)—in his early teens, and treated with multiple stimulants. Some of the medications provided brief periods of relief; the majority disrupted Jeremy's appetite and sleep, worsening his obsessions and compulsions. In his late twenties, after nearly fifteen years on medication for ADHD, Jeremy stopped taking any prescribed pills. "I was sick of taking them and felt like they were making everything worse," he said.

Since then, Jeremy sometimes kept his symptoms under check through distraction and sheer will, telling himself he risked losing the things that mattered most to him. But inevitably the symptoms would return. The fear of germs (and the associated handwashing) had persisted from his childhood, but the obsessions and compulsions related to hitting a pedestrian had been the strongest recent symptoms. Increasingly, Jeremy had been giving in to his fears by engaging in prolonged and intense compulsive behavior, like circling the block ten times or more. It was clear he couldn't continue living the way he had been. "I need to do something about this," Jeremy said, "before it's too late."

## CLUES TO LOOK FOR

As for most patients, Jeremy's history was crucial to understanding his symptoms and making a diagnosis and treatment plan. Particularly noteworthy in his case was what he *hadn't* shared with previous physicians he had seen: information about his obsessions and compulsions. Many patients are reluctant to share such symptoms, as they feel the symptoms are "all in their heads" and that they should have better control over them. People are especially concerned about sharing obsessions and compulsions with others, even medical professionals, for fear that they will be judged negatively.

While Jeremy seemed to qualify more clearly for an anxiety-related disorder than anything else, it was important to rule out all explanations for his symptoms. For example, Jeremy's hearing, vision, and blood test results were in the normal range, and he didn't report any other conditions that might have explained his distractibility and poor concentration. That left the obsessive and compulsive symptoms as the best explanation. Specifically, he had "textbook" symptoms of obsessive-compulsive disorder, as discussed in the next section. The long-standing obsessions and compulsions caused Jeremy's poor concentration and distractibility, among many other challenges for him.

## Main Clue

The main clue to an obsessive-compulsive diagnosis underlying attention-deficit symptoms is the presence of hallmark symptoms including obsessions (for example, fear of germs) and the compulsions (for example, hand-washing) that patients use to relieve these. Note that many patients may be reluctant to discuss their OCD symptoms directly, so it's important to supplement their provided history with careful observation and discussions with family members if possible.

Moreover, there were clues to an anxiety-related diagnosis in Jeremy's family history. Though no one in his nuclear family had been diagnosed with or treated for an anxiety disorder, Jeremy had an uncle who had been treated for panic disorder, and a first cousin who had been diagnosed with generalized anxiety disorder. Jeremy admitted that he had heard about OCD and knew his symptoms sounded consistent with the disorder, but that it had been "easier" to deny that he qualified for the diagnosis and to continue believing that he had ADHD, as he had been told decades earlier. Jeremy said, "I wanted to believe it was just ADD, but realized I was just fooling myself."

## WHAT IS OBSESSIVE-COMPULSIVE DISORDER?

OCD is a mental disorder marked by obsessive thoughts and compulsive behavior aimed mostly at reducing the obsessions. Not surprisingly, the symptoms of OCD interfere with patients' concentration and other elements of functioning, sometimes resulting in the misdiagnosis of ADHD. According to the fifth edition of the *Diagnostic and Statistical Manual of Mental Disorders*, OCD involves recurrent obsessions and/or compulsions.[2] Specific criteria for diagnosing OCD include:

- The presence of either obsessions, compulsions, or both; obsessions are recurrent, persistent thoughts or images that are unwanted and usually cause distress, and are difficult to suppress; compulsions are repetitive behaviors or mental acts the individual feels he or she must perform to reduce distress or prevent some feared outcome.
- The obsessions and compulsions must be time-consuming (over an hour a day) and cause significant impairment in functioning.
- The symptoms are not better explained by another condition (see below).

While the *DSM* is a helpful reference source that provides such criteria, it's important to include broad clinical judgment in making a diagnosis, given the implications for the patient's treatment and self-perception. As illustrated by Jeremy's case, the most frequently occurring obsessions have to do with contamination (that is, fear of germs or other contaminants), doubts (for example, whether one has left a door unlocked or accidentally driven into a pedestrian), a need for rigid order, or violent or sexual images. The obsessions are typically not related to real-life issues.

Consistent with the obsessions noted above, among the most common compulsions are hand-washing, checking (for example, whether a door has been left unlocked), and praying or silent repetition of words. That the obsessive-compulsive symptoms must be time-consuming (requiring at least one hour per day) and/or cause significant impairment in functioning helps distinguish true OCD symptoms from normal superstitious behavior (for example, carrying a good-luck charm) or reasonable checking behavior (for example, confirming that one has turned off an oven before leaving the house). In most cases of OCD, the patient has recognized that their obsessions and/or compulsions are unreasonable or excessive, and are likely to have tried to suppress them. It's also important to differentiate OCD from mood disorders, which may involve rumination about negative thoughts or images; generalized anxiety disorder, which involves excessive worry about *real-life* circumstances (for example, losing one's job); and specific phobias, characterized by preoccupation with a feared situation or object (for example, spiders).[3] Finally, OCD is different from the *DSM-V* diagnosis of obsessive-compulsive personality disorder, which involves excessive focus on orderliness and control across settings, but includes no specific obsessions or compulsions.

Jeremy's symptoms fit the diagnostic criteria for OCD perfectly. From childhood, he'd had a history of obsessions and compulsions, starting with a fear of germs (and compulsive hand-washing) and most recently expressed as excessive concern about having hit a pedestrian with his car (and driving around the block to check). Jeremy's symptoms took up a significant amount of his time, often making him late, even for important appointments. The symptoms had clearly caused impairment in his functioning across academic, occupational, and social settings. Also consistent with the *DSM-V* definition, Jeremy knew his obsessions and compulsions were unreasonable, and had even hidden them from his parents and doctors when he was younger because of this insight.

According to the *DSM-IV*, OCD has an estimated lifetime prevalence of 2.5 percent—meaning that two or three people out of every one hundred will be diagnosable with OCD at some point in their lives.[4] The *DSM-V* only presents the likelihood that a given person will report OCD symptoms in the last year, which it lists as 1.2 percent.[5] Among adults, about half of all OCD cases could be considered severe, with dramatic impairment of functioning.[6] While children as young as three can show signs of OCD, the disorder usually starts in adolescence or early adult years, and is equally common in males and females. As was the case for Jeremy, stress (for example, job-related) typically makes OCD symptoms worse.

## RELATION TO ATTENTION-DEFICIT/HYPERACTIVITY SYMPTOMS

Both core elements of OCD, obsessions and compulsions, would likely result in attention deficits. Individuals thinking excessively about whether they have come into contact with dangerous contaminants or wondering if they have unintentionally run a pedestrian over with their car will almost definitely have trouble concentrating on anything else, like schoolwork or job responsibilities, and appear highly distractible. Similarly, attempts to suppress the OCD symptoms by distracting oneself would also disrupt the ability to concentrate significantly and stay on task.

OCD and ADHD have been linked in large-scale academic research. For example, researchers studied nearly one thousand people from childhood (starting at one to ten years of age) and found that ADHD symptoms in adolescence predicted OCD symptoms in adulthood.[7] While the researchers considered the disorders separate diagnoses, the pattern they uncovered fits my argument here: that early ADHD symptoms may be the result of early but not yet full-blown OCD symptoms.

Other, more informal but widely read sources have also linked OCD and the disorder called ADHD. A physician writing for a popular ADHD website cautions readers about the possibility of OCD being mistaken for ADHD.[8] The doctor highlights the case of "Franklin," a fifteen-year-old diagnosed with ADHD and treated with a stimulant because of fidgeting and an inability to complete his class work. It turned out Franklin's "ADHD" symptoms resulted from obsessions and compulsions: He had to have his paper and pencil positioned perfectly, along with writing each letter as carefully as possible. Franklin's parents, teachers, and doctors had never asked him *why* he was having so much trouble in the classroom. Once diagnosed with OCD, Franklin was taken off the stimulant (which had worsened his symptoms, as was the case for Jeremy) and treated with nonstimulant medication and psychotherapy. Finally, one high-profile physician has argued that some cases of OCD may result from ineffective attempts to cope with early attention-deficit/hyperactivity symptoms; that is, some individuals unconsciously deal with uncontrollable shifts in attention (as is the case with ADHD) by adopting repetitive thoughts and behaviors that grow into the obsessions and compulsions associated with OCD.[9] While this is an interesting hypothesis, my experience is that early OCD symptoms are likely to be misdiagnosed as ADHD, rather than the former resulting from symptoms of the latter.

## TREATMENT FOR OBSESSIVE COMPULSIVE DISORDER

OCD is usually treated with a combination of medication and psychotherapy. Medications that have been used for successful treatment of OCD symptoms include selective serotonin reuptake inhibitor (SSRI) antidepressants. Other medications have been used "off-label" for OCD—meaning that they are not specifically indicated for the disorder but can help alleviate its symptoms in some patients. Cognitive-behavioral therapy, often in conjunction with medication, has also helped individuals with OCD. The most common form of cognitive-behavioral therapy for OCD is called "exposure and response prevention." As the name implies, patients are exposed to the items or activities they fear (for example, dirt, driving) and then prevented from engaging in the compulsions (for example, hand-washing, checking for accident victims) they use to reduce their anxiety. OCD can be a chronic, long-term disorder, and some cases are very difficult to cure.[10] But high levels of motivation on the part of the patient and their supporters can help lead to better outcomes.

Jeremy agreed to try a combination of medication and psychotherapy for his OCD. He began taking an SSRI and started cognitive-behavioral treatment on an outpatient basis. After making minimal progress, we replaced his SSRI with a different drug from the same class. Now Jeremy made faster progress, with a steady reduction in his OCD symptoms, including a marked decrease in the driving-related checking behavior. He reported improvement in every area of his life: work, relationship, friendships, hobbies. "I thought I'd have to live with the symptoms forever," he said. "Now I know I don't have to." Perhaps one of the best indications of Jeremy's improvement was that he was no longer late for appointments with me, as he had been able to drive directly from his home to my office, with no need to circle back due to the OCD.

# CHAPTER 15

# Tourette's Syndrome

## The Big Point

Childhood fidgeting, distractibility, and impulsivity are often viewed as signs of ADHD. But these early symptoms, combined with a family history of tics, are usually better explained by a diagnosis of Tourette's syndrome, a condition involving significant motor and vocal tics.

In the United States, awareness of Tourette's syndrome—a neuropsychiatric condition marked by motor and vocal tics—has grown quickly in recent years, with greater coverage of the syndrome across media outlets. While stereotypical views of the disorder focus on its more severe and disruptive symptoms (for example, the shouting of obscenities or inappropriate phrases), the general public has come to understand that patients with Tourette's may display a wide range of tics with varying severity, and that these symptoms may be more manageable than previously thought. Some studies estimate that as many as 90 percent of those with Tourette's will also qualify for an "ADHD" diagnosis.[1] The further challenge is that early signs of Tourette's may include fidgeting, distractibility, and impulsivity, rather than obvious tics. (By definition, Tourette's will typically emerge by age eighteen.) These early symptoms are much more likely to appear in Tourette's than in other tic disorders. Moreover, the symptoms may be misdiagnosed as ADHD, resulting in negative consequences for young patients and their families. This was the case for Max, one of my child patients.

## PERPETUAL-MOTION MAX

When I first saw eight-year-old Max at my office, he was like a perpetual-motion machine. He tapped his fingers on the waiting room table and swung his legs back and forth, shaking his feet violently. Max's parents reported that the fidgeting was becoming a problem in school. "His teacher says he's academically on track," his mother said, "but he just can't stop moving around. He's distracting himself and everyone else." His parents also noted his "incredibly short attention span." At home, he would struggle to sit at the table to do his homework or eat dinner with the family, impulsively rising to engage in other activities (for example, watching TV). At school, he had trouble concentrating on in-class work and the teacher's presentations. When I asked Max about his fidgeting and impulsive behavior, he said he "didn't know" he was doing it so much. He also reported that his neck was sometimes stiff or sore.

Six months earlier, based on Max's fidgeting and distractibility, his pediatrician had diagnosed him with ADHD and started him on a stimulant. Max's symptoms didn't improve much and, within two months of starting on the medication, the boy had developed mild tics, including blinking his eyes, rolling his head, and grunting. His mother said, "At first we thought it was just part of his fidgeting. And sometimes he went weeks without doing it." But Max's parents began to believe the stimulant may have caused the tics, and mentioned this concern to the pediatrician. The doctor suggested Max try a different stimulant, but the family decided to hold off on any medications before seeking a second opinion. On his first visit to my office, Max showed no signs of the tics his family reported.

We decided to observe Max's symptoms over the next months, rather than making a diagnosis or starting the boy on a new medication. Soon his fidgeting and tics worsened, affecting Max's behavior at home and school. The tics had become especially more pronounced, with more intense and prolonged blinking and head rolls, and louder, more frequent grunting. Beyond affecting Max's performance, the symptoms had social repercussions for the boy. His father said, "Some of the kids are teasing him about it and imitating him." Tearfully, Max agreed, and the family reported that the social stress seemed to have made the boy's tics even worse, along with his problems with distractibility and impulsiveness.

It was clear the family needed relief from Max's symptoms as quickly as possible.

## CLUES TO LOOK FOR

Max's symptom picture and family history helped us develop a more effective diagnosis and treatment plan. To start, it was important to rule out simple explanations for the symptoms. While he was struggling with increasing fidgeting and tics, Max had no vision or hearing issues, and his parents reported that he had no sleep disturbance or other conditions that can contribute to attention-deficit/hyperactivity symptoms. During his office visits, despite his fidgeting, occasional tics, and concern about social issues (for example, teasing), Max appeared well rested and alert. Moreover, his blood test results were all in the normal range.

Over time, Max's full symptom picture—marked by ongoing fidgeting and distractibility and the more recently developed tics—fit diagnostic criteria for Tourette's disorder (also called Tourette's syndrome or just Tourette's). As discussed in the next section, Tourette's is marked by intermittent physical and verbal tics that may be exacerbated by stimulants.

> **Main Clue**
>
> Patients who have Tourette's syndrome often have an early history of fidgeting, impulsivity, and distractibility—which may be mistaken for a symptom of ADHD—followed by the development of physical and/or verbal tics. The tics may first appear or worsen when the patient takes stimulant medications. A thorough medical history (including family input) and careful observation can help confirm the diagnosis.

Max's family history also supported the Tourette's diagnosis. His father and grandfather had mild, intermittent tics—hand movements and shoulder shrugging, respectively—that had remained undiagnosed and untreated. "I thought it was just the way we were," Max's father said. I also helped the family understand that starting Max on the stimulant may have *accelerated* the appearance of the tics, rather than causing them in the first place. Had Max not taken the medication, the tics most likely would have emerged a bit later. Moreover, the head-rolling tic helped explain Max's occasional experience of a stiff or sore neck. Relieved to have a diagnosis that seemed more accurate, Max's family began reading about Tourette's and thinking about the treatment plan.

## WHAT IS TOURETTE'S SYNDROME?

Tourette's is a neuropsychiatric "tic disorder" involving specific motor movements or vocalizations that seem uncontrollable. The early fidgeting and subsequent tics associated with Tourette's may be misdiagnosed as ADHD. While Tourette's and other tic disorders tend to be chronic, effective treatment can reduce the tics and the attention-deficit/hyperactivity symptoms they may contribute to.

According to the fifth edition of the *Diagnostic and Statistical Manual of Mental Disorders*, Tourette's is one of four diagnosable tic disorders.[2] Because the other three conditions tend not to be preceded by the degree of fidgeting, distractibility, and impulsivity (which tend to be mistaken for ADHD) that Tourette's is, we will focus on Tourette's in this chapter. A tic is a "sudden, rapid, recurrent, nonrhythmic, stereotyped motor movement or vocalization."[3] Simple motor tics include blinking, grimacing, and head-rolling; complex motor tics include jumping and grooming behaviors. Grunting, barking, and throat-clearing are examples of simple vocal tics; complex vocal tics include the repetition of words or phrases (sometimes inappropriate or obscene ones) out of context and "echolalia," or the repeating of words or phrases spoken by others. According to the *DSM-V*, Tourette's syndrome may be diagnosed when an individual (under age eighteen) has multiple motor tics and at least one vocal tic that are present (constantly or intermittently) for at least a year. In my experience, the tics associated with Tourette's tend to intensify or weaken, depending on patients' situations and how they perceive them; more stress generally equals more frequent and intense tics.

The *DSM-IV* (published in 1994) required significant impairment in social or occupational functioning for a Tourette's diagnosis, but the subsequent revision of the manual removed this criterion, as practitioners had observed many patients who displayed all symptoms of the syndrome without suffering noticeable impairment in these domains.[4] The *DSM-V* continued the relaxing of this criterion by not requiring impairment for a

Tourette's diagnosis. As noted in earlier chapters, this development reflects the *DSM*'s status as an evolving reference source, rather than the final authority on diagnostic criteria.

It's important to differentiate diagnosable tic disorders from what many physicians think of as "tics of childhood," or motor tics (for example, blinking) that last only briefly during an individual's early years and stop without intervention—in such cases, the best treatment is time. Also, some tics may be caused by medication only, rather than reflecting an underlying disorder such as Tourette's. Tic disorders may also be differentiated from abnormal movements caused by medical conditions such as stroke, multiple sclerosis, and head injuries. So it's important to gauge whether the tics are associated only with a specific medicine or medical condition. Tics should also be differentiated from compulsions associated with obsessive-compulsive disorder; as discussed in a previous chapter, compulsions are specific actions (for example, hand-washing) performed in response to obsessions (for example, fear of germs). Tics, in contrast, are not triggered by specific thoughts or images.

Max's symptoms fit the diagnostic picture for Tourette's syndrome well. He displayed at least two motor tics—blinking and head-rolling—and one vocal tic (grunting). Blinking and other facial tics (for example, mouth twitches) tend to be among the earlier tics to appear.[5] Though he had sometimes gone weeks without tics, Max had experienced them at least once every three months for a year. Moreover, the tics tended to worsen with stress, such as when Max was teased by classmates. Although impairment is no longer required for a Tourette's diagnosis, the symptoms were clearly disrupting Max's functioning in academic and social settings.

According to the *DSM-V*, Tourette's occurs in three to eight school-age children per ten thousand, or .03 percent to .08 percent of the entire child population, a very small proportion. Other studies suggest a much higher rate; for example, the Centers for Disease Control and Prevention noted that survey research has shown a 3 percent rate of Tourette's among some populations.[6] The CDC points out that differences in study methods may explain the wide gap between estimates. There is better evidence for the disparity of Tourette's diagnoses by gender: The disorder is up to four times more common in males than females, according to the *DSM-V*. The average age at which Tourette's has been observed to start is around six and a half years.[7] Most cases of the disorder have been identified by adulthood. The *DSM-V* also points out that Tourette's has a strong hereditary component: Vulnerability to the syndrome (and other tic disorders) is transmitted genetically. However, not everyone who inherits the vulnerability will develop a tic disorder, and the expression and severity of the disorder may differ significantly across generations. In Max's case, both previous generations of men in his family displayed symptoms of tic disorders, though neither his father nor grandfather had been diagnosed or treated. Tourette's is usually a lifelong condition, though it is not considered degenerative (that is, it causes no decline in function over time) and its symptoms often diminish during adolescence or adulthood.

## RELATION TO ATTENTION-DEFICIT/HYPERACTIVITY SYMPTOMS

The disorder known as ADHD and Tourette's have been linked on several levels. Tics have been estimated to occur in as many as 50 percent of children diagnosed with ADHD; as many as 90 percent of children diagnosed with Tourette's may also be diagnosed with ADHD.[8] So while about half of children diagnosed with ADHD may also have tics, the vast majority of kids with Tourette's diagnoses are told they have ADHD. This has certainly been my experience, as it is nearly impossible to find a case of Tourette's that doesn't involve attention-deficit/hyperactivity symptoms. Recall from the first chapter that the diagnosis of multiple disorders in the same person is known as "comorbidity"; in fact, the *DSM-V* suggests that ADHD is particularly likely to be comorbid with tic disorders.[9] My argument is that comorbid ADHD does not exist, and the non-ADHD diagnosis can account fully for the attention-deficit/hyperactivity symptoms. That is the case for Tourette's. This opinion is not mine alone: There is significant debate in the scientific community about whether ADHD and Tourette's are separate disorders.[10]

As far as overlap in symptoms between Tourette's and ADHD, in my experience strong precursors to Tourette's include fidgeting (for example, finger and toe-tapping), an inability to stay seated, and impulsivity. While the *DSM-IV* noted that hyperactivity, distractibility, and impulsivity are associated with Tourette's disorder, the *DSM-V* no longer makes this relation. These may be easily mistaken for ADHD symptoms, especially early in the course of Tourette's, before motor and vocal tics become full-blown.

## TREATMENT FOR TOURETTE'S SYNDROME

Treatment for Tourette's typically involves some combination of medication and behavioral treatment. Prescription medicines that have demonstrated success reducing tics include tricyclic antidepressants and neuroleptics (that is, antipsychotics), the latter of which are also used to treat schizophrenia.[11] As noted earlier, I've observed that stimulants used to treat an assumed ADHD diagnosis can often elicit or exacerbate the tics associated with Tourette's, potentially accelerating their appearance. This link remains controversial. For example, a review study of Tourette's,

ADHD, and stimulants found that while there is no evidence for a significant link between stimulant use and worsening of tics on a group level, individual patients may definitely see their tics increase if they start on a stimulant.[12] Moreover, as with any drug treatment, it's important to balance treatment benefits with side effects. For example, side effects of neuroleptics can include sedation, weight gain, and neurological symptoms such as tremor and twisting movements/postures.[13] No medicine has been proven to completely eradicate tics (for most patients, some observable tics will persist over their lifetime), but many Tourette's patients can function very well without medication. Thus generating a thoughtful treatment plan on a case-by-case basis is important.

Behavioral treatments for Tourette's include habit-reversal training and other behavioral modification programs. Habit reversal is based on the idea that those suffering from Tourette's are often unaware of their tics and thus can be taught to increase their awareness of the symptoms and replace them with other behaviors.[14] Special logs are given to patients and their families to record tic-related behaviors, and patients are shown how to replace tics with less obtrusive behaviors (for example, replacing a shoulder shrug with a lengthening of the neck and movement of the shoulder downward). Another behavior modification program that can be used to diminish Tourette's syndrome includes rewarding patients for gaining control over their symptoms. Such programs work particularly well with children in home or classroom settings, where parents or teachers can monitor behaviors and provide rewards.

In Max's case, we decided to try a behavioral modification program at home and at school, along with reducing some of the academic pressure he faced in the classroom. He received a meaningful reward (stickers related to his favorite TV show) for staying in his seat and keeping his tics under control. He was also given extra time for in-class assignments. Though it was challenging at first, Max soon learned to control his tics much better at home and at school, and his parents and teacher reported significant improvement in his mood and academic performance. We decided he could continue without medication as long as his symptoms stayed under control. Perhaps best of all, the boy learned how to explain his Tourette's symptoms to his peers, and began to make more friends in his school and neighborhood. Though Max would likely have some tics for most of his life, it was clear he and his family could manage them better than they had imagined.

# CHAPTER 16

# Asperger Syndrome
# (An Autism Spectrum Disorder)

## The Big Point

Problems related to social interactions—especially difficulty connecting with others—when combined with attention-deficit/hyperactivity symptoms may be diagnosed mistakenly as ADHD when Asperger disorder (a formerly common diagnosis that the *DSM-V* now considers to be a form of mild autism) is a better explanation.

Everyone knows someone who seems a bit "odd," socially. Medical practitioners and laypeople have paid increasing attention to Asperger syndrome, a condition marked by difficulty with social interactions, including challenges responding to social cues (for example, maintaining eye contact) and, sometimes, an obsessive interest in things to which others pay little attention. As we will discuss in this chapter, Asperger syndrome has been a commonly accepted diagnosis and appeared in the fourth edition of the American Psychiatric Association's *Diagnostic and Statistical Manual of Mental Disorders*.[1] While the current (fifth) edition of the *DSM* no longer includes a separate diagnosis for Asperger syndrome, and considers the symptom picture a mild form of autism,

I and many of my colleagues continue to view many patients as meeting criteria for Asperger syndrome.

Because Asperger syndrome involves difficulty paying attention—especially in social interactions—and occasional impulsivity, it has been easy to mistake the syndrome for the disorder called ADHD, or to assume that the two conditions occur together. But for those who qualify for an Asperger syndrome diagnosis, typical stimulant-medication treatment may not be helpful. That was the case for my patient Donald.

## THE FRIENDLESS TEMP

In his first visit to my office, Donald made almost zero eye contact. The twenty-four-year-old had come to see me because his parents "made" him, due to increasing difficulties at work. When I asked Donald what he meant by that, he said, "My supervisor says I don't listen very well." The young man was working as a temporary employee with a manufacturing company, with responsibilities including filing paperwork and helping to maintain a large customer database. He admitted that he often forgot his supervisor's instructions but didn't ask for clarification of tasks at the time he was given them or afterward. Instead, he "tried to remember" what he was supposed to do, usually making mistakes. Donald also said that he sometimes listened in on other employees' conversations, which distracted him from his work and sometimes annoyed his colleagues. When they confronted him, he usually walked away without saying anything.

Donald had attended a small private school in the Midwest, where he had majored in political science and earned A and B grades consistently, with aspirations of becoming a lawyer. He had worked as an intern at two law firms, but had received negative evaluations at both, again due to his distractibility and poor social skills. He had chosen not to apply to law school—"It seemed like too much work"—and, due to the poor job market, had been temping since graduating from college. Donald noted that he had switched temp agencies twice so far, due to poor performance. "I guess I'm not a very good employee," Donald said. In general, eliciting responses from him was difficult, often requiring repetition of my questions.

Donald's social challenges were even more evident outside the workplace. "I have lots of friends," he said early in our session. When I asked for details, he admitted that the "friends" to which he was referring were fellow players of a medieval-themed online role-playing game, and that he'd never met any of them. Donald said that he played the game for hours daily, and for long stretches of the weekend, taking breaks only to eat or to use the bathroom. He said he was particularly interested in the game's "scenery," and spent a lot of time wandering the virtual forest in which it was set, rather than trying to score points. In our session he was wearing a T-shirt with the game's logo, and the conversation about this interest was the only time he showed any emotion, with a half smile and slightly more animated gestures.

In elementary school, high school, and college, Donald had struggled to fit in, saying silly things or acting impulsively—including making inappropriate jokes. As an adult he seemed to have given up on normal in-person social interactions, eavesdropping (as mentioned above) and acting oddly in other ways, including laughing too loudly when others made jokes (though he admitted to not understanding most of them) or even when they spoke about nonhumorous issues (for example, a family member's illness). "I get a lot of weird looks," Donald said, but seemed unfazed by this. He stated that he had never had a girlfriend, and had rarely attempted to ask anyone out in school or since then.

Due to his attention deficits and impulsivity, Donald had been diagnosed with ADHD in elementary school and started on stimulant medication. Since then, he had tried multiple stimulants, with little success. "They don't make me feel any different," he said. While Donald himself expressed little concern about his condition, his parents were worried. "He's always had trouble finding his way," his mother said in a phone conversation. She added that he had been a "healthy but strange" child, including his obsessive interest in model-car tires, a pursuit on which he spent hours at a time. His mother said, "We just want him to have a good life."

While Donald may have been less likely to have what his parents considered a "good life"—a conventional definition including satisfying work and social interactions—it was clear that his diagnosis of ADHD and treatment for it had done little to improve his situation. Determining a more appropriate diagnosis was the first step to helping him.

## CLUES TO LOOK FOR

As with all my patients, I deepened my understanding of Donald's symptoms with a full physical exam and history, including a family history. According to his parents, Donald's childhood growth and development had been normal, with no motor or speech delays, or hearing or vision difficulties. As noted earlier, he had few friends and tended to act oddly in social situations. Donald reported no sleep disturbance, which ruled out that factor as an explanation. His blood test results were all in the normal range.

Thorough questioning revealed no medical conditions that could account for Donald's symptoms, except one: Asperger syndrome, a condition including significant challenges in social functioning and a restricted range of interests and activities. As discussed in the next section, Asperger syndrome often involves noticeable impairment in occupational functioning as well.

> **Main Clue**
>
> Patients with Asperger syndrome (or what could be considered mild autism), while able to function well cognitively, have markedly poor social functioning, including an inability to make and keep friendships, and a tendency to become preoccupied with a narrow range of interests (for example, games, collections) or to engage in repetitive motor activities (for example, hand-flapping).

As is often the case, Donald's family history included evidence of Asperger syndrome. "Two of his uncles are a lot like him," his mother said, pointing out the relatives' difficulty with social interactions, including a tendency to keep to themselves and avoid family gatherings. Donald seemed unsurprised by the Asperger diagnosis—but that was often his reaction to other aspects of his life.

## WHAT IS ASPERGER SYNDROME?

Asperger syndrome is most evident in patients' social interactions—including failure to develop meaningful relationships with others. Though many Asperger's patients will face lifelong challenges, their symptoms can often be improved by targeted intervention. The fourth edition of the *Diagnostic and Statistical Manual of Mental Disorders* groups Asperger syndrome (also known as "Asperger's disorder," "Asperger's syndrome," or just "Asperger's") with disorders first diagnosed in infancy, childhood, or adolescence. According to the *DSM-IV*, Asperger's involves "severe and sustained impairment in social interaction . . . and the development of restricted, repetitive patterns of behaviors, interests, and activities."[2] The handbook considers Asperger's a "pervasive developmental disorder," or one that affects multiple aspects of development and functioning.

To qualify for the diagnosis, patients must demonstrate significant impairment in social, occupational, or other aspects of functioning. Such impairment is not surprising, given the typical type and degree of Asperger's symptoms. The *DSM-IV*, for example, requires that at least two of the following social-interaction patterns be present for the diagnosis: impairment related to eye contact, facial expression, body posture, and/or gestures related to maintaining appropriate social interactions; failure to form developmentally appropriate relationships; lack of interest in sharing with other people or discussing common interests; and lack of social reciprocity, such as responding to a greeting. The Mayo Clinic describes Asperger's social-interaction symptoms as including "engaging in one-sided, long-winded conversations, without noticing if the listener is listening or trying to change the subject" and "having a hard time 'reading' other people or understanding humor," along with speaking in a monotone voice.[3]

The second cluster of symptoms associated with Asperger syndrome involve "restricted repetitive and stereotyped patterns of behavior, interests, and activities."[4] Symptoms fitting this criterion include preoccupation with a narrow interest that is odd in focus or intensity (for example, spending forty hours a week on a stamp collection). Other signs—potentially related to the interest in question—include rigid adherence to rituals or routines, and repetitive movements (for example, shrugging).

There is significant controversy surrounding the diagnosis of Asperger syndrome. It is considered by many health-care practitioners to be on the mild end of a spectrum of conditions that includes autism.[5] As mentioned earlier, the fifth edition of the *Diagnostic and Statistical Manual* does away with the Asperger syndrome diagnosis, while expanding the scope of the autism diagnosis to "autism spectrum disorder." I (and many others in the medical field and general public)[6] disagree with the removal of the Asperger syndrome diagnosis, for multiple reasons. First, those diagnosed with what we once called Asperger's show no significant delays in acquiring language skills, whereas most autistic patients show significant delays in these and other cognitive capabilities. In fact, Asperger syndrome patients generally have no history of cognitive impairment, other than with regard to the development of social skills.[7] The *DSM-IV* also notes that Asperger's symptoms are likely to be observed later in childhood than signs of autism. Perhaps more importantly, what I still think of as Asperger's is highly consistent with the definition of autism spectrum disorder in the current version of the *DSM*. Specifically, diagnosis of autism requires the same hallmark symptoms the Asperger's definition formerly required:[8]

- Deficits in social communication/interaction across settings, including an "abnormal social approach," problems with non-verbal interaction (such as poor eye contact), and challenges developing and maintaining relationships
- Restricted, repetitive behavior and interests, including repetitive movements or speech, abnormally intense interests, and insistence on sameness (such as an inflexible routine or diet)

As you'll note, these are pretty much the same symptoms required for an Asperger's syndrome diagnosis in the *DSM-IV*. The *DSM-V* also provides specifiers of the severity of the autism spectrum disorder—Level 1, the mildest level, suggests that the diagnosed individual requires support for social interactions; Levels 2 and 3 require "substantial" and "very substantial" support, respectively.[9] The *DSM* also suggests that the level of symptoms may even fall below Level 1. Thus Asperger syndrome could be seen as a mild (or very mild) form of autism spectrum disorder. I will use the term "Asperger's" here, given my belief that this diagnosis is still valid.

It's just another example of the need to view the *DSM* as a set of guidelines for diagnosis, rather than as the final authority. Additionally, while obsessive-compulsive disorder (also detailed in the *DSM-V* and in another chapter of this book) and Asperger's share patterns of obsessive, repetitive behavior, Asperger's is marked by more difficulty with social interactions. Similarly, Asperger's and Tourette's disorder both involve repetitive movements, but the former diagnosis requires social impairment.

Donald's symptoms met criteria for a diagnosis of Asperger disorder (and mild autism spectrum disorder). He had trouble using nonverbal gestures (for example, eye contact) as part of social interactions and had long-standing trouble forming friendships and romantic relationships. His trouble recognizing and expressing humor was also a typical Asperger's symptom. As far as abnormal interests or activities, as a child Donald had been preoccupied with model-car parts. In adulthood he played an inordinate amount of an online role-playing game. While it was unclear if that time he spent on the game was beyond what would be considered normal for his age group,[10] his interest in less central aspects of the game (that is, the scenery) was consistent with a diagnosis of Asperger's.

## PREVALENCE OF ASPERGER'S (OR AUTISM SPECTRUM DISORDERS)

Epidemiological data on Asperger's is limited, but a Swedish study in the early 1990s found the rate of Asperger syndrome in children ages seven to sixteen years to be 3.6 per 1,000, or a little under 0.4 percent, with 4 cases in males for every 1 in females.[11] That general gender pattern is also pointed out by the Mayo Clinic.[12] The *DSM-V* suggests that autism spectrum disorder affects about 1 percent of the population.[13] As far as the course the disorder takes, the *DSM-IV* noted that motor delays or clumsiness may be evident in preschool years, with the social-interaction symptoms of Asperger's more apparent in the context of school. My experience of children with Asperger's is that they are very smart, sometimes in narrow subject areas, but tend to show poor social judgment and face multiple challenges engaging others, which is consistent with the diagnostic criteria.

The *DSM-IV* and *V* also point out that Asperger's and autism spectrum disorder tend to run in families, as it appeared to in Donald's, given the evidence provided by his mother regarding his uncles' symptoms. According to the *DSM-IV*, the duration of Asperger's for the "vast majority" of patients tends to be lifelong.[14] Recent research, in contrast, suggests that as much as 20 percent of children with Asperger's diagnoses may outgrow their symptoms and no longer qualify for the diagnosis in adulthood, though they may continue to face social and communication challenges.[15] As discussed in the treatment section below, there is increasing evidence that Asperger's patients can learn to develop better social and emotional sensitivity, which helps them engage in more normal interactions.

## RELATION TO ATTENTION-DEFICIT/HYPERACTIVITY SYMPTOMS

"Is it Asperger's or ADHD?" reads the title of a physician-authored article for a U.S. regional Asperger's association; the article goes on to discuss the "muddy territory" shared by Asperger syndrome and the disorder known as ADHD, pointing out the challenges in diagnosing and treating patients with

attention-deficit/hyperactivity and social-interactions symptoms.[16] The author cites anecdotal evidence that up to 70 percent of children diagnosed with Asperger's will have symptoms
compatible with ADHD as well. He also notes that a "sizeable
portion" of Asperger syndrome patients won't respond well to
stimulant medications, as has been my overwhelming experience.
Interestingly, the article suggests that the attention-deficit/hy-
peractivity symptoms associated with Asperger's may be driven
more by anxiety than by understimulation, helping to explain the
medication-related pattern; in fact, the author argues that some
Asperger's patients may respond better to anti-anxiety medications (for example, selective serotonin reuptake inhibitors), which
lends support to this hypothesis. I have also observed this firsthand in my practice.

The overlap between Asperger's and ADHD diagnoses is also
confirmed by larger-scale, more academic research. A 2008 study
found significant correlations—based on parent and teacher observations of symptoms—between "autistic traits" (presumably including those associated with Asperger's, which can be considered
part of the autism spectrum) and attention-deficit/hyperactivity.[17]
The study concludes that "common genetic influences" affect
symptoms related to autism and ADHD. More recent, larger-
scale research out of Harvard also found genetic overlap among
ADHD, autism, and several other conditions.[18] A separate, broad
review of the literature on the diagnosis of Asperger's, autism,
and other conditions argued that overlap among such diagnoses
is very common, and that the exclusion criteria (that is, those used
to rule out diagnoses beyond the one of focus) used by all versions
of the *DSM* and other references could be improved to promote
better differentiation.[19] Other researchers have studied different
elements of the overlap between Asperger's and attention-deficit/

hyperactivity. For example, a 2007 study showed that the logical reasoning ability of Asperger's patients tends to diminish with age, but that this is less the case for others with attention-deficit/ hyperactivity symptoms.[20] In general, these findings speak to the high overlap between Asperger's and attention-deficit/hyperactivity symptoms, which increased the likelihood that Asperger's may be mistaken for ADHD.


## TREATMENT FOR ASPERGER SYNDROME

The Mayo Clinic describes treatment for Asperger's as follows: "The core signs of Asperger's syndrome can't be cured. However, many children with Asperger's syndrome grow into happy and well-adjusted adults."[21] That's in line with the earlier part of this chapter, which noted evidence that many kids diagnosed with Asperger's no longer meet criteria for the disorder in adulthood, though they may continue to face social and communication challenges.

Beyond hoping that age will temper some of the symptoms of Asperger's, there are multiple routes to treatment, again summarized well by the Mayo Clinic.[22] Among relevant interventions— which may be used in combination—are social skills training, cognitive-behavioral treatment, and medication. Skills training helps Asperger's patients—usually children—learn how to carry on social interaction in a more "normal" and effective way, including as related to speaking tone/rhythm, nonverbal gestures, and the interpretation of cues related to emotion and humor. Such training can be part of a broader cognitive-behavioral intervention, which helps children and adults with Asperger's recognize and anticipate situations that cause adverse reactions for them (for example, loud social situations) and develop strategies (such as generating behavior options and choosing the best one) for coping with these.

Finally, while no medications have been developed specifically for Asperger's, some pharmaceutical treatments can help alleviate symptoms of the disorder. For example, as mentioned earlier, selective serotonin reuptake inhibitors may be able to alleviate anxiety associated with Asperger's, while some antipsychotic drugs can be used to relieve patients' obsessive behaviors. In general, a large part of practitioners' approach to helping those with Asperger's is to help patients and their families understand that while some core symptoms will likely be lifelong, most of those with the diagnosis have the potential for a very high level of functioning, especially compared to more severe developmental disorders such as autism.

For my patient Donald, one of the challenges was understanding the degree to which he was motivated to improve. After all, he was an adult who was able to live and work on his own, and his condition, unlike a more physiologically based one such as high blood pressure, had few implications for his physical health. Still, it was clear that without intervention Donald would face ongoing challenges related to work and social functioning. He was more concerned about his work situation—partly because his parents were also worried about this aspect of his life—than his social life. Together we agreed to focus on his work life, and through my network I found a psychologist who specialized in skills training for individuals with Asperger's and other conditions affecting social functioning. Donald began attending individual and group treatment with that practitioner. Because he showed no significant anxiety or mood symptoms, we decided not to start him on a medication.

In the meantime, I helped Donald's parents—especially his mother—to be more realistic about their expectations. It was clear they believed their son could have as full a life as most people in their early twenties, including his sister, a twenty-six-year-old with a successful career as an accountant and a long-term romantic relationship (she was engaged to be married). I explained that while it wasn't impossible for Donald to enjoy a similar future, his Asperger's would make key aspects of life more challenging, and that the most important thing was to understand what would make him most happy, and how he could achieve it. The parents agreed to leave more space for their son, and to support him in any way they could.

Over time Donald did make progress, though not in leaps and bounds; that was to be expected. Through his therapy he learned to use nonverbal cues better, and made noticeably more eye contact with me in later sessions. He also became more adept at reading social signals by attending to others' reactions more carefully, such as knowing whether a comment was meant to be humorous. These skills helped him perform better at work, to the point that he was able to stay on the same temp assignment for several months—a first. Donald also reported that he had made progress with friendships, due in part to his improved social skills. He had met two neighbors who played the online game he enjoyed, and they sometimes met to play the game or watch TV.

Perhaps Donald's mother summarized his progress best when she said, "He may not have the kind of life we wish for him, but he's found the kind of life that works for him."

# CHAPTER 17

# Neurochemical Distractibility/Impulsivity

## The Big Point

Sometimes ADHD symptoms can result from abnormal levels of the neurotransmitters serotonin and epinephrine/norepinephrine in the nervous system. In these cases, stimulant medication or a reuptake inhibitor may be the best method of treatment, provided the severity of the symptoms are such that they interfere substantially with the patient's everyday functionality.

This chapter is different from any other condition chapter in this book because it is the only condition that is not a formal diagnosis accepted by the medical community; rather, it is based on my clinical experience. Also, while other conditions in this book are associated with a multitude of symptoms, NDI exclusively captures the symptoms of attention deficit and hyperactivity. You may be wondering, why not just call this ADHD? The reason for calling this NDI is precisely that ADHD is defined only by the expression of these symptoms, which, as we've seen, may occur alongside many other conditions, while we define NDI by its root cause: the presence of abnormal levels of specific neurotransmitters—the chemicals that relay messages in the nervous system. Furthermore, unlike an "ADHD" diagnosis, the type of neurotransmitter in question determines the medical treatment that is most likely to be effective.

## THE BOY WITHOUT AN OFF SWITCH

Peter literally ran into my office the first time I met him. The eight-year-old had arrived with his mother, who looked exhausted from chasing after him. "I know boys can be really active, but he's an extreme case," she said. She told me he had also run through the parking lot outside the clinic, nearly being hit by a car. Her son, a smiling boy with dark hair, interrupted her by asking me, "How long do I have to stay here? We're playing soccer at school and I don't want to miss it."

Peter's mother described how he was a "fanatic" about sports, and played on hockey, soccer, basketball, and baseball teams. She said, "His coaches all say he has great ability, but they're concerned that he doesn't listen and take directions well. They told us he sometimes disrupts his teammates, too, by yelling or horsing around." When I asked her about school she said his teachers said the same kinds of things: The boy was clearly smarter than average, but he had trouble sitting still, talked excessively, and often disrupted his class by blurting out answers and nudging or talking to his classmates during lessons or quiet times.

At home, Peter showed much of the same distractible, impulsive behavior. "He turns on the TV for five minutes then turns it off and says he's bored," his mother said. "Then he goes outside and comes back in because he can't find anyone to play with or they don't want to play what he does. During mealtimes he talks nonstop, often spills his drink, and pokes at his younger sister." When I asked Peter about school, he said he "liked sports more" and that he "just gets bored" with a lot of his activities, including schoolwork and sports practices.

When I asked his mother about Peter's social life, she said he made friends quickly at school and in the neighborhood, but that some of the children seemed less willing to play with him than they had been at first—"I assume it's because he just can't control himself sometimes," she said. Peter said he "had fun" with friends but that he often felt they didn't want to do the same things he did. He described how the previous week he had tried to get some neighborhood boys to play a game that was a combination of hockey and baseball (he called it "hockey-ball"), but they said that was a "crazy" idea. "I think they were just worried they would lose," Peter said.

As far as sleeping and eating, Peter's mother said that his behavior was "mostly normal." Sometimes he had trouble sleeping and came out of his room multiple times—she thought it was mostly because he didn't want to miss anything—and he often left the table before finishing his meal, though he usually came back to complete it.

Peter's teacher and family doctor were both concerned that he had ADHD. "His symptoms seem to match that pretty well," his mother said, "but I wanted to get another opinion to be sure." She added, "I feel like he just got too much of the 'boy gene,' and he doesn't have an 'off' switch."

I told her I'd do my best to help her get to the bottom of her son's behavior.

## CLUES TO LOOK FOR

What I knew about Peter after the first session led to very few hypotheses about the root of his symptoms. As his mother said, it seemed that his behavior was mostly an exaggerated version of a normal boy's. This was further supported by the testing I did with Peter in later sessions, including physical, neurological, and hearing and vision tests. None of these revealed an alternate explanation for the symptoms. Nor did questions about psychological conditions such as mood and anxiety disorders—Peter met *DSM-V* criteria for none of these conditions. Similarly, his age-appropriate academic performance suggested he had no issues with learning disabilities.

What finally helped me figure out Peter's symptoms were the results of his blood test: He had significantly lower than normal levels of the neurotransmitter serotonin. Serotonin and other neurotransmitters help transmit messages within the nervous system, and changes in their levels can result in many different types of symptoms, including those like Peter's. In Peter's case, the low levels of naturally occurring serotonin in his bloodstream were responsible for his distractibility and impulsivity.

> **Main Clue**
>
> The symptoms of neurochemical distractibility/impulsivity (NDI) include inattention, distractibility, and difficulties with self-control in multiple settings (such as home and school). The only way to confirm this condition is through blood tests showing low serotonin (which results in the consistent manifestation of distractibility and/or impulsivity) or high epinephrine/norepinephrine (which results in similar symptoms, but the symptoms tend to appear inconsistently).

## WHAT IS NEUROCHEMICAL DISTRACTIBILITY/ IMPULSIVITY?

Neurochemical distractibility/impulsivity, or NDI, results from abnormal levels of specific neurotransmitters, resulting in symptoms like poor attention, distractibility, and impulsivity. As we've noted, NDI is *not* a formal diagnosis. NDI, in contrast to the other conditions I cover, does not appear in medical textbooks or reference materials, and you won't find any information about it online at sites like WebMD or the Mayo Clinic's. Instead, I base my definition of NDI on the more than five thousand cases of patients diagnosed with ADHD that I've seen, and the symptom set consistently related to abnormal levels of the two neurotransmitters, serotonin and epinephrine/norepinephrine.

These patients exhibit symptoms of inattention and hyperactivity-impulsivity. Among these are difficulty sustaining attention and following through on instructions, easy distractibility, forgetfulness, fidgeting, running about (in inappropriate situations), leaving one's seat, interrupting, and blurting out answers. Once I confirm these patients don't show signs or symptoms related to other conditions, I check their brain chemistry patterns to conclude that these symptoms are indeed a result of abnormal neurotransmitter levels.[1] In almost all cases, these people show one of two neurotransmitter patterns: 1) *low* measurable levels of whole-blood *serotonin*; 2) *high* levels of whole-blood *epinephrine/norepinephrine*. For readers who aren't familiar with these two chemicals, the roles that these neurotransmitters play in the body, while very complex, can be simplified as follows: Both serotonin and epinephrine/norepinephrine, like all neurotransmitters, work at the synapses within the nervous system, or the small gaps between nerve fibers. Specifically, the neurotransmitters help neural messages make the jump across the synapse. Serotonin can act to have a calming effect and is associated with a general feeling of well-being. On the other hand, epinephrine/norepinephrine are colloquially known as "adrenaline," the hormone that activates our nervous system and makes us feel more alert—whether in a positive way (as when we need to focus on a challenging task like a test) or a negative way (as when we feel afraid).

The two types described show subtly different symptom patterns (and respond to different treatments, as discussed in the following section). The low-serotonin group tends to look more like what people think of when they think of the disorder called ADHD. The high-epinephrine/norepinephrine group is "consistent in its inconsistency": Sometimes these patients can concentrate well, and sometimes they can't; sometimes they engage in impulsive, hyperactive behavior, and sometimes they don't. The different symptom patterns have to do with physiological processes that are beyond the scope of this book.[2]

Peter's symptoms were very consistent with the low-serotonin form of NDI. He displayed many signs of distractibility and impulsivity, including poor listening (to his teacher, coaches, and parents), fidgeting, talking excessively, blurting out answers, and having difficulty sustaining attention in school, at home, and during sports practices and games. Moreover, his symptoms appeared consistently, over both time and setting. Again, this fits with the low-serotonin form of NDI, rather than the high-norepinephrine version, which involves less consistency of symptoms—sometimes they appear, and sometimes they don't. Peter's symptoms were resulting in multiple consequences for the boy, including the frustration of his parents, teachers, and coaches, along with increasing social challenges with his peers (such as their reduced interest in playing with him, as his mother had noticed). So it was important to get the right diagnosis and treatment for him quickly. As with all the conditions I describe in this book, *treatment delayed is treatment denied.* A correct diagnosis is important for securing the most effective intervention and preventing ongoing suffering for the patient, their family, and those around them.

## PREVALENCE OF NDI

The prevalence of NDI in the population is difficult to quantify precisely because it is not a recognized condition, and there have been no systematic studies about the levels of serotonin and epinephrine/norepinephrine in the population. Overall, I would estimate that about 1–2 percent of all people—children and adults— have the symptom and neurotransmitter pattern associated with NDI. Of course, that doesn't mean that everyone who may qualify for the diagnosis is aware of their symptoms or has tried to get treatment for these. That's true of all the conditions in this book. I've also noticed no specific demographic patterns for NDI: It seems equally common among children and adults (many of whom have probably had the condition since childhood), among males and females, and across ethnic groups that I see. In my experience, NDI does run in families: Those qualifying for the condition tend to have family members with similar symptoms— blood tests for the family members would likely reveal consistent neurotransmitter patterns. Peter's family history included several relatives with significant distractibility and impulsivity, including a grandmother and two uncles. None of these members had sought medical help for their symptoms, partly because there had been less concern about such symptoms in their generations, compared to Peter's.

## RELATION TO ATTENTION-DEFICIT/HYPERACTIVITY SYMPTOMS

As we saw early on in this chapter, while the symptoms associated with NDI are generally the same as those linked to the disorder called "ADHD" (through the *DSM-V* criteria), the conditions are very different. NDI is defined by its *cause* (neurochemical imbalances related to serotonin and norepinephrine/epinephrine, as confirmed by blood tests), whereas ADHD is defined only by its *symptoms*. As I've said throughout this book, ADHD simply does not exist in the way that most people, including medical practitioners, believe it does. For example, NDI would not even be included in any version of the *DSM*, because its diagnosis is based not on specific symptoms but on a deficit or excess of neurotransmitters in the body. In that way, the NDI diagnosis is more like hyperthyroidism (discussed later, in the chapter on "Other Conditions"), which is based on an excess of thyroid hormone but then causes symptoms including poor attention. Similarly, it's important to note that the neurotransmitters involved in NDI are also related to other conditions, such as mood disorders. For example, studies show that serotonin and epinephrine/norepinephrine levels (the neurotransmitters themselves and/or their activity levels) are low in those diagnosed with depression.[3] Note that if one of my patients shows symptoms of both depression and NDI, I tend to focus treatment more on the NDI. That's because 1) I don't like loading my patients up with multiple medications, which makes it difficult to understand exactly what pharmaceutical has what effect, and 2) with successful treatment of NDI, the depression symptoms often disappear—because they are generally related to the NDI, whether reflecting the symptoms of NDI itself (such as poor concentration) or consequences of the NDI symptoms (such as sad mood due to chronic distractibility).

## TREATMENT FOR NEUROCHEMICAL DISTRACTIBILITY/ IMPULSIVITY

Treatment for NDI also involves some overlap with the way ADHD is usually approached by medical practitioners. However, it is important to weigh the risks of stimulant medication with the benefits before prescribing this medication. For many reasons alluded to earlier in this book, prescribing stimulant medication should not be taken lightly. First, as with all conditions discussed in this book, the symptoms of NDI should have a significant impact on your life for medical treatment to be warranted. It should affect your well-being in one or more areas of functioning: work, school, social relationships, or others. Second, the dosage of any medication prescribed should be monitored carefully, to prevent significant side effects. As discussed elsewhere in this book, side effects of stimulants like Ritalin include disturbed sleep and appetite, irritability, and even depression. When patients experience these or other side effects, I lower their stimulant dosage, try a different stimulant (there are often subtle differences in side-effect profiles even among medications of the same general type), or take them off the medication (that is, when the side effects outweigh any benefits of the treatment). After taking all of the above into account, NDI patients may benefit from taking certain medications. The low-serotonin group, which tends to look more like what people think of when they think of the disorder called ADHD, responds well to stimulants like Ritalin, Adderall, and Vyvanse, which are often used in the treatment of "ADHD." The high-epinephrine/norepinephrine group—whose members have inconsistent symptom patterns—tend to respond well to norepinephrine reuptake inhibitors, such as Strattera. A reuptake inhibitor aimed at any neurotransmitter prevents that chemical from being taken back into the nerve fiber after it has been used to facilitate message transmission in the synapse; in patients with high levels of norepinephrine, the reuptake inhibitor can have a paradoxical effect of lowering the overall neurotransmitter levels in the blood, thus improving NDI symptoms. These treatment patterns help explain why some people diagnosed with ADHD respond well to stimulant medication. In other words, they got lucky by targeting the hidden chemical abnormalities within their nervous system.

Choosing a specific treatment depends on securing a comprehensive blood screening for patients, given that the two types of NDI respond differently to different medications. As far as time-release stimulants go (such as Adderall XR and Vyvanse), I typically prescribe a short-acting stimulant first as a test dose to gauge the patient's response to the medication and side effects. Assuming the patient responds well, I then recommend an extended-release stimulant. As we saw in the chapter on stimulants, the short-term side effects can be less severe with these slow-acting verions. Beyond choosing the right medication, I monitor my NDI patients' symptoms and potential side effects carefully to make sure we find the right dose. As noted above, excessive dosages or use of pharmaceuticals like Ritalin can result in significant side effects like sleeplessness, excitability, and reduced appetite, which can make distractibility and impulsivity even worse. Norepinephrine reuptake inhibitors (used for the high-norepinephrine/epinephrine form of NDI) can also have side effects; these include cold-like symptoms or stomach aches, if the medicine is not taken with food.

My NDI patients tend to respond very well to treatment with any of the above medications. Some need reduced dosages of the medicines over time, and may eventually stop taking them, without a significant increase in symptoms. This is particularly true in child patients, who sometimes seem to "grow out of" the NDI, most likely reflecting an age-associated change in their neurotransmitter patterns; our bodies sometimes adjust to more normal states of functioning over time. Other NDI patients, especially adults, may need to stay on the medication for longer periods. In every case, I balance the benefits of the medication with the costs (such as side effects) of staying on it.

After explaining Peter's NDI diagnosis to his parents, I decided to start him on a low dose of Ritalin. We also agreed that if his symptoms didn't improve significantly in the near future, his parents would also look into more behaviorally oriented treatments—both for Peter and themselves (to improve their parenting skills). While the boy's symptoms showed mild improvement within the first month of Ritalin use, I believed it was worth increasing the dose slightly. At the higher dose, Peter quickly showed marked improvement across his distractibility and impulsivity symptoms. Peter's mother noted that her son's behavior at home, in school, and on the playing field had improved dramatically. "He's still a very active little guy," she said, "but he seems much better able to rein it in and show some self-control." This included fidgeting and blurting out less in school, paying more attention and poking his sister less at home, and listening more carefully to his coaches in the multiple sports he played.

When I asked Peter how he liked school and practice these days, he said, "They're not as boring as they used to be." His mother also reported that he was getting along much better with friends at school and in the neighborhood. By talking to his neighborhood friends more nicely and agreeing to play the games they wanted to play, too, Peter had finally engaged them in a few games of "hockey-ball," his own creation. "It was a lot of fun," he said.

I noticed that Peter no longer ran into my office for appointments, but walked (quickly) instead. And his mother reported no near accidents in the parking lot due to his running. "I can finally keep up with my son," she said, "most of the time."

# CHAPTER 18

# Schizophrenia

## The Big Point

Schizophrenia is a disorder that can occur in children and adults and is marked by visual and auditory hallucinations, delusional (for example, paranoid) beliefs, and other symptoms. Patients experiencing these symptoms often demonstrate impulsivity, distractibility, and short attention spans, which may be mistaken for ADHD. Careful assessment, especially for children, can yield the correct diagnosis of schizophrenia and help determine the best approach to treatment.

Schizophrenia is one of the most sensationalized mental disorders, with extreme depictions of the condition in books, movies, and other media, and widespread misconceptions, including the confusion of schizophrenia with multiple personality disorder. In reality, schizophrenia is a serious illness that occurs on a range from mild and treatable to severe and requiring lengthy hospitalization. The hallmark symptoms of schizophrenia include hallucinations such as hearing voices in one's head and delusions such as believing that one is the target of government conspiracies. Understandably, such symptoms take up significant mental capacity, often leading to symptoms including attention deficits, distractibility, and even hyperactivity.

When those consequent symptoms are misdiagnosed as ADHD, schizophrenic patients are likely to be treated with stimulants, which fail to alleviate the symptoms and may even make them worse. This was the case for my patient Matt.

## THE BOY WHO MUMBLED TO HIMSELF

Matt was having trouble in school. The ten-year-old—a dark-haired boy with piercing green eyes—was performing well academically in his private elementary school, but his teacher reported that he was increasingly distractible and "hyperactive," including whispering to himself during class and scuffling with other students in the classroom and on the playground.

Matt's mother brought him to see me after two previous physicians had diagnosed the boy with ADHD and started him on stimulant medications over the past year. "The medicine made it harder for him to sleep and eat," she said. "And it didn't seem to help his symptoms, either." When I asked Matt if he thought the medication had helped, he shrugged and said, "I guess not." He expressed very little emotion during their first visit, avoiding eye contact and sometimes mumbling to himself. "He does that more and more," his mother whispered to me midway through the session.

She also mentioned that Matt had exhibited "odd" behavior, such as keeping to himself and saying things that didn't make sense, since about age five, but that it had worsened in the past year. For example, at the dinner table he sometimes blurted out statements (for example, "I think squirrels don't like our yard!") that had nothing to do with the conversation around him. He had been keeping to himself more at home as well, often sitting quietly or whispering to himself. Also, while he'd never had many friends, he had never gotten into fights with other children—until recently. His mother said, "Matt says the other children pick on him a lot, but the teacher seems to think he's the one starting fights." When I asked Matt if he felt picked on by his classmates, he frowned—one of the only times he showed emotion—and said, "Why do you care?" After that he refused to speak for the duration of the visit, with the exception of some mumbling to himself.

After my first session with Matt and his mother I had some hypotheses about what was going on with the boy. I told his mother I was confident we could get Matt better help for his symptoms after doing more comprehensive testing.

## CLUES TO LOOK FOR

As I expected, the physical, neurological, educational, and hearing and vision tests I ordered for Matt over subsequent sessions were all negative; that is, they revealed no evidence of a specific condition that would explain his attention-deficit and behavioral symptoms. His strong academic performance also helped us rule out a learning disability as a possible root cause.

In fact, the first solid clue to Matt's underlying condition was his answer to a question I asked in our second session: "Do you ever hear voices in your head—other than your own?" He shrugged (his usual first response) and said, "Yeah. Doesn't everybody?" Now I knew the likely cause of the boy's symptoms. Auditory hallucinations, including voices in one's head, are symptoms of schizophrenia and other psychotic disorders. I conducted a more comprehensive psychological examination of Matt to understand the extent of his symptoms and determine the most appropriate diagnosis. As suspected, he met diagnostic criteria for schizophrenia, with symptoms including auditory hallucinations, paranoid delusions, and flattened affect.

Schizophrenia is one of a number of mental disorders marked by hallucinations, delusions, and/or odd behavior. It is typically treated with a combination of medication and psychotherapy, as discussed in detail in the next sections.

### Main Clue

Schizophrenia and other diagnoses involving psychotic symptoms (such as hallucinations and delusions) can be difficult to determine due to patients' limited communication skills or guardedness about their symptoms. People with these conditions, especially children, will rarely volunteer information related to them. Direct questioning (for example, "Do you hear voices in your head, other than your own?") can help uncover such symptoms—which often relate in turn to attention-deficit/hyperactivity symptoms—and lead to an accurate diagnosis.

## WHAT IS SCHIZOPHRENIA?

Schizophrenia is an often-sensationalized and misunderstood condition that can range from mild and easily controlled with medication, to truly debilitating. Schizophrenia is the most well-known mental disorder among a set of conditions marked by *psychotic* symptoms. According to the fifth edition of the *Diagnostic and Statistical Manual of Mental Disorders*, "schizophrenia spectrum" and other psychotic disorders are those that include delusions, hallucinations, disorganized thinking/speech, disorganized/abnormal motor behavior, and "negative" symptoms; we'll discuss these in more detail below.[1] Diagnosis of schizophrenia, specifically, requires:

- Two or more of the following for the better part of at least a one-month period: delusions, hallucinations, disorganized speech (at least one of these first three symptoms

is required), disorganized or catatonic behavior, negative symptoms
- Impaired level of functioning related to work, social relations, and/or self-care
- At least six months of continuous signs of the disturbance (with at least one month where symptoms are present for the majority of the time)

The *DSM-V* also points out that to be diagnosed, schizophrenia and other psychoses should not be better explained by substance use or another diagnosis. As always, the *DSM-V* should be viewed as providing good clues to likely diagnoses, rather than the final authority.

As noted above, several types of symptoms are considered characteristic of schizophrenia. Many practitioners view the two main categories of schizophrenia symptoms as "positive" and "negative." Positive symptoms involve distortions of normal functions, while negative symptoms involve the loss or absence of normal functions.

Positive symptoms include distorted thinking (delusions, including those based in paranoia), false perceptions (hallucinations), "disorganized" speech—or bizarre, nonsensical communication patterns—and disorganized behavior, as described below, based on the *DSM-V* and my own experience with patients:

- Persecutory *delusions* are the most common type of distorted belief; patients feel they are being followed, watched, ridiculed, or picked on. They may also believe that newspaper or online articles, overheard conversations, song lyrics, or other environmental phenomena refer to them, despite a lack of evidence. Bizarre delusions (for example, that the government has programmed one's thoughts) are especially likely to be part of a schizophrenia diagnosis.

- *Hallucinations* can involve any of the five senses: sight, hearing, taste, smell, touch. But auditory hallucinations are most common, usually occurring as voices in one's head. Sometimes these take the form of a single voice; other times the hallucinations can involve a conversation between two or more voices.

- *Disorganized thinking* can include "loose associations," or rapidly moving from one topic or idea to another, with only the most tangential links, or even nearly incomprehensible speech—what has been termed a "word salad" for its jumble of phrases and ideas.

- *Disorganized behavior* in schizophrenia ranges from silliness (such as singing a children's song in an inappropriate context) to agitation (for example, shouting obscenities) to various forms of catatonia (rigidity, strange postures, etc.).

Negative symptoms include an excessively low range of emotional or verbal expression, and sometimes the absence of goal-directed behavior. According to the *DSM-V*, negative symptoms related to schizophrenia include:

- *Diminished emotional expression*, including reduced eye contact, variation in speech tone, and hand/head movements
- *Avolition*, which is a lack of goal-directed activity, including as related to academic, occupational, and social pursuits
- *Alogia*, another symptom of the disorder, meaning decreased speech (that is, saying little, including in response to questions or attempts at conversation), but not due to a voluntary restriction of speaking

- *Anhedonia*, or the decreased ability to enjoy normally positive events and activities
- *Asociality*, an observable lack of interest in social interactions (which may be related to avolition)

Negative symptoms can be difficult to diagnose accurately because many normal people display elements of them in various settings and situations.

The *DSM-IV* (the *DSM-V's* predecessor) presented several subtypes of schizophrenia.[2] The main ones are paranoid type (marked by persecutory and other delusions), disorganized type (involving disorganized speech and behavior), and catatonic type (lack of, excessive, or peculiar movement). Diagnosable schizophrenia that falls outside those types was called undifferentiated type. As mentioned earlier, it's important to distinguish schizophrenia from other medical conditions that include psychotic symptoms. Among these conditions are medical disorders (for example, brain tumor), substance abuse (for example, involving hallucinogenic drugs), and mood disorders (for example, bipolar disorder). All of these conditions are discussed elsewhere in this book. It's also important to note that schizophrenia is *not* synonymous with multiple personality disorder, though many people confuse the two conditions. According to the *DSM-V*, multiple personality disorder, or "dissociative identity disorder," involves the presence in one person of at least two separate personalities capable of taking full control of that person's thoughts and actions for prolonged periods, whereas schizophrenia rarely involves the full control of the patient by a separate personality or identity. Nonetheless, it can be challenging to differentiate schizophrenia from dissociative identity disorder, especially when the schizophrenia is characterized by deep and sustained identity-related delusions.

As mentioned earlier, the symptoms of schizophrenia should collectively interfere with functioning in at least one of these areas: self-care, social activities, academics, and occupational performance. Underlying this interference are the symptoms' effects on areas including communication, perception, self-awareness, and attention, as discussed in later sections.

My patient Matt showed multiple signs of schizophrenia, including the positive symptoms of auditory hallucinations (the voices he heard in his head) and persecutory delusions (he believed his classmates were constantly picking on him or thinking negatively of him), and the negative symptom of diminished emotional expression (silence, poor eye contact, indifference to emotional issues such as an injury in the family). Further testing revealed that the hallucinations and delusions were linked: Over time Matt admitted to his parents and me that the voices he heard often told him that his classmates didn't like him and talked about him behind his back, and that he should "get back" at them for how they treated him; sometimes the voices even accused others of stealing from Matt. Those hallucination-fueled beliefs had motivated almost all of the fights his teacher said he'd gotten into at school. Moreover, Matt's mumbling and whispering to himself was now explained: He was talking back to the voices, sometimes disagreeing with them, sometimes asking them questions, sometimes just conversing.

It wasn't surprising that Matt was distractible in school and at home, given that he was consumed with his increasingly frequent hallucinations and delusions. Also not surprisingly, Matt's previous diagnosis of ADHD—and resultant treatment with stimulants—had failed to improve his symptoms, because those medications have no proven effects on hallucinations, delusions, or the negative symptoms of schizophrenia. As in many other cases, *treatment delayed due to the misdiagnosis of ADHD was again treatment denied*, resulting in deep frustration for Matt's family and teachers.

## PREVALENCE OF SCHIZOPHRENIA

The *DSM-IV* estimates the lifetime prevalence of schizophrenia as up to 0.7 percent across the population, though this figure may vary across countries. So, about 7 out of 1,000 people would be diagnosed with schizophrenia at some point in their lives. There are also cultural and religious factors that should be taken into account when considering a diagnosis of schizophrenia, as some cultures hold what might be considered delusional beliefs (for example, witchcraft) and some religions accept or even revere what might be considered hallucinations (for example, seeing or hearing God) outside of that context.

Schizophrenia most commonly starts in teenage years or early adulthood; it is first observed more rarely in younger children (such as my patient Matt) or older adults (for example, in their fifties). The disorder's typical course includes an initial phase involving gradual withdrawal from school, work, or social activities, followed by positive symptoms including hallucinations and/or delusions. The longer-term course of the disorder is difficult to assess, but the *DSM-V* reports that only a small number of individuals with schizophrenia can be expected to recover completely. The *DSM* also mentions that about 5 percent of those with schizophrenia may commit suicide, with as much as 20 percent attempting suicide at least once.

Some studies suggest a higher rate of schizophrenia in males, whereas others find no difference between genders. There is a strong familial pattern associated with schizophrenia, such that blood relatives of schizophrenic patients have a much higher likelihood of diagnosis with the disorder. At the same time, twin studies show that environmental factors also play a significant role, as genetically identical individuals often have different outcomes (that is, one develops schizophrenia while the other does not).

Upon completion of a full family history, we understood that Matt was at slightly increased risk for schizophrenia based on his genetic heritage. His paternal great-grandfather and a maternal uncle (who had committed suicide in his fifties) had been "odd" individuals with some evidence of positive (for example, delusional thinking) and negative (for example, keeping to themselves) symptoms, but neither had been formally diagnosed with schizophrenia or another psychotic disorder.

## RELATION TO ATTENTION-DEFICIT/HYPERACTIVITY SYMPTOMS

The symptoms of schizophrenia are likely to result in attention-deficit/hyperactivity symptoms that might be mistaken for the disorder called ADHD, especially in less severe cases of schizophrenia. Delusions and hallucinations take up significant brain-processing capacity, leaving less "bandwidth" for everyday tasks such as attending to conversations or paying attention in class. Similarly, talking to oneself (including to the voices in one's head) or accusing others of teasing may potentially be viewed as hyperactive behavior. Nonetheless, few studies have examined how frequently ADHD and schizophrenia are diagnosed together.

Some studies have examined the physiological factors underlying attention deficit in schizophrenia. A Norwegian study, for example, found that adolescents with schizophrenia had more trouble completing memory tasks than their nondiagnosed peers, which could relate to attention deficits.[3] A Canadian researcher has argued that neurons (nerve cells) in the prefrontal part of the brain's cortex act as information filters or gatekeepers, and that these cells may be damaged or dysfunctional in disorders like schizophrenia, resulting in "brain clutter," or the presence of too much information, including irrelevant material.[4] The brain clutter that schizophrenic patients experience would likely result in noticeable attention deficits. Finally, as discussed in the introductory chapter, researchers have demonstrated significant overlap in the genetics of schizophrenia, ADHD, and multiple other conditions, further suggesting a link among them.[5]

Schizophrenia can be treated with medication and nonpharmacological treatments, as discussed in the next section.

## TREATMENT FOR SCHIZOPHRENIA

According to the National Institute of Mental Health (NIMH), "Because the causes of schizophrenia are still unknown, treatments focus on eliminating the symptoms of the disease."[6] Two generations of antipsychotic medications—the older ones are called "typical" and the newer ones "atypical"—have been developed to reduce hallucinations, delusions, and agitation. Documented side effects include drowsiness, dizziness, and uncontrolled mouth movements (the last one is associated with long-term use of typical antipsychotics and known as "tardive dyskinesia"). More severe cases of schizophrenia often require inpatient treatment, to provide patients basic care (that is, nutrition, sleep, hygiene) when they can't provide this for themselves and to prevent them from harming themselves or others. It's important to note that violence associated with schizophrenia, while not insignificant, represents only a very small fraction of the overall level of violence in a given population.[7] Schizophrenia is generally considered a chronic disorder requiring lifelong treatment, even if most symptoms have abated.[8]

Psychosocial treatments can be used to supplement drug-based intervention, especially once more significant symptoms are under control. According to the NIMH, these interventions include illness management skills (for example, strategies for monitoring symptoms and preventing relapse), social and vocational training (since schizophrenia often affects people during key formative periods), family education and treatment (because the disorder's severity can affect families significantly and families are often the ones taking care of schizophrenic patients), and self-help groups for patients and their families.

Upon confirming the schizophrenia diagnosis, we started my patient Matt on a low dose of an antipsychotic. His hallucinations and delusions improved quickly, but his negative symptoms—including emotional flatness and social withdrawal—remained noticeable both at school and at home. I helped Matt's family understand the long-term nature of his condition but reassured them that many patients diagnosed with schizophrenia lead full, healthy lives. I also referred them to a psychologist who specialized in family treatment for schizophrenic patients diagnosed at a young age. In addition to working with them, the therapist helped the family find a group facing similar issues. Matt's mother said, "Seeing that other families are going through exactly what we are has been very helpful."

The diagnosis of schizophrenia meant that Matt and his family faced a long road ahead. But by seeking out the correct diagnosis, they ensured that Matt was receiving the best possible treatment much earlier than he might have.

# CHAPTER 19

# Fetal Alcohol Syndrome

### The Big Point

Fetal alcohol syndrome, or a set of symptoms that results from excessive drinking during pregnancy, has lifelong effects on a child, including challenges related to attention, impulsivity, and hyperactivity. Children and adults displaying these symptoms may be diagnosed mistakenly with ADHD. Making an accurate diagnosis of fetal alcohol syndrome can help patients and their families find the best treatment.

For decades, there was little understanding that drinking alcohol during pregnancy was harmful for the fetus and would likely result in lifelong developmental problems. While our understanding of the harmful link between alcohol and pregnancy has improved dramatically, fetal alcohol syndrome remains a problem in countries worldwide, including the United States. The condition has a wide range of symptoms including physical characteristics (for example, small head), coordination problems (for example, fine-motor skills), cognitive challenges (for example, learning disabilities), and attention-deficit/hyperactivity. The latter symptoms may be mistakenly diagnosed as ADHD, resulting in the wrong treatment for the condition, which can fail to alleviate and/or worsen the symptoms. This was the case for my patient Victor and his family.

## WHAT'S WRONG WITH VICTOR?

On their first visit to my office, nine-year-old Victor's parents told me how excited they'd been when they first met him: not in the delivery room, but at an orphanage in Romania. The couple, now in their early fifties, had tried for years to have a child but eventually decided to adopt. They'd been overjoyed to win approval to adopt Victor, who was three years old at the time. "He smiled at me as soon as he saw me," his mother said. "It was like we were meant to be his parents." They'd brought him to the United States and kept his Romanian name.

For their first years together, the family had done well. Victor, who'd always had a smaller-than-average head and small eyes with skin folded over the inner corners, displayed some of the difficult behaviors normally seen among toddlers, including occasional temper tantrums. But his preschool and early elementary school teachers had reported no problem behaviors, and he'd kept pace academically with his peers, having learned English quickly and made several friends.

"That changed last year," Victor's father said. The boy's behavior became a problem. For example, he had frequent temper tantrums: "He gets these unstoppable rages," his mother said, "and it can be frightening." Both parents described how Victor would scream, throw things, and punch and kick them when they tried to set limits with him, such as asking him to turn off the TV. Further questioning revealed the parents had good intentions but only limited parenting skills. As Victor's behavior worsened, they often let their son "have his way," rather than taking a stand, as confirmed by the father: "We walk on eggshells around him, for fear of setting him off." Victor's mother added that the boy had cuddled with her frequently in their early years together, but that he no longer showed signs of affection, usually pushing her away when she tried to hug him. In my office, both parents seemed intimidated by their son, often whispering their answers to my questions. Victor himself only answered me with shrugs and single syllables. The boy had trouble staying still during the visit, walking or even running around my office. He ignored his parents when they asked him to sit.

The situation at school wasn't any better. Victor's third-grade teacher reported that he had been having frequent outbursts and picking fights with classmates. He was also having trouble paying attention in class, frequently rising from his seat, interrupting the teacher, and disrupting classmates. He refused to answer questions in class. Several visits to the principal had failed to improve Victor's behavior. His parents said the teacher had also expressed concern that Victor was slipping well below his grade level in reading, math, and other subjects, with difficulty learning new concepts. "It's like he's going backward," his father said, referring to Victor's earlier academic progress. Both parents admitted that Victor, unlike most of his peers, was unable to tie his shoes—"We tried to teach him, but he kept getting mad"—and had struggled to learn how to ride a bike, eventually giving up. Though Victor had played soccer and baseball in earlier grades, he had never enjoyed the sports or showed talent for them. The boy had also stopped socializing with neighborhood and school friends, and expressed no interest in being with other children. "He just fights with other kids, anyway," his mother said with a sigh.

Since his behavior had worsened, Victor's parents had taken him to three physicians; I was the fourth. The first doctor said the boy would "grow out of" his symptoms. The next two diagnosed

Victor with ADHD and suggested stimulant medication. The physicians had tried three stimulants so far, with no success. The first two had failed to improve any of Victor's symptoms, and the last one had improved his impulsiveness slightly but failed to enhance his focus and disrupted his sleep and appetite significantly. "We told the doctor we wanted to stop the medication," Victor's father said. I told them I understood their motivation.

Near the end of their first visit Victor's mother tearfully said, "We just want to know what's wrong with Victor." I asked the parents to get as much information about Victor's background as possible from the orphanage where he'd spent his early years, as that could provide more clues to his condition.

## CLUES TO LOOK FOR

To understand possible causes for Victor's symptoms I ran multiple tests with the boy: full physical and history, as well as vision, hearing, cardiac, and neurological exams. I also referred him for more in-depth educational testing. As expected, the physical exam showed that Victor had a smaller head circumference than average. Basic coordination tests (for example, walking a straight line forward and backward, transferring small screws from the table to a cup) showed that he struggled with both gross- (large muscle) and fine-motor coordination, again as expected from initial information and observation. The heart exam showed a slightly defective valve, but there was no evidence that this affected the heart's functioning significantly. Victor also showed evidence of both verbal and math-related learning disabilities, consistent with his recent academic performance.

While these test results may have yielded some clues to Victor's condition (for example, learning disabilities can lead to attention-deficit/hyperactivity symptoms, as discussed in another chapter), the best evidence arrived in the information his parents were able to secure from the Romanian orphanage. The orphanage director confessed that the facility had little information about Victor's biological mother, but said she was "young and troubled" and that many of the women who gave their children up for adoption in that region had substance-related issues, especially with alcohol.

Now we had a better explanation for Victor's symptoms. It was likely the boy suffered from the longer-term effects of fetal alcohol syndrome (FAS), a condition resulting from excessive alcohol consumption by the mother during pregnancy. FAS remains a problem worldwide, and its signs and symptoms include developmental delays, coordination problems, learning challenges, and attention-deficit/hyperactivity.

> ### Main Clue
>
> Fetal alcohol syndrome (FAS) in children usually presents as a condition including developmental and learning delays, along with some physical characteristics (such as small head size) and behavioral symptoms (for example, attention-deficit/hyperactivity). Confirming the diagnosis requires evidence that the mother consumed alcohol excessively while pregnant—information that can be secured from the mother (for example, oral history or blood alcohol tests during pregnancy) or other observers (the child's father, medical practitioners, adoption agency staff, etc.).

## WHAT IS FETAL ALCOHOL SYNDROME?

FAS has a clear cause and can include symptoms ranging from mild to severe. FAS occurs when a pregnant woman uses or abuses alcohol regularly.[1] The problem is that the alcohol passes easily through the placenta (the organ that connects the fetus to the mother's uterine wall, allowing passage of nutrients and waste) to the fetus, harming its development. It is unknown exactly what level of alcohol intake will leave the baby's development unaffected, but larger amounts of alcohol are associated with more serious FAS symptoms. While drinking alcohol at any time during pregnancy can be harmful to the fetus, drinking during the first three months is particularly so.

Signs and symptoms of FAS include:

- Delayed development both in the womb and after birth
- Poor muscle tone and coordination
- Distinct physical characteristics such as a small head, small upper jaw, thin upper lip, and narrow eyes with large epicanthic folds (that is, covering the inner corner of the eye)
- Specific heart defects such as a heart murmur (loud heart sounds that can be benign or harmful) or weak or absent atrial septum, which can result in lower oxygen levels in circulating blood
- Intellectual/learning disabilities including as related to verbal and quantitative skills, with severe cases involving significant mental disability
- Attention-deficit, hyperactivity, and impulsivity, along with other behavioral problems such as difficulty managing anger and frustration
- Death of the fetus or infant (in extreme cases)

Tests for FAS include those related to the mother, the fetus, and the affected child. In the mother, consistently high blood alcohol results during pregnancy (for example, a pregnant woman charged with driving under the influence of alcohol based on blood-alcohol levels) or observable evidence of intoxication (for example, slurred speech, difficulty walking) can serve as evidence of likely FAS. A pregnancy ultrasound can confirm delayed development in the fetus when FAS is suspected. Finally, brain imaging such as a CT (computed tomography) or MRI (magnetic resonance imaging) scan can show evidence of the effects of FAS on the brain of an affected child.

Victor clearly showed many of the signs and symptoms of FAS. Physically, he had a small head and eyes, with distinct epicanthic folds. Developmentally, he showed delays and disabilities related to his cognitive (for example, difficulty with reading and math) and motor (for example, difficulty tying his shoes and riding a bike) functioning. His attention, impulsivity, and anger/frustration management problems (getting out of his seat, starting fights, etc.) had become more pronounced over the last year, causing problems for Victor, his classmates, his teacher, and his parents. He also showed evidence for a benign heart valve defect. Overall, Victor's FAS symptoms were in the mild to moderate range. It is not clear why Victor's symptoms had worsened over time, but I've observed many FAS patients who follow a similar pattern: They seem to develop at a normal pace initially, but quickly decline in early or later childhood.

## PREVALENCE OF FAS

A study cited by the National Institute on Alcohol Abuse and Alcoholism estimates that FAS occurs in 0.5 to 2 births out of every 1,000 in the United States.[2] *Fetal alcohol spectrum disorder* refers to the broad range of cognitive, physical, and/or behavioral conditions and disorders—including FAS—caused by drinking during pregnancy; about 1 percent of all U.S. births are estimated to involve a condition on this spectrum.[3] Drinking while pregnant is common in the United States. A CDC study conducted in the late 2000s showed that 7.6 percent of pregnant women had drunk alcohol in the past thirty days; rates were higher than that among pregnant women age 35–44 (14.3 percent) and those who were college graduates (10.0 percent) and/or employed (9.6 percent).[4] Among women at risk for significant alcohol consumption, estimated rates of FAS run as high as 44 percent. Similarly, in countries with higher rates of drinking (for example, Russia, South Africa), the prevalence of FAS is thought to be higher than in the United States, though few formal epidemiological studies have been conducted internationally.[5]

Children adopted from countries with a higher rate of drinking are at greater risk for developing FAS and related conditions. For example, a study of children adopted into Sweden from Eastern European countries (including Romania) showed that 30 percent were diagnosable with FAS and a full 44 percent qualified for a fetal alcohol spectrum disorder (that includes the 30 percent diagnosed with FAS).[6] Adoptions from Eastern Europe peaked in the 1990s, with more than forty-seven thousand children adopted from Russia alone in the late 1990s and early 2000s; researchers have noted that alcohol consumption is higher in Eastern Europe, and that many children in orphanages there came from parents with substance abuse issues.[7]

Victor's case reflected many of the trends above, as he was adopted from a country known for problems with drinking during pregnancy. Though the details of his mother's drinking were unclear, it was likely that she consumed excessive alcohol. As noted above, FAS has been identified as occurring with high frequency among children adopted from Romania. For children like Victor, FAS is a lifetime condition; there is no cure. Moreover, problems tend to compound over time. For example, studies have shown increased rates of school-related problems (suspensions, expulsions, etc.), trouble with the law (for example, arrests for fighting), inappropriate sexual behavior (such as making unwanted advances), employment problems, and alcohol and drug abuse (including a severity requiring inpatient treatment) among those diagnosed with FAS.[8] However, targeted treatment, especially when conducted early in life, can improve patients' development and quality of life.[9] Treatment options are discussed later in this chapter.

## RELATION TO ATTENTION-DEFICIT/HYPERACTIVITY SYMPTOMS

As mentioned earlier, FAS is associated with attention deficits, impulsivity, and hyperactivity. In line with this, a 2006 study found that 41 percent of children with fetal alcohol spectrum disorders qualified for a diagnosis of ADHD.[10] Other studies have suggested that ADHD is the most commonly diagnosed additional disorder with FAS and fetal alcohol spectrum conditions, and that it is difficult to determine the exact relationship between the disorders.[11] It's not surprising that what we call ADHD would be diagnosed frequently with FAS, given the cognitive and behavioral symptoms associated with FAS, including attention/learning challenges and problems managing frustration and anger.

However, as discussed throughout this book, the idea is that diagnosing ADHD on top of a fetal alcohol condition is erroneous: Managing the effects of the FAS will generally help address the attention-deficit/hyperactivity symptoms. That idea is reinforced by a late 1990s study that found that children diagnosed with FAS had different types of attention problems (for example, they had less trouble sustaining attention but more trouble shifting attention) than those meeting criteria for ADHD.[12] Another study found that children with FAS had unique difficulty handling overstimulation compared to their peers diagnosed with ADHD.[13] Such evidence points to the importance of providing an accurate diagnosis of FAS as quickly as possible for patients, to get them the most helpful treatment. As for all the conditions discussed in this book, *treatment delayed is treatment denied*, with significant negative consequences for patients and their families, including increased symptom severity, stress, and financial costs.

## TREATMENT FOR FAS

As mentioned earlier, FAS is a lifelong condition, with no available treatment to cure it completely. But a range of interventions can improve symptoms related to FAS.[14] Early intervention—including speech and physical therapy from a child's first year to three years old—can be especially important in improving development. For FAS-diagnosed children and adults alike, treatment options should be considered in several categories.

While no medication is indicated specifically for FAS, pharmaceuticals can be used to address specific symptoms. Among the possibilities are antidepressants for mood-related symptoms and irritability, anti-anxiety agents, and neuroleptics, which are often used to treat symptoms like hallucinations but can reduce aggression and other behavior problems. These medications must be administered by a qualified physician, with careful monitoring of their effectiveness and potential side effects, and adjustment of dosage as necessary.

Other important approaches to FAS include physical and occupational therapy. For example, physical therapy can be aimed at improving coordination problems (both gross- and fine-motor). Occupational therapy is used to improve patients' abilities to carry out activities of daily living—allowing them to "engage in occupations of life."[15] Child-focused occupational therapy might include help with activities such as feeding, handwriting, and social interactions.

Specific forms of training for FAS patients and their families may be included as part of or independently from physical or occupational therapy. Education-focused training is especially important for addressing FAS. Among the interventions that have been shown to be effective in this area are social skills training, executive functioning training, parent-child interaction therapy, and parenting training. Social skills training would likely focus on teaching children (and adults) how to interact appropriately with others, including how to enter a new group and avoid conflicts. Executive functioning training is aimed at improving skills such as problem-solving, memory, logical reasoning, and planning. Parent-child interaction therapy helps families create programs that consistently reward positive behaviors (for example, complying with requests) and discipline negative ones (for example, temper tantrums). Parents of children with FAS can also undergo separate training to help them become more thoughtful and consistent in their approach to caregiving and discipline; components of the training might include accepting the child's condition and limitations, concentrating on the child's strengths and talents, and creating more stability and structure within the home.

I encouraged Victor's parents to explore several of these treatment options. We agreed that the boy should stop taking the stimulant medication, as it had failed to improve his symptoms significantly. Instead, I referred Victor for physical and occupational therapy, and the family for a behavioral training program that included a family component and separate sessions for the parents. We also agreed that Victor should take part in the special education program at his school to address his cognitive and behavioral symptoms more completely.

A year later, the family reported significant improvement in Victor. "He has gotten much better," his mother told me excitedly. The boy's symptoms had improved at both home and school. At home, the behavioral interventions had helped Victor's parents cope with his anger more effectively. "He knows that temper tantrums mean time-outs and less TV time," his father said. Both parents said that Victor had far fewer outbursts, and that they had seen him stop himself from acting out in situations (such as having to come to dinner) that would have set him off in the past. The parents' consistency in handling such situations had clearly made a difference. "We feel much more effective as parents now," his mother said. She also reported that while Victor rarely initiated displays of affection, he no longer pushed her away when she hugged him, and that he said "You, too" when she said "I love you."

The boy's improvements were even more pronounced at school, where he spent part of the day in the special education program but much of it in his original classroom. "His teacher says he seems much happier," his father said. Clearly the teacher was more satisfied with Victor's behavior, too, because he was no longer disrupting the class routinely. For example, he had learned to ask permission before rising from his seat, and to accept that there were times when he had to stay seated. Victor had also learned to manage his anger at classmates much more effectively. His mother said, "The teacher says he still gets frustrated with things sometimes, but he uses words instead of his fists." With special tutoring in math and reading, Victor was making gains in these areas, as well, though he remained behind his grade level overall.

There were two especially bright spots in Victor's improvement. The first was that his physical therapy and special education programs had helped uncover his talent and passion for art. The boy was especially capable with drawing and painting, and enjoyed rendering animals; his work improved quickly as the physical therapy addressed his fine-motor coordination. "I've never seen this level of quality from a student his age," his art teacher told his parents. Victor concentrated especially well when immersed in his art. The second bright spot was that Victor had used what he learned through his social skills training to make a friend at school—a girl who also enjoyed art. "She comes over once a week and they just sit and draw together," his mother said. "It's wonderful."

Both parents agreed that they had unprecedented hope about Victor's future now. "We know we'll have to work even harder than we thought to help him have a good life," they said. "But the joy of seeing his smile motivates us every day."

# CHAPTER 20

# Fragile X Syndrome

## The Big Point

Fragile X syndrome, a genetic syndrome with physical, intellectual, and behavioral symptoms, is likely to include attention deficits, distractibility, and hyperactivity that can be misperceived as ADHD. While there is no specific treatment for fragile X syndrome, individuals with the disorder and their families can benefit from customized education and training.

Fragile X syndrome is a genetic disorder that is the leading cause of inherited intellectual disability, with severity ranging from mild to profound deficits. Fragile X is also marked by attention deficits, impulsivity, and hyperactivity—partly from the disorder itself and partly as products of its core symptoms, such as social interaction challenges. Aside from causing distress for fragile-X patients and those in their environments, the attention-deficit/hyperactivity symptoms may easily be mistaken for signs of the disorder called ADHD, resulting in suboptimal understanding of the condition and treatment. That was the case for my patient Byron.

## THEY CALLED HIM AN ALIEN

"The other kids call him an alien," Byron's mother said on their first visit to my office. She'd brought her fourteen-year-old son to me because he had been displaying a range of symptoms, including distractibility and impulsivity. A freshman in high school, Byron was short for his age, with a large head and prominent, pointy ears—his physical appearance made him the target of name-calling and other taunts at school.

According to his mother, Byron had a lot of trouble with social interaction, both at home and in school. He tended to avoid eye contact, spending most of the time staring at his hands or the floor—something that was immediately evident in my office. When faced with social interaction, he displayed significant anxiety, and often removed himself from the situation if possible. His mother said, "He even acts shy around me and his father," and noted that he spent most of his time in his room, playing with action figures or reading books well below his grade level. When I asked the boy about what activities he enjoyed, he was silent. But when his mother told him to talk about his favorite comic books, he became excited. "I like *Batman* a lot!" he said. "*Batman* is really cool!" Byron flapped his arms as he spoke, and tended to repeat himself, discussing his interest in *Batman* at length before lapsing into silence again.

"He's falling more and more behind in school," his mother said. While Byron had never performed at his grade level in math, reading, and other subjects, his performance had been within one grade level of his peers in most areas, until recently. Though he was working with a special tutor at the high school, the boy had become more distractible and impulsive, often rising from his chair or asking the teachers and tutor to repeat themselves. His mother said, "It's becoming disruptive for the other students," explaining that his teacher had suggested he be "tested" for ADHD.

The family's doctor had already mentioned that Byron may

suffer from ADHD, and had suggested trying stimulant medication for him. Byron's mother said they were reluctant to start the medication without securing a second opinion. "We're anxious to find something that will work for him," she said.

Byron's mother also talked about how affectionate he was. "He's such a loving boy," she said, mentioning that one of his favorite times was when she held him in the evenings while they watched TV together. "He's getting too big to sit in my lap," she said. "But he still tries to." Even in my office Byron showed a lot of affection for his mother, sitting close to her and smiling while she rubbed his arm and shoulder. Byron's mother reported that her son also showed affection for his younger sister, hugging her often, though he was sometimes shy around her as well.

Based on everything I observed on their first visit, I had a good hypothesis about the explanation for Byron's symptoms. I told the family I wanted to run more tests on their son, and that I should have some better answers for them soon.

## CLUES TO LOOK FOR

Over the next sessions I conducted physical, neurological, educational, and hearing and vision tests with Byron to determine his full medical picture. As expected, he showed mild developmental delays in most academic areas. However, these did not explain his full symptom picture sufficiently; given my hypothesis, I also wanted to run genetic testing on Byron.

The results of the genetic tests came back as expected: The boy tested positive for a genetic mutation that results in fragile X syndrome, a disorder that is the most common form of inherited intellectual disability in boys. The syndrome explained most of Byron's symptoms, including those related to attention-deficit/hyperactivity.

> **Main Clue**
>
> While attention-deficit/hyperactivity, learning disabilities, and repetitive movements/speech may be observed in multiple diagnosable disorders (for example, autism), when these occur in conjunction with physical features including an elongated face and protruding ears, a diagnosis of fragile X syndrome may be warranted. Genetic testing can confirm the fragile X diagnosis and help set direction for treatment.

## WHAT IS FRAGILE X SYNDROME?

Fragile X syndrome—also known as Martin-Bell syndrome or FXS—is an inherited genetic disorder with multiple associated symptoms caused by a problem on the X chromosome that prevents expression of a protein required for normal neural (that is, the brain and other parts of the nervous system) development. Specifically, the problem results from mutation of the X chromosome's FMR1 gene, causing a repeated DNA sequence that disrupts production of the crucial protein.[1]

The mutation in question can be full or partial, resulting in varying degrees of disruption of the nerve development protein. Males with the full mutation typically show multiple symptoms of FXS, with greater severity; females with the full mutation generally have less severe symptoms. As mentioned earlier, symptoms take several forms:

- *Physical* symptoms include a longer face than average, large and/or protruding ears, flat feet, low muscle tone, and larger than average testes (in men).
- *Intellectual* symptoms range from mild learning disabilities to severe cognitive disability preventing normal functioning.

Again, males are more likely than females to fall into the
latter category.

- *Social* symptoms include many difficulties with social interaction. Among these are poor eye contact, social anxiety,
and problems communicating with and forming relationships
with peers. While social withdrawal is common among individuals with FXS, this symptom can again range from mild
(for example, shyness) to severe (for example, nearly complete
avoidance of social interactions).

- *Behavioral* symptoms can include repetitive speech patterns,
such as repeating the same words/phrase and/or discussing
the same subject repeatedly.

Some females with a partial mutation of the FMR1 gene will
develop fragile X–associated primary ovarian insufficiency, which
in adulthood can result in infertility, irregular or missed men-
strual cycles, and early menopause. Some older adults with the
partial mutation may develop fragile X–associated tremor/ataxia
syndrome, which includes problems with movement and memory.
These disorders are considered part of the "fragile X family" of
conditions.

My patient Byron displayed most of the symptoms associated
with FXS in childhood; his symptoms ranged from mild to moderate. As mentioned earlier, he had an elongated face and prominent ears. A physical examination revealed larger-than-average
testes and poor general muscle tone. Byron's cognitive functioning was below his grade level; though he had been able to advance
in school with his same-age peers, the gap between his academic
performance and theirs had been widening. Still, he performed
much better than many peers with FXS, who were profoundly

cognitively disabled. Byron's social interaction symptoms were also prominent: He had difficulty maintaining eye contact and answering questions, along with forming friendships with his peers at school. Some researchers have shown that individuals with FXS are interested in social interaction, despite their challenges with this area.[2]

Byron also showed several symptoms related to autism, a developmental disorder characterized by repetitive behavioral patterns and impairment in social interaction and communication.[3] My patient's repetitive arm-flapping was consistent with autism, which is diagnosable in up to 33 percent of people with FXS.[4] FXS is seen as the cause of approximately 5 percent of all autism cases, making it the leading genetic cause of that condition.[5] Note that an earlier chapter discusses how Asperger's syndrome, which can be considered a mild version of autism, may be confused with the disorder called ADHD.

As far as transmission, fragile X is an inherited genetic disorder, meaning that it is passed from one generation to the next. A small percentage of the total population carries the X-chromosome-based FMR1 "premutation," which can expand to the full mutation in subsequent generations of their family.[6] Estimates of the proportion of carriers in the population vary. The National Fragile X Foundation suggests that about 1 in 250 females and 1 in 800 males are carriers. The Centers for Disease Control and Prevention places the number at 1 in 151 females and 1 in 468 males.[7] Females can pass the premutation on to their sons or daughters, since mothers always pass along an X chromosome to their children of either gender. Men can only pass a Y chromosome to their male children, so they can't transfer the premutation to their sons; moreover, when a father passes a premutation to his daughter, it typically doesn't expand to a full mutation. Genetic testing for the pre- or full FMR1 mutation is highly accurate.

## PREVALENCE OF FRAGILE X SYNDROME

Partly because males are more likely to have or express the full mutation than females, FXS is estimated to occur in about 1 in 4,000 males and 1 in 6,000 females.[8] The CDC reports that FXS occurs in about 1 in 5,000 males, and that the average age of diagnosis for boys is 35–37 months and for girls about 42 months.[9] The CDC also notes that most families have to make multiple visits to practitioners before the FXS diagnosis is confirmed; more than a third of families surveyed reported making more than ten visits to doctors before confirmation. Byron's family fell into this category, as they had seen multiple practitioners without hearing the FXS diagnosis. Part of the reason for the delay was that Byron's symptoms (for example, cognitive, social) weren't as severe as those of others meeting the criteria for FXS. Because of its prominent symptoms, full-blown FXS is most likely to be diagnosed and addressed in childhood; however, less severe cases (such as in females) could persist undetected into adulthood, causing attention-deficit/hyperactivity symptoms, among others.

Upon hearing the diagnosis of FXS, Byron's mother underwent genetic testing. She was found to have the X-chromosome premutation, as expected. Byron's younger sister was also tested but showed no evidence of the FMR1 mutation; that's possible because her mother only had the premutation on one of her two X chromosomes (a common condition in females), meaning that she could pass along either a mutated or nonmutated X chromosome to each of her children. Moreover, as mentioned earlier, even if Byron's sister had displayed a premutation or full mutation, she likely would have suffered less severe symptoms than her brother did. There was also no history of FXS or significant development problems in Byron's family. He was just unlucky. Because Byron's parents planned to have no more children, there were no implications of the genetic testing results for family planning.

## RELATION TO ATTENTION-DEFICIT/HYPERACTIVITY SYMPTOMS

There is significant overlap between the FXS diagnosis and attention-deficit/hyperactivity symptoms. A CDC survey of parents of children with FXS found that a significant proportion of diagnosed children had been diagnosed with and/or treated for attention problems (84 percent for boys; 67 percent for girls) and hyperactivity (66 percent for boys; 30 percent for girls).[10] An academic study in the early 1990s found that 31 percent of girls with FXS displayed significant attention difficulties requiring diagnosis or treatment.[11]

Given the overlap between FXS and attention-deficit/hyperactivity symptoms, a large percentage of those with FXS are likely to be diagnosed with ADHD, as well. In fact, I've observed that attention-deficit/hyperactivity symptoms can be precursors to other symptoms associated with FXS. Moreover, the core symptoms of FXS—including intellectual deficits and social withdrawal—are likely to result in attention problems that can be mistaken for ADHD; for example, a child struggling to understand a new type of math problem due to intellectual challenges may be misperceived as lacking focus or attention. Some researchers have even found that children with FXS are likely to have more severe distractibility, fidgeting, and impulsivity than children diagnosed with ADHD in the general population.[12] As discussed in other chapters, if ADHD is diagnosed without looking deeper for other conditions, such as FXS, that can explain the attention-deficit/hyperactivity symptoms, the patient will fail to receive the most effective treatment, and they and their families will suffer on multiple dimensions, including physically, psychologically, and financially. Indeed, there is evidence that fragile-X patients treated with stimulants—the treatment of choice for ADHD—can experience increased irritability, anxiety, and mood swings.[13] *As with any disorder mistaken for ADHD, treatment delayed is treatment denied.*

## TREATMENT FOR FRAGILE X SYNDROME

There is no specific treatment that can "cure" FXS. As such, the emphasis is on treating the symptoms of the syndrome and trying to ensure that patients reach their full potential. For example, FXS patients with severe anxiety symptoms (i.e., panic attacks, obsessive-compulsive symptoms) can be given anti-anxiety medication. Similarly, mood-influencing medication can be used to alleviate symptoms of depression. Selective serotonin reuptake inhibitors, for example, can reduce both anxiety and mood symptoms.

Much of the treatment for FXS takes place outside the realm of pharmacology. Intervention modes include special education and behavioral therapy, among others.[14] Many if not most children with FXS qualify for legally mandated special education programs to address cognition, speech, learning, sensory motor skills, and other areas related to academic settings. Various forms of therapy can be used in conjunction with or independent of special education, as well. For example, patients can benefit from social-skills training, which helps them learn appropriate ways of approaching and responding to other people, often using rewards to shape behavior. Once they leave the school system, adults with FXS can benefit from life-planning assistance provided by public or private sources. In the United States, services vary by state but are likely to include assistance with planning for college (if that's a viable option for the patient), career options, and residential choices such as community living.

As with most conditions, the prognosis for individuals with FXS varies significantly by the severity of the syndrome: Patients with less severe symptoms have much brighter futures. A national survey by the CDC provided a view of what can be expected for adults with FXS: While about 44 percent of women with FXS enjoyed a good quality of life (for example, living independently, working full-time, and enjoying multiple friends and leisure activities) overall, only 9 percent of men achieved a similar level of independent functioning, with most requiring significant assistance with daily living and fewer than one-third reporting that they enjoyed friendships and leisure activities.[15] These findings are in line with the earlier suggestion that females with FXS tend to have much milder symptoms than their male counterparts.

My patient Byron's treatment plan included several of the approaches mentioned above. An early objective was making sure that the family understood Byron's condition and had reasonable expectations for his future. Unlike many patients with FXS—especially males—he had displayed a high level of functioning, especially in school. That meant his prognosis was much better than average, and that he had a higher chance of enjoying a more independent life than most who shared his diagnosis. At the same time, Byron's academic performance had been declining, and it was likely that the gap between him and his classmates would widen further over time. With this in mind, I suggested that his parents look into an individualized education program at his school, given that his diagnosis qualified for this under federal guidelines.[16]

I also discussed Byron's social interactions with his parents, suggesting they observe whether he seemed interested in playing with other children occasionally, especially those who shared his interests (for example, comic books, action figures). We agreed that it would be harmful to "force" Byron to interact with other children, but that occasional interaction could boost his quality of life significantly. The family also agreed to look into behavioral training (with a focus on social skills), and to consider anti-anxiety medication on an as-needed basis, especially for anxiety related to social situations, such as playing with another child. Finally, we located a local support group for families dealing with FXS, and the family planned to attend their first meeting.

As hoped, Byron made good progress with his early treatment. He began an IEP at his school, with a focus on keeping him as close to his grade level as possible in all academic areas. The IEP also included a component of helping him interact with classmates in way that felt more comfortable for him. Byron also continued working with his tutor, as they had developed a good working relationship previously.

Progress was slower for Byron on the social front. "It seems like he wants to make friends but doesn't know how," his mother said after observing him for several months. The family had worked with a behavioral therapist who had developed a series of gradually more challenging "assignments" for Byron, such as saying hello to three people at school and initiating a conversation during recess. The boy had avoided completing most of these, expressing significant anxiety about each. His parents had opted not to start him on anti-anxiety medication, but they were still willing to consider this measure if he didn't show improvement. For example, his behavioral assignment to invite a friend over to read comic books seemed unachievable given his current level of anxiety about social situations.

The brightest spot in Byron's treatment was his family's participation in a local support group for FXS. There the boy and his parents found a warm community of supporters dedicated to helping individuals with FXS live full lives and reach their potential. His mother said, "They understand what we're going through better than anyone." She also noted that seeing how severe the symptoms of many of the other children were helped her to be thankful for Byron's level of functioning, and to maintain hope for the future.

"He's still the same loving boy I've always known," she said at one of our later sessions, holding her son's hand as he sat beside her, "but now I feel like I know him even better and can help him in the right way."

# CHAPTER 21

# Other Conditions

Multiple conditions beyond those discussed in previous chapters involve attention-deficit/hyperactivity symptoms, resulting in misdiagnosis of ADHD and the wrong treatment approach, which in turn increase stress and other costs for patients and their families. This chapter explores several of these other conditions in depth.

1. Poor diet (iron deficiency and excess sugar)
2. Allergies
3. Overactive thyroid (hyperthyroidism)
4. Pituitary tumor
5. Prematurity
6. Heavy metal poisoning

So far I've taken you through many disorders and conditions that can be misdiagnosed as ADHD, from simple vision or hearing problems to complex, often chronic conditions like schizophrenia, obsessive-compulsive disorder, and sensory processing disorder. I like to think of the previous chapters as covering the "greatest hits," or the conditions *most likely* to be seen— and treated—as ADHD, when in reality there's no such thing as ADHD as we know it. This chapter also covers conditions that are mistakenly diagnosed as ADHD, resulting in the wrong treatment. I've grouped these disorders together because they tend to occur less frequently than some of the others or may be somewhat less likely to be diagnosed and treated as ADHD than the other conditions I've covered, given the symptoms they involve. But the risk of misdiagnosis remains significant, leading to multiple problems for patients and their families.

Whereas in previous chapters I devoted more space to a case example of someone with the condition in question, along with a definition and description of the condition, its prevalence and demographics, its relation to ADHD, and treatment options, in this chapter I'll present more abbreviated versions of these sections. As with any of the conditions presented earlier in this book, my goal is not to have readers diagnose themselves or others based on the material here, but to gain a sense of how certain attention-deficit/hyperactivity symptoms may be related to specific diagnosable conditions, and to seek further medical help in a more informed way.

## POOR DIET (IRON DEFICIENCY AND EXCESS SUGAR)

Trey, a thirteen-year-old boy, was brought to my office by his mother, who was raising him alone. The boy was referred to me after being diagnosed with ADHD and started on a stimulant about a year before, with no visible improvement. His teachers reported that the eighth grader was "sluggish and distracted" in class. Since he had started elementary school, previous teachers had said similar things to Trey's mother, but his academic and behavioral performance had declined rapidly over the last year, and he was at risk of being held back. "It's like he just doesn't care about his schoolwork or anything else anymore," she said. For example, though he had enjoyed baseball when he was younger—and showed talent for the sport—the boy had stopped playing two years ago, claiming he was "too tired." Trey was also fidgety in class, sometimes squirming in his chair to the point that it distracted other students. "That started after he went on the medication," his mother said. In my office, the boy appeared uninterested, responding to my questions by shaking or nodding his head or providing one-word answers. I observed his fidgetiness, too: He shifted uncomfortably in his seat for the duration of his visit.

My initial physical exam of Trey showed no specific condition that could have explained his symptoms, and he did not meet criteria for vision or hearing problems or depression. He also showed no evidence of learning disabilities. But the blood tests I ordered for the boy as part of my standard examination provided a good explanation for his symptoms: He had low serum iron, or an iron deficiency (anemia). Further questioning revealed that Trey, who spent significant time alone before and after school while his mother was at work, was eating junk food (potato chips, doughnuts, and soda) almost exclusively, instead of more nutritious meals, resulting in the deficiency.

Iron deficiency is a problem because our bodies use iron for multiple important purposes, including helping to digest food, carrying oxygen through the blood, and enabling muscles to store and use oxygen. Iron deficiency is the most common type of nutritional problem in the United States.[1] Given its relation to poor nutrition and parasitic infection, low serum iron is particularly common in developing countries. Significant iron deficiencies delay infant brain and motor development, along with causing physical fatigue (like Trey's sluggishness), poor attention/concentration, and memory problems. Infants (because they are growing) and pregnant women (because they are nurturing a baby) have higher iron needs than others. Heavy blood loss can also result in an iron deficiency. While symptoms associated with iron deficiency may be more obvious in children (as in a school setting), attention deficits and other problems caused by this condition are common in adults as well.

There is a clear link between iron deficiency and attention-deficit/hyperactivity symptoms. As mentioned above, low serum iron can result in poor attention and memory, which can be viewed mistakenly as evidence of ADHD, as was the case for Trey. I've also observed significant hyperactivity in children with iron deficiencies; in Trey's case, his fidgetiness could have resulted from the low serum iron, the stimulant he was taking, or some combination. A 2004 study in France found that 84 percent of children diagnosed with ADHD had low serum iron, compared to only 18 percent of nondiagnosed children.[2] Similarly, iron supplementation was found to improve attention-deficit/hyperactivity symptoms significantly in children.[3]

As would be expected, treatment for iron deficiency involves improving iron intake levels through diet and/or supplementation. In Trey's case, we used a combination of these approaches. He stopped taking the stimulant and started taking iron pills, along with improving his diet—I recommended more fruits and vegetables, low-fat milk and cheese, fish, whole grains, eggs, and nuts. The vitamin C in certain foods like oranges can also help the body absorb iron better. Making the changes was difficult for Trey and his mother at first—especially because the boy was unsupervised after school—but they soon improved his diet significantly. As a result, his attention and performance improved in school. He also stopped fidgeting (beyond what was normal for a boy his age). Once I saw proof of his dietary improvement, I took him off the iron supplement. As an added bonus, Trey had more energy for sports, and he made the ninth-grade baseball team as a starter.

What about sugar? Sugary foods have a reputation for making children "wild" and are often associated with hyperactivity, so it's important for me to address the role of sugar with regard to symptoms of ADHD. First, is sugar truly a stimulant? The answer: not in the way that we've defined stimulants in earlier chapters, as agents that affect the neurotransmitters that help our nervous system function. Sugar, like other simple carbohydrates, does provide fast energy to our bodies, and an excess of it can cause a temporary rise in feelings of alertness and activity levels, as anyone who's around young children can attest to. But the key word here is "temporary"—the effects of high sugar intake tend to be short-lived, and are often followed by a period of diminished activity or a "crash."

More generally, there continues to be controversy over the link between sugar, additives (such as the coloring and flavoring added to foods and even toothpaste), and other dietary elements in attention-deficit/hyperactivity.[4] My experience is that there is very little evidence linking sugar or other dietary elements to attention-deficit/hyperactivity. I am far from alone among medical practitioners in taking this viewpoint.[5] Beyond my experience with patients, I helped conduct an informal study on this topic at Children's Memorial Hospital in Chicago in the 1980s: We found that only 1–2 percent of hyperactive children responded favorably to dietary changes (for example, less sugar and artificial colors/flavorings), a number no better than in a control group (that is, at least 1–2 percent of children who underwent *no* dietary changes also improved on hyperactivity over time).[6] The bottom line is that while a very small percentage of the population may experience attention-deficit/hyperactivity symptoms, almost always temporary ones, due to food elements, the vast majority does not. So, while I continue to advocate a healthy diet for children and adults, I don't see any link between sugar or other dietary elements and *chronic* attention-deficit/hyperactivity.

## ALLERGIES

Leigh, eight years old, was a bright-eyed girl with a big smile. Her father brought her to my office early one fall, telling me that she was having a very difficult time at school. "Her teacher says she's distracted all the time and doesn't pay attention," he said. "She wanted to have her tested for ADD." While he spoke, Leigh watched us, sniffling. She didn't seem unhappy, so I asked about her congestion. Both Leigh and her father said she'd had trouble with nasal symptoms starting the previous spring, when the weather had changed; since then, she'd had steadily increasing problems with a runny nose, itchy eyes, and sinus pain, with flare-ups around seasonal weather changes. When I asked her if the symptoms bothered her in school she said "yes" very quickly. "I have to wipe my nose all the time," she said. I asked her if her nose, her eyes, and her head all bothered her at the same time and she said, "Sometimes, but not always." For example, she sometimes had only a runny nose or headache.

To be safe, I conducted a full assessment with Leigh. But the source of her attention-deficit problems seemed clear from the start: She had seasonal allergies. Leigh's parents already knew she had allergy trouble; they had tried her on antihistamine medication several months before, with some success. But her symptoms had worsened recently, disrupting her ability to pay attention in school. The reason her parents and teacher had failed to link her allergies directly to her attention problems was that she didn't have all the allergy symptoms all the time. Sometimes she had only the sinus pain, which, though invisible to others, made it very difficult to concentrate in school. And it seemed the recently increased severity of her symptoms had lessened the effectiveness of the antihistamine, compounding the problem. Multiple child patients I've treated were mistakenly diagnosed (prior to my seeing them) with ADHD before we discovered they suffered from allergies.

In general, allergies are the result of an immune system response to nonharmful "allergens" including chemicals, dust, certain foods (peanuts, milk, wheat, etc.), drugs (for example, antibiotics), perfumes, plants, and pollen. Specifically, when people with allergies encounter specific allergens, their immune system responds to the allergens in multiple ways, including releasing histamines (which inflame surrounding tissue as a means of protection).[16] A given person of any age may have no allergies, or one or more. Symptoms of allergies depend on the specific kind of allergen and range from mild to life-threatening. For example, allergens that are breathed in can cause nasal congestion and itching, sinus pain, coughing, and wheezing (as Leigh experienced). Food allergens can cause vomiting, cramping, abdominal pain, and diarrhea. As a group, allergies are extremely common: An estimated 40–50 million people suffer from allergies in the United States alone.[17] One of the most common allergies is "allergic rhinitis," also called hay fever, or the development of nasal congestion and other symptoms in response to pollen, dust, and other airborne allergens. This is what my patient Leigh had.

Treatments for allergies include avoidance, medications, and allergy shots. Some allergens (for example, foods, drugs) may be easier to avoid than others (for example, pollen, dust). Allergy medications include over-the-counter and prescription antihistamines, decongestants, and corticosteroids (to reduce inflammation). Allergy shots involve regular injections of the allergen in question (in steadily increasing doses) to help diminish the immune system's response. No specific treatment will work for every person. In Leigh's case, we first tried an increased dose of antihistamine, followed by a prescription corticosteroid. These reduced her symptoms to the point that she had only occasional, milder symptoms (for example, lasting days versus weeks), and she was much better able to pay attention in class.

"She's so much happier," Leigh's father said, "and so are we and her teacher!"

## OVERACTIVE THYROID (HYPERTHYROIDISM)

Yoko's parents were very concerned when they brought the eleven-year-old girl to my office. "She has always been a very good student," her mother said, "We don't know what happened." Yoko's school records showed that she had indeed excelled in school and on standardized tests from early elementary school. Her parents, an engineer mother and chemist father, had emigrated from Japan to the United States several years before Yoko was born, and had always emphasized the value of a good education. Based on her academic performance, Yoko had been able to skip third grade, and she was currently a year or more younger than her peers in seventh grade.

But things had changed quickly in the new grade, as Yoko appeared inattentive and distracted much of the time, at school and at home. "Her teachers are very puzzled," her father said. The girl's grades had dropped quickly, from placing her at the top of her peer group to near the middle. Her standardized test scores had also declined across subjects. Her mother said, "It's like she's not trying anymore." Both parents were concerned that the social challenges of being a younger student in middle school were simply too much for Yoko, and were interfering with her academics, along with making their daughter appear nervous and restless. The girl's teachers thought that perhaps the level of work was too hard for her, and that maybe the pressure her parents placed on her to excel was also a factor. Yoko's pediatrician thought she qualified for a diagnosis of ADHD, but her parents brought her to me for a second opinion. In my office, Yoko appeared polite but distractible (for example, asking me to repeat my questions) and restless. She also appeared

thinner than she should have been for her age, and her parents confirmed she'd lost weight in recent months.

My physical exam of Yoko revealed no medical explanation of
her symptoms, but the blood tests I ordered did: She tested positive for an overactive thyroid, a condition that can result in several
types of symptoms, including attention-deficit/hyperactivity. The
thyroid gland, part of the endocrine system, is located in the neck,
and it produces hormones that control how our bodies use energy,
including our metabolic rate (how fast we "burn" the food we
consume).[7] Hyperthyroidism is another name for an overactive
thyroid, a condition where the gland produces too great a volume
of hormones. It can be caused by multiple factors including infection or inflammation of the thyroid, Grave's disease, some tumors
or benign growths, and overexposure to iodine. Common hyperthyroidism symptoms include fatigue, poor concentration, ner-
vousness and restlessness, weight loss, and increased sweating—
symptoms that can affect hyperthyroid patients of any age. Yoko
displayed many of these symptoms at home and at school.

As suggested above, an overactive thyroid leads to multiple
attention-deficit/hyperactivity symptoms, including poor concentration and restlessness, which can be misdiagnosed as ADHD.
One academic study showed that even children with "subclini-
cal" (low, not obvious) levels of hyperthyroidism displayed significant attention-deficit/hyperactivity symptoms, and that these
improved with treatment (medication).[8] Other researchers have
pointed out that hyperthyroidism can also lead to misdiagnosis of
ADHD in adults.[9] So it's not surprising that Yoko's pediatrician
viewed her symptoms as likely signs of ADHD.

Treatment of hyperthyroidism is usually approached with
antithyroid medications that lower the gland's output of hormones. In extreme cases, surgery or a technique involving radio-
active iodine can be used to stop the thyroid from functioning

altogether; patients undergoing those procedures must take thyroid hormone replacement pills for the rest of their lives. In Yoko's case, a low dose of antithyroid medication soon improved her symptoms dramatically. She became much more attentive at home and at school, and her grades improved "overnight," according to her parents. Soon she was on the school's honor roll, with all A's and participation in multiple academic extracurricular activities, to her parents' delight. "It's like our daughter is back again," her father said.

## PITUITARY TUMOR

On Marilyn's first visit to my office she said her medical symptoms were "ruining" her marriage. The thirty-seven-year-old woman, an office assistant at a law firm, had come in because her husband was convinced she had ADHD. "I think he just wants me to pay more attention to him," she joked. Joking aside, Marilyn described symptoms including fatigue, stress, negative mood, frequent severe headaches, and poor concentration at home and at work. She also noted that she recently had been having trouble with her sense of smell, including feeling that food "smelled strange." Past doctors had medicated Marilyn for depression (with little improvement in her symptoms), and a recent physician had suggested she might qualify for ADHD and that she try a stimulant "just to see if it works." She was considering the suggestions seriously but wanted my input before filling her prescription.

Marilyn's history suggested she had no past medical condition that could have explained her symptoms. While she clearly had symptoms of depression, she also didn't qualify for a formal mood disorder diagnosis. Her blood tests revealed slightly elevated hormone (for example, thyroid hormone) levels. Moreover, because she reported frequent headaches and a disrupted sense of smell, I ordered an MRI scan for her, and that provided a clear explanation: Marilyn had a noncancerous pituitary tumor. The pituitary gland, located at the base of the brain, regulates multiple hormones in the body. Up to about 20 percent of people of any age may have a pituitary tumor, but most such tumors are noncancerous and never even cause noticeable symptoms.[10] When symptoms do occur, they include headaches, fatigue, trouble with vision (such as double vision) and smell, and nausea. Because the pituitary gland regulates hormone production, tumors in that area can also cause conditions like hyperthyroidism (which also results in attention-deficit/hyperactivity symptoms), discussed earlier in this chapter. Marilyn's symptoms (including fatigue, headaches, difficulty with her sense of smell) were consistent with the effects of a pituitary tumor.

The symptoms associated with pituitary growths—especially headaches, fatigue, and vision difficulties—can easily cause attention deficits that may be mistaken as ADHD. While there have been no formal studies linking pituitary tumors to ADHD diagnoses, I have seen multiple cases where a pituitary problem was behind symptoms that were mistaken by other physicians and the patients themselves as ADHD.

Treatment for pituitary growths includes surgery, radiation, or medication to shrink or remove the tumor. When tumors in that area are fast-growing, it's usually best to remove them, to avoid their damaging important nearby structures such as the optic nerve. In Marilyn's case, the tumor appeared to be growing slowly (if at all), so we opted to reduce it with medication. The treatment was successful; with the reduction of her tumor came significant improvement in symptoms: Her headaches and energy levels improved, and her difficulty with smell abated. "Who would have thought such a small growth could cause such big problems," she said. Unfortunately, Marilyn's marital challenges continued, as she and her husband continued to argue frequently, contributing to her ongoing negative mood and stress. When we last spoke, they had agreed to try couples counseling to work on their relationship.

## PREMATURITY

No one would have guessed that Elizabeth had been born three months before her due date, weighing in at just over three pounds. The baby girl had to spend two weeks in the hospital for observation. By age three, Elizabeth had caught up on most developmental milestones, and she appeared no different from her peers on most measures. But when she was ten years old her parents brought her in to see me because she was struggling academically and behaviorally at school. "Things are going downhill fast," her mother said, noting that Elizabeth's fourth-grade teacher was frustrated with her inability to pay attention in class and her frequent disruptions of other students by blurting out answers or trying to talk to her table mates during quiet times. The girl's mother said, "She feels like everyone is against her and that people are always looking for something wrong with her." Elizabeth's behavior at home also reflected increasing distractibility. The family's pediatrician had diagnosed the girl with ADHD and started her on a stimulant, but there had been little improvement in her symptoms, and her sleep and appetite had been disturbed.

When full testing revealed no specific medical conditions for Elizabeth, I helped her parents understand that the explanation had been there all along: The girl's premature birth likely explained most of her symptoms. Premature (or "preterm") birth is defined as any birth that takes place three or more weeks before the due date. Rates of premature birth range from 5 percent to 18 percent across countries.[11] Early consequences of prematurity include small head size, difficulty with reflexes (for example, sucking, swallowing), susceptibility to infection, and even death.[12] A National Institutes of Health study showed that even births that took place two to four weeks early could result in various developmental delays in early childhood.[13] Elizabeth had caught up to her peers at an early age, but the predisposition toward developmental challenges persisted and was realized later in her life—a phenomenon I've seen in multiple patients. A large-scale Norwegian study confirmed that children born prematurely were more likely to have multiple problems that extended into adulthood, including a lower likelihood of completing high school.[14]

Problems related to premature birth can take the form of attention-deficit hyperactivity symptoms, as well. Not surprisingly, then, children born prematurely have been found to have significantly increased risk of an ADHD diagnosis than their full-term peers. For example, a 2011 Swedish study found that the likelihood of being diagnosed with ADHD was correlated with prematurity, such that the more premature a child was, the greater his or her chance of receiving the diagnosis—babies born four to seven weeks early were up to 60 percent more likely to be diagnosed with ADHD later in life.[15] Elizabeth, like many of her premature peers, helped contribute to that statistic.

Naturally, there is no "cure" for the condition of prematurity. However, specific symptoms associated with prematurity can be treated successfully in most cases, through a combination of behavioral treatment, academic interventions, and medication, if needed. For Elizabeth, I recommended tutoring to address her academic challenges and behavioral therapy (for example, using rewards to reinforce appropriate behavior) to help her control her classroom behavior better. The combined approach helped her make slow improvement, and she was able to maintain academic performance close to her grade level. I helped her parents under-stand that she might face lifelong challenges, but that targeted treatment—like what I'd recommend—could help her manage specific symptoms effectively.

## HEAVY METAL POISONING

Alex's problems started in kindergarten, where he was unable to pay attention as well as his classmates, becoming easily distracted and sometimes disrupting the class. The five-year-old's mother brought him in because of his teacher's consistent reports of dif-ficult behavior; the school had recommended testing for ADHD. At home, Alex also had difficulty paying attention, but there was less need, as his parents—a writer and freelance graphic designer—both worked from home and let the boy wander the large old Victorian house they had been renovating for three years. Alex played make-believe in the long hallways and hid in the fort he had built behind his bed out of pillows and blankets.

Alex's parents had no explanation for the boy's short attention span and distractibility. But the blood tests I ordered as part of my full examination did: Alex had lead poisoning. The result was confirmed by further tests including X-rays. Hearing these re-sults, the parents looked more carefully at Alex's habits and found that he had been peeling and eating chips of lead-based paint from the walls of their home, likely for years. For example, he'd peeled paint from much of the wall behind his bedroom fort.

Lead poisoning is one specific form of heavy metal poi-soning, or the toxic accumulation of specific metal elements within the body.[18] Arsenic, cadmium, mercury, and lead are the most likely metals to cause this condition. Exposure to these substances can take place through pollution, specific foods, metal-lined food containers, specific industries (for example, chemicals, manufacturing), and, as in Alex's case, lead-based paint. Symptoms associated with heavy metal poisoning can relate to the nervous system, digestive system, cardiovascular system, reproductive system, and renal (kidneys) system. Specific symptoms include confusion, memory loss, muscle/joint pain, headaches, upset stomach, vision problems, and fatigue. Diagnosis can be made by a combination of personal history, lab tests (for example, blood, urine, hair), and X-rays. While heavy metal poisoning can happen anywhere in the world, risk is much higher in developing countries, which still allow lead and other metals in some products (for example, leaded gasoline). In the United States, the risk of poisoning is greatest among lower-income urban populations. Children are at particularly high risk for heavy metal poisoning, given their tendency to eat items like paint. Moreover, the cognitive symptoms (for example, confusion, memory loss) associated with heavy metal poisoning can result in attention deficits that could be mistaken for symptoms of ADHD, as was the case for Alex. Recent studies have found that children diagnosed with ADHD had lead levels up to 30 percent higher than those of undiagnosed children.[19] While most of these children didn't qualify for a diagnosis of lead poisoning, the link between that condition and attention-deficit/hyperactivity symptoms was clear.

Treatment of heavy metal poisoning usually involves the use of "metal-chelating" drugs or an intravenous chelating procedure that bonds and removes metal molecules from the body. Patients undergoing such processes may receive vitamin C and other mineral supplements. Ongoing lab tests are used to monitor metal levels. The treatment can take years to reduce metal levels. While a complete cure is possible, some patients may suffer life-long symptoms due to residual damage to organs including the brain and liver. In Alex's case, I referred him to a doctor with expertise treating heavy metal poisoning. While the expert was hopeful about reducing the boy's lead levels, he was guarded about achieving a full cure, given that Alex had likely been living with the condition for a long time. Several months later, the boy's lead levels had come down significantly, and his attention had improved moderately, but it appeared that he would face some ongoing effects of the poisoning. Again the story points out that *treatment delayed is treatment denied*, with potentially lifelong consequences.

PART III

# TAKE ACTION

# CHAPTER 22

# When There's No Diagnosis

**The Big Point**

The majority of this book is about the many disorders and conditions that are misdiagnosed as ADHD because their symptoms or effects include attention-deficit/hyperactivity. But sometimes no diagnosis is warranted, and attention-related or hyperactivity symptoms are related only to a given phase of life or specific circumstances. Let's consider the cases of a child and an adult that fit this pattern.

## JUSTIN JUST CAN'T CONCENTRATE

When his mother brought him into my office for the first time, eleven-year-old Justin looked like he'd rather be anywhere else. The boy thumbed through a sports magazine while his mother described the situation. "He's been having trouble focusing in school," she said, "and I'm worried he may have ADD." The sixth grader attended a private school where he had always earned satisfactory grades and behavioral evaluations. Justin tested at above-average levels in reading and math, and he excelled at the drums, playing with a band he and several friends had formed. He had also recently taken up lacrosse, on top of his deep involvement in hockey and soccer. But his mother was concerned that he was losing focus, and several notes home from school (about his occasional lapses of attention and disruption of other students) seemed to confirm her fears. A physician neighbor of the family had suggested Justin might have ADHD. "His attention and behavior at home are fine overall, but I sometimes feel like he's not listening to me," his mother said. She mentioned that she and Justin's father had recently divorced, and that she had her hands full as a single mother to Justin and his younger sister. When I asked Justin about school, he said it was "okay," and that his teachers were a little harder on him this year than last year.

I suggested that we test Justin thoroughly to rule out any specific condition, but also mentioned to his mother that there wasn't a lot of evidence to suggest a medical issue. As expected, none of the tests—including for vision and hearing, mood symptoms, and learning issues—came back positive. Talking more to Justin and his mother, it became clear that the boy's attention challenges and occasional impulsivity were well within a normal range for his age. For example, he was part of a very close group of friends (including his bandmates) that tended to get in trouble for talking in class and had to be seated at some distance from one another to prevent them from disrupting the class. Similarly, Justin and his friends were flirting with their female classmates more (two of them even had girlfriends), and this was causing further distractibility and occasionally impulsive behavior. Furthermore, Justin's concentration and behavior were excellent in music and sports. He attended very carefully to his music teacher and coaches, and practiced diligently, earning praise from all of them. "I enjoy music and sports a lot more than school," the boy said. Finally, Justin had been given his first cell phone recently, and, like most of his peers, he spent a lot of time calling, texting, and surfing, along with staying up late at night to communicate with friends (his parents had recently discovered this). Collectively, these factors explained Justin's attention-deficit/hyperactivity symptoms, and highlighted that they were specific to contexts where he felt bored or unengaged, rather than affecting his life across the board.

When I explained my take on the situation to Justin and his mother, they seemed relieved. "I guess he's just a normal kid," his mother said. I assured her that this was the case, but added that it would be a great idea to help Justin develop healthy habits that could serve him well into adulthood. For example, while it was understandable that Justin felt less engaged in school, it was also important for him to develop good listening skills there and to avoid disrupting his classmates. Similarly, he would have benefited from finding a way to apply some of the focus and drive he demonstrated in sports to more academic pursuits. I suggested these general ideas to the boy and his mother, along with some tips for implementation (such as providing rewards when Justin went long periods without notes home) and they agreed to apply them the best they could. Over the next year Justin's mother sent occasional updates suggesting that he was doing much better on all counts, continuing to excel in music and sports while focusing better in the classroom and on assignments. "He even listens to me better than before," she added happily.

## YVETTE'S BUSY LIFE

"Nothing is working," Yvette said to me the first time she came to my office. The twenty-five-year-old was juggling part-time jobs as a restaurant server and teacher's aide while she studied for her education certificate. "I want to be a teacher," she said, "but I'm beginning to wonder if I can handle a whole classroom of kids." The problem, according to Yvette, was that she couldn't keep track of her life—responsibilities, finances, social engagements, etc. Convinced she had ADHD (her boyfriend was convinced, too), Yvette had asked her doctor for a prescription for a stimulant, because she had "read a lot" about how it could help. After asking a few questions, the doctor had agreed it was worth trying the medication. Unfortunately, Yvette had found the stimulant only made her feel "even more scattered and nervous" and disturbed her sleep and appetite.

My full history and medical examination of Yvette—including lab tests—revealed no specific condition that could explain her symptoms. She met criteria for none of the disorders or conditions described in this book. Moreover, when I asked her to detail her "symptoms," it was clear that she was experiencing a normal level of stress for someone with as many roles and activities as she had: employee, trainee, student, significant other, friend, daughter, sister, among others. For example, despite her perception of stress, Yvette's job and academic standing had never been in jeopardy as a result of her difficulty remembering and carrying out her responsibilities. She just felt overwhelmed by her daily life.

As I told Yvette when sharing the results of my assessment, "Not every set of symptoms is a diagnosis." I explained that she was justified to feel stress, but that the best approach to her symptoms was to consider lifestyle changes and to keep everything in perspective. For example, though formerly a fitness enthusiast who ran and biked regularly, she had stopped exercising due to her many commitments, and couldn't imagine finding the time to return to those activities. I challenged her to carve out at least three hours total per week to exercise, promising her it would be worth it. Similarly, I suggested she try yoga, as many of my patients had found it to be relaxing. We also discussed the need to keep a better schedule (she tried to keep everything in her head) to help her organize her day. We agreed that she would try to cut back on her hours at the restaurant or as a teacher's aide, as she had overcommitted to both. Finally, I suggested Yvette consider cognitive-behavioral therapy (which helps patients reach goals by adjusting their thoughts and behaviors) if she felt she was still struggling to cope with daily life.

Yvette took on the challenge of managing her activities better with enthusiasm. Over the next months she returned to the gym for biking and yoga, averaging four hours of exercise weekly. She tried a number of different schedule-minders, including paper-and-pencil and online versions, settling for the online one because she could change it more easily. While she hadn't been able to cut back on her hours at work or as an aide, she was able to take time off for important activities by trading shifts with others, which helped her feel less stressed. Because of the progress she was making, Yvette had decided not to pursue any medication or therapy. In our last session she told me, "I realize now it wasn't ADHD. It was just life."

## IT'S NOT YOU, IT'S THE ENVIRONMENT

As I've mentioned in detail in Part I of this book, there is an epidemic of ADHD misdiagnosis, and that's the result of the motivations and activities of several groups: medical practitioners, pharmaceutical companies, and patients themselves. Ongoing media attention devoted to ADHD has made it easy for people to "diagnose" themselves with the disorder, and for physicians to diagnose ADHD too easily (as Justin's neighbor did) or prescribe stimulants after asking just a few questions (as Yvette's doctor did). Moreover, we as a society are much busier than previous generations were, between the demands of school, work, "leisure" activities, family (with individuals' responsibilities mounting due to the high rate of divorce and blended families), and other aspects of modern life, leading people to perceive their attention, rightfully, as scattered and their activity as "hyper." Many of these trends were reflected in the cases of Justin and Yvette—challenges of everyday life were bringing out attention-deficit/hyperactivity symptoms that easily could have been mistaken for, and treated as, ADHD. The reality is that many children grow out of such symptoms (as Justin did) as their brains mature, especially with proper attention from their caregivers, and many adults can improve the symptoms with lifestyle changes (as Yvette did).

## HOW DO YOU KNOW WHEN ATTENTION-DEFICIT/ HYPERACTIVITY SYMPTOMS ARE NORMAL?

As I discuss at length in this book's last chapter, it's mostly about how much the symptoms are affecting your life. A child who fidgets a lot but pays attention in class and is able to complete assignments effectively is a child who probably doesn't need medical attention. Similarly, an adult who may occasionally lack focus at work or elsewhere or feel they are always in motion taking care of their responsibilities (but is getting everything done reasonably well) is one who probably doesn't qualify for a diagnosis based on attention-deficit/hyperactivity symptoms. On the other hand, children who are consistently unfocused and disruptive, and adults who are losing jobs and relationships due to their attention-related or behavioral challenges, are experiencing a level of impairment that requires further investigation of their symptoms and, ideally, development of a diagnosis and treatment plan. In the next chapter I present a lot more information about evaluating your symptoms and understanding the line between normal and diagnosable.

# CHAPTER 23

# Evaluating and Managing Your Symptoms

**The Big Point**

People are often very good at understanding and describing what symptoms bother them most—whether related to attention-deficit/hyperactivity or not. This chapter helps you learn to look for symptom patterns in a more systematic way, with a better "vocabulary," so that you can help your doctor determine the most helpful diagnosis and treatment. I also discuss how to manage attention-deficit/hyperactivity symptoms that aren't explained easily by diagnoses like those featured earlier in this book or don't respond to early treatment efforts.

Over many years of medical practice, I've come to rely substantially on a very specific source of information when helping my patients: the patients themselves. Of course, there is valuable information in medical textbooks and other written and online documents, and, like most doctors, I also rely on regular discussions with colleagues who have complementary areas of expertise to keep up with new developments in diagnosis and treatment, and to consider especially tricky patient cases. But usually the most potent clues to what's going on with a person who walks into my office are provided by that person themselves. The description of their symptoms as well as their medical history is the most valuable evidence. Even children are surprisingly good at understanding and describing their symptoms, though they often need their parents or guardians to assist their explanations, as we saw in some earlier chapters. For example, I rely heavily on parents' observations when a child shows evidence of a mood disorder, given that the child may be unaware of symptoms or reluctant to discuss them.

Although a patient's testimony of symptoms is essential in determining a diagnosis, it is especially important that the patient not have predetermined notions about their condition. As we've seen, cultural bias may lead a patient to believe they have "ADHD" when in fact their distractibility and/or impulsivity is experienced at normal levels. Part of my motivation for writing this book is to level this bias so that patients and physicians don't jump to conclusions about their symptom patterns.

If you or your child is struggling with symptoms of attention deficit/hyperactivity, this chapter will help you understand how to assess your symptoms carefully, arming you for a comprehensive discussion with your medical care providers to help determine the most appropriate diagnosis and the most effective treatment. If you are a medical professional, this chapter can help you take an even more objective and informed approach to diagnosis. At the chapter's end I will provide some tips for dealing with attention-deficit/hyperactivity symptoms that persist despite attempts at diagnosis and treatment.

## THE FOUR QUESTIONS

My initial approach to evaluating anyone who walks into my office is very simple: I ask the patient (and their parent or guardian, in the case of a child) to write brief answers to these questions:

1. What are your biggest problems and challenges, in your view?
2. What do you think other people see as being your problems and challenges?
3. What things do you feel you are very good at (your strengths)?
4. What are your weaknesses?

This very simple form generates surprisingly honest and accurate information about my patients, whether related to attention-deficit/hyperactivity, anxiety, depression, school-related challenges, or more traditional medical complaints. It also provides a great starting point for the more thorough history and physical exam (and lab tests, if needed) I conduct in initial sessions.

So a good starting point for anyone dealing with medical/behavioral symptoms is with those simple questions above. They just need to be as honest as possible in answering, and to view the answers (especially to questions 1 and 2) as entry points for exploring symptom patterns and possible explanations with a qualified medical practitioner. The answers to questions 3 and 4 can help people understand the assets (for example, resourcefulness, discipline, organizational skills) they have to tackle medical and other types of problems, along with any potential obstacles (such as quitting easily) to making progress. That information is important for the practitioner to know as well.

## EVALUATING YOUR ATTENTION–DEFICIT/HYPERACTIVITY SYMPTOMS

Attention-deficit/hyperactivity symptoms may be obvious (as in a child who can't sit still for more than one minute at a time) or subtle (as in a student who's struggling to focus on difficult study material). One way to understand the extent to which attention-deficit/hyperactivity symptoms are a problem for a given person is to read the description of the specific criteria—as related to inattention and hyperactivity-impulsivity—provided in the first chapter of this book. Do those descriptions sound like you or the person in question? Again, most people are surprisingly good at identifying their symptoms and weaknesses (though it's easy to go "overboard" with self-diagnosis, as I describe later in this chapter).

Another way to identify attention-deficit/hyperactivity symptoms is to take "self-tests" that appear online or elsewhere. One online test aimed at adults, for example, asks you to rate yourself (from "not at all" to "very much") on twenty-two items (for example, "I tend to fidget with my hands or feet, or squirm in my seat," "I tend to lose things") related to attention-deficit/hyperactivity, providing a total score for the extent to which the symptoms represent a problem.[1] As with any such test, these are *screening* instruments only, and are not designed to provide an actual diagnosis, though some may claim to. Indeed, much of my motivation for writing this book came from my observation that practitioners and patients alike are much too willing to diagnose a set of symptoms as ADHD when there's usually something else going on. Your goal for any kind of self-test, whether for attention-deficit/hyperactivity or other symptoms, should be to gain important information about yourself to share with your practitioner.

## EVALUATING OTHER SYMPTOMS

When people come to see me I ask them to fill out the form (on what they see as their primary problems) mentioned above and evaluate them on multiple other dimensions, depending partly on the types of symptoms they describe as most prominent. On my "checklist" of problems to look for are those related to the conditions I've outlined in this book. These include:

- Short attention span
- Distractibility
- Hyperactivity
- Impulsive behavior
- Lack of motivation
- Learning challenges
- Negative mood
- Excessive anxiety
- Behavioral problems (for example, disruption of school, family)
- Eating problems

Besides probing in these areas, I consider whether to test hearing and vision, especially in children—even if recent tests have been conducted, sensory problems (for example, nearsightedness) can develop quickly and result in multiple symptoms including attention-deficit/hyperactivity. When child patients who come to see me show evidence of school-based problems (learning-related and/or behavioral), I send a short form for their teachers to fill out, including questions about their academic performance and general behavior. The answers provide additional evidence to help diagnose and treat the patient. Sometimes what's going on at school (for example, disruptive behavior) is very different from what parents observe at home.

Because symptoms related to anxiety and depression are very common among the general population, I assess these carefully, as well. That means using a combination of established tests (one example is the Hamilton Anxiety Rating Scale)[2] that I complete based on my observation of and questions for the patient, and self-rating scales that I may ask the patient to fill out or that they have already completed online.[3] As we saw in earlier chapters, depression and anxiety symptoms can easily result in attention-deficit/hyperactivity and be mistaken for ADHD.

As alluded to earlier, I often use lab tests and other types of medical evaluations to gain additional insights into a patient's condition. These are on top of the complete physical examination that I perform. Sometimes I refer my patients for additional testing by a specialist such as an educational psychologist. All inputs help determine the most accurate diagnosis and best treatment plan. A table of the medical evaluations I conduct, in relation to their corresponding conditions or disorders, will follow later in this chapter.

The table below presents the conditions covered in earlier chapters (in the order in which they appear in the book), along with the main symptoms they involve. I present this here to help readers understand the wide range of conditions that can result in attention-deficit/hyperactivity symptoms, and to allow them to compare their own symptoms to the ones below. It's important to emphasize, again, that I'm not providing this information to enable self-diagnosis, but rather to help readers get a better handle on their symptoms and a larger vocabulary to describe them, in order to help their practitioner reach the best diagnosis and treatment. I should also caution you to be conservative in "owning" the symptoms or conditions below. It's well-known that medical students, health-care journalists, and others involved in the medical field become susceptible to believing they have the disorders they're learning about (for example, a mild headache becomes evidence of a cancerous brain tumor). I don't mean hypochondriasis—the often debilitating conviction that one has one or more diseases despite a lack of evidence—but a milder concern about specific symptoms and conditions. The easy access the Internet provides to comprehensive but sometimes erroneous information about medical symptoms and conditions has complicated this problem to the point that the word "cyberchondriasis" was coined to describe the tendency for people to self-diagnose, typically without adequate justification, based on what they read online![4] You should listen to your body, but also seek the guidance of a medical professional to confirm your symptoms and their causes.

Note that attention-deficit and/or hyperactivity can be primary or secondary symptoms for all of the conditions (hence their inclusion in this book), but in the table below I've noted these only where they are part of the condition's medically established diagnostic criteria or particularly likely to appear.

| CONDITION | MAIN SYMPTOMS |
|---|---|
| VISION PROBLEMS | • Trouble seeing at near or far distances<br>• Blurred vision<br>• Headaches from eyestrain |
| SLEEP DISTURBANCE | • Sleeping less than the recommended number of hours<br>• Waking up multiple times during the night<br>• Fatigue<br>• Poor attention/distractibility |
| SUBSTANCE ABUSE | • Excessive consumption of alcohol and/or drugs<br>• Development of tolerance for alcohol and/or drugs<br>• Withdrawal symptoms<br>• Difficulty discontinuing use of substances<br>• Impaired judgment |
| BIPOLAR DISORDER OR DEPRESSION | Specific periods marked by:<br>• Negative mood/low self-worth<br>• Sleep/appetite disturbance<br>• Low energy level<br>• Inflated self-esteem (bipolar only)<br>• Racing thoughts (bipolar only)<br>• Risky behaviors (bipolar only) |

| CONDITION | MAIN SYMPTOMS |
| --- | --- |
| HEARING PROBLEMS | • Limited hearing or unresponsiveness to sound<br>• Asking people to repeat themselves<br>• Favoring one ear over another (for example, by turning one's head) |
| LEARNING DISABILITY | • Difficulty with math, reading, or writing inconsistent with one's apparent level of intelligence<br>• Frustration related to learning challenges<br>• Distractibility related to learning challenges |
| SENSORY PROCESSING DISORDER | Difficulty integrating sensory information as suggested by:<br>• Poor physical coordination<br>• Excessive sensitivity to environmental stimuli (for example, loud noises, uncomfortable clothing)<br>• Poor social skills |
| GIFTEDNESS | • Superior talent in one or more academic/ non-academic domain<br>• Aptitude-related boredom/distractibility (for example, due to mastery of the material)<br>• Impatience |
| SEIZURE DISORDERS (ESPECIALLY ABSENCE SEIZURES) | • Brief loss of sensory input<br>• Unresponsiveness (even to hearing one's name or being tapped on the shoulder) |
| OBSESSIVE-COMPULSIVE DISORDER | • Obsessions related to contamination, order, or other areas<br>• Compulsive behavior related to or independent of obsessions<br>• At least one hour a day spent on obsessions/ compulsions |
| TOURETTE'S SYNDROME | • Excessive fidgeting (before development of other symptoms)<br>• Physical (for example, blinking) and verbal (for example, grunting) tics |

| CONDITION | MAIN SYMPTOMS |
|-----------|---------------|
| ASPERGER SYNDROME (MILD AUTISM) | • Poor social skills<br>• Preoccupation with a narrow interest (for example, coin collection)<br>• Repetitive motor movement (for example, hand-flapping) |
| SCHIZOPHRENIA | • Hallucinations (for example, hearing voices)<br>• Delusions (for example, belief that one is being followed)<br>• Disorganized speech/behavior<br>• Lack of emotion |
| FETAL ALCOHOL SYNDROME | Alcohol consumption during pregnancy that results in these symptoms in the child:<br>• Physical features (for example, smaller head, narrow eyes)<br>• Developmental/learning delays<br>• Poor physical coordination<br>• Attention deficits<br>• Impulsivity |
| FRAGILE X SYNDROME | • Physical features (elongated face, protruding ears)<br>• Mild to severe intellectual disability<br>• Poor social skills<br>• Repetitive speech |
| IRON DEFICIENCY | • Fatigue<br>• Poor attention/concentration<br>• Memory problems |
| ALLERGIES | Depending on the specific allergy type:<br>• Nasal congestion<br>• Coughing/wheezing<br>• Sinus pain<br>• Vomiting/abdominal pain |
| OVERACTIVE THYROID | • Fatigue<br>• Poor concentration<br>• Restlessness<br>• Weight Loss |

| CONDITION | MAIN SYMPTOMS |
|---|---|
| PITUITARY TUMOR | • Frequent headaches<br>• Fatigue<br>• Trouble with vision or smell |
| PREMATURITY | • Small head size (as infant)<br>• Developmental delays |
| HEAVY METAL POISONING | • Confusion/memory loss<br>• Muscle/joint pain<br>• Headaches<br>• Vision problems<br>• Fatigue |

Here I list the multiple potential medical exams I conduct when evaluating a patient with ADHD symptoms. As the table suggests, each test can contribute important information related to the conditions above. Some of the conditions can't be "tested" for, and need to be evaluated by other means. It's important to note, however, that a *careful and thorough* history and physical exam should lead most practitioners to the right diagnosis or diagnoses. However, the tests below can be very useful to confirm the diagnosis and/or to illuminate conditions that may not be apparent from the history and physical exam.

| TEST | WHAT IT TESTS FOR | CONDITIONS IT CAN HELP UNCOVER |
|---|---|---|
| Vision/hearing tests | Vision/hearing functioning | • Vision/hearing disturbance |
| Urinalysis | Proteins/enzymes, blood cells, trace metals, and other substances in the body | • Substance abuse<br>• Iron deficiency<br>• Heavy metal poisoning |

| TEST | WHAT IT TESTS FOR | CONDITIONS IT CAN HELP UNCOVER |
|---|---|---|
| Blood tests<br><br>• Complete blood count (CBC)<br><br>• Specific blood tests | Blood components and chemistry including as related to neurotransmitters (especially dopamine, serotonin, epinephrine/norepinephrine), thyroid hormone (T4/TSH), heavy metals, iron, and specific substances of abuse | • Neurochemical distractibility/impulsivity<br>• Substance abuse<br>• Overactive thyroid<br>• Iron deficiency<br>• Heavy metal poisoning |
| Electrocardiogram (EKG) | Baseline and in-treatment heart function/activity | • Potential effects of medications used for mood disorders, OCD, and NDI |
| Electroencephalogram (EEG)/Brain electrically activated mapping (BEAM) | Brain-based electrical activity/wave patterns | • Seizure disorders<br>• Pituitary (and other) tumors<br>• Learning disabilities (a somewhat controversial use of these tests) |
| CT Scans/MRI | Images of anatomical structures throughout the body | • Pituitary (and other) tumors |
| Genetic testing | Chromosome patterns including mutations | • Fragile X syndrome |
| Allergy tests | Sensitivity to allergens including pollens and foods | • Allergies |
| Intelligence/ Educational testing | Cognitive functioning— overall and as related to specific academic subjects like math and reading | • Learning disabilities<br>• Giftedness |

| TEST | WHAT IT TESTS FOR | CONDITIONS IT CAN HELP UNCOVER |
|---|---|---|
| Self-rating scales | Patients' (or guardians'/teachers') perceptions of symptoms related to mood, anxiety, attention-deficit/hyperactivity, and other areas | • Sleep disturbance<br>• Mood disorders (bipolar disorder, depression)<br>• Obsessive-compulsive disorder<br>• Asperger's<br>• Sensory processing disorder<br>• Schizophrenia |

## MANAGING ATTENTION-DEFICIT/HYPERACTIVITY SYMPTOMS

Most of this book has been devoted to helping you understand the conditions that are often misdiagnosed as ADHD, leading to costly treatment delays or even the denial of treatment. My hope is to help as many people as possible avoid being diagnosed with "ADHD" when a different condition can explain their attention-deficit and hyperactivity symptoms fully; successful treatment of the other condition usually takes care of the  symptoms. Recall also from the chapter on neurochemical distractibility/impulsivity that in a minority of patients attention-deficit/hyperactivity symptoms are based on very specific patterns related to a body's neurotransmitters. For those patients a prescription medication (stimulant or norepinephrine reuptake inhibitor) may be helpful. However, there remains the possibility that even the most accurate diagnosis and thoughtful treatment plan will fail to relieve all attention-deficit/hyperactivity symptoms, or that a given person may qualify for no diagnosis at all, as was the case for my patients Justin and Yvette. For such cases, I wish to offer a set of general recommendations for symptom management below.

## HOW TO KNOW IF YOUR SYMPTOMS ARE CONSEQUENCES OF A CONDITION OR ARE NORMAL

One of the simplest indications of the need for intervention is the degree to which symptoms affect your functioning at school, work, and with family and other relationships. In other words, medical treatment is probably unnecessary if your symptoms aren't disrupting your life in a meaningful way. Many people who are convinced they have ADHD or some other diagnosable condition are simply dealing with a normal level of stress in a faster-paced world. In such cases, simple lifestyle changes make up the best approach. Most of us know how to live healthier lives but struggle to put this knowledge into action. Among the basic suggestions I make to patients, in no particular order:

- *Improve diet* by eating more nutritious foods and eating less if you're prone to overeating. While *specific* ingredients like sugar don't have a long-term effect on attention-deficit/hyperactivity, chronically poor diets definitely do (in general, healthy people have better attention spans and activity levels)
- *Exercise more*, especially by finding an activity that you enjoy and/or can do with others
- *Reduce harmful habits* like smoking and illicit drug use
- *Take up healthy habits* like exercise (as mentioned above) and meditation
- *Sleep more*, because most of us aren't getting enough (see the chapter on sleep disturbance for specific tips)
- *"Practice your passion"* by doing at least one thing that you really enjoy regularly, whether it be something creative, athletic, or otherwise
- *Invest in fulfilling relationships* by spending time with people you care about and making an effort to share more of your life with them (the converse works, too: avoid or find a better way to be part of stressful relationships)

Of course, there are other ways of living a healthier life, but those are the things that work best for my patients, usually in combination. I'll leave you with the idea that in dealing with any kind of symptoms, one of the hardest things to do is to keep the big picture in mind. How much do the symptoms really bother you? Are there simple steps you can take to improving them? How much is your attitude or mind-set affecting the symptoms, positively or negatively? As humans, we are all susceptible to thinking the worst, and that sometimes becomes a "self-fulfilling prophecy," or a reality that we've helped make happen. Attention-deficit/hyperactivity symptoms are troublesome for many, and they are often the result of a diagnosis you may not even realize you have, including one of the many I've detailed in this book. What I hope this book has taught you is what attention-deficit/hyperactivity symptoms are *not*: They are not part of the disorder known as ADHD, a diagnosis that has become far too large and all-encompassing, resulting in too many people suffering from stimulant use and the delay or denial of the treatment that's actually right for them. I hope this book is a step in the right direction, away from our overreliance on the ADHD diagnosis, and toward a better understanding of the symptoms associated with it for my readers and the broader community.

# Acknowledgments

First and foremost, Yolanda. You are my muse, companion, best friend, confidante, and lover.

A big thanks to Karen Rinaldi and everyone at HarperCollins. A special thanks to Jake Zebede, my editor, for the guidance and insight.

Thank you, Sheree Bykofsky, the best agent that I could have hoped for, and Sachin Waikar, PhD, for all his help.

# Notes

## CHAPTER 1: WHERE WE ARE AND HOW WE GOT HERE

1. http://www.nichq.org/toolkits_publications/complete_adhd/03VanAssesScale
   Parent%20Infor.pdf.
2. American Psychiatric Association, *Diagnostic and Statistical Manual of Mental
   Disorders*, 5th ed. (Washington, DC: American Psychiatric Association, 2013).
   The abbreviation *DSM* is also used throughout these notes in reference to the
   manuals.
3. Edward M. Hallowell and John J. Ratey printed "The Story of Fidgety Philip"
   in *Driven to Distraction* (New York: Touchstone, 1994), attributing it to a 1904
   issue of the British medical journal *Lancet*. "The Story of Johnny Head-in-Air"
   appears online and has been attributed to Dr. Heinrich Hoffman, who wrote the
   verse in 1884 (retrieved April 15, 2012, from http://home.earthlink.net/~mishal/
   Poem2.html).
4. Ronald C. Kessler, Lenard Adler, Russell Barkley, Joseph Biederman, C. Keith
   Conners, Olga Demler, Stephen V. Faraone, Laurence L. Greenhill, Mary J.
   Howes, Kristina Secnik, Thomas Spencer, T. Bedirhan Ustun, Ellen E. Walters,
   and Alan M. Zaslavsky, "The Prevalence and Correlates of Adult ADHD in the
   United States: Results from the National Comorbidity Survey Replication,"
   *American Journal of Psychiatry* 163, no. 4 (April 2006): 716–23.
5. Edward M. Hallowell and John J. Ratey, *Driven to Distraction* (New York:
   Touchstone, 1994).
6. American Psychiatric Association, *Diagnostic and Statistical Manual of Mental
   Disorders*, 2nd ed. (Washington, DC: American Psychiatric Association, 1968).
7. American Psychiatric Association, *Diagnostic and Statistical Manual of
   Mental Disorders*, 3rd ed. (Washington, DC: American Psychiatric Association, 1980); American Psychiatric Association, *Diagnostic and Statistical*

*Manual of Mental Disorders*, 3rd ed., rev. (Washington, DC: American Psychiatric Association, 1987).

8.  American Psychiatric Association, *Diagnostic and Statistical Manual of Mental Disorders*, 4th ed. (Washiongton, DC: American Psychiatric Association, 1994); J. Biederman, S. V. Faraone, W. Weber, R. L. Russell, M. Rater, and K. S. Park, "Correspondence Between DSM-III-R and DSM-IV Attention-deficit/hyperactivity Disorder," *Journal of the American Academy of Child and Adolescent Psychiatry* 36, no. 12 (December 1997): 1682–87.

9.  Gina Kolata, "5 Disorders Share Same Genetic Risk Factors, Study Finds," *New York Times*, February 28, 2013, retrieved March 21, 2013, from http://www.nytimes.com/2013/03/01/health/study-finds-genetic-risk-factors-shared-by-5-psychiatric-disorders.html.

10. *DSM*, 5th ed.

11. *DSM*, 4th ed., p. 78.

12. *DSM*, 5th ed., p. 59.

13. *DSM*, 4th ed., p. 84.

14. *DSM*, 5th ed., p. 60.

15. Ibid., p. 65.

16. Ibid.

17. *DSM*, 4th ed., p. 82.

18. Centers for Disease Control and Prevention, ADHD Home Page, retrieved April 15, 2012, from http://www.cdc.gov/ncbddd/adhd/data.html.

19. Teal Ruland, "The 'Hidden' Costs of ADHD," *NEA Today*, January 9, 2012, retrieved April 29, 2012, from http://neatoday.org/2012/01/09/the-hidden-costs-of-adhd/.

20. Brian Wymbs, William Pelham, Brooke Molina, Elizabeth Gnagy, Tracey Wilson, and Joel Greenhouse, "Rate and Predictors of Divorce Among Parents of Youth with ADHD," *Journal of Consulting and Clinical Psychology* 76, no. 5 (October 2008): 735–44.

**CHAPTER 2: AN EASY ANSWER: THE ROLE OF CULTURAL BIAS**

1.  American Psychiatric Association, *Diagnostic and Statistical Manual of Mental Disorders*, 5th ed. (Washington, DC: American Psychiatric Association, 2013).

2.  "ADHD May Be Misdiagnosed in Youngest Classmates," CBC News, March 5, 2012, retrieved April 29, 2012, from http://www.cbc.ca/news/health/story/2012/03/05/adhd-schoolchildren-birth-month.html.

3.  *DSM*, 5th ed.

4.  "Men, Women, and ADHD," *New York Times,* Consults blog, February 11, 2011, retrieved April 26 from http://consults.blogs.nytimes.com/2011/02/11/men-women-and-a-d-h-d/.

5. See, for example, Margarita Tartakovsky, "ADHD Affects Girls and Boys at Roughly the Same Rate," *SpecialEd Post*, December 24, 2012, retrieved March 20, 2013 from http://specialedpost.com/2012/12/24/adhd-affects-girls-and-boys-at-roughly-the-same-rate/.

6. Alan Schwarz, "Attention Disorder or Not, Pills to Help in School," *New York Times*, October 9, 2012, retrieved March 21, 2013, from http://www.nytimes.com/2012/10/09/health/attention-disorder-or-not-children-prescribed-pills-to-help-in-school.html?pagewanted=all.

7. "Overview of ADHD," Centers for Disease Control and Prevention, retrieved April 29, 2012, from http://www.cdc.gov/ncbddd/adhd/research.html.

## CHAPTER 3: THE STIMULANT EPIDEMIC AND SIDE EFFECTS

1. For an overview of stimulants, including their effects and side effects, see "ADD and ADHD Health Center," WebMD, retrieved May 6, 2013, from http://www.webmd.com/add-adhd/stimulants-for-attention-deficit-hyperactivity-disorder.

2. Alan Schwarz, "Risky Rise of the Good Grade Pill," *New York Times*, June 9, 2012, retrieved March 21, 2013, from http://www.nytimes.com/2012/06/10/education/seeking-academic-edge-teenagers-abuse-stimulants.html?pagewanted=all.

3. Alan Schwarz and Sarah Cohen, "ADHD Seen in 11% of US Children as Diagnoses Rise," *New York Times*, March 31, 2013, retrieved April 2, 2013, from http://www.nytimes.com/2013/04/01/health/more-diagnoses-of-hyperactivity-causing-concern.html?ref=todayspaper&_r=1&.

4. William Graf, Saskia Nagel, Leon Epstein, Geoffrey Miller, Ruth Nass, and Dan Larriviere, "Pediatric Neuroenhancement: Ethical, Legal, Social, and Neurodevelopmental Implications," *Neurology* 80 (March 2013): 1251–60.

## CHAPTER 5: VISION PROBLEMS

1. For more information on these and other vision problems and their causes, see online resources including the National Institutes of Health's Medline Plus, http://www.nlm.nih.gov/medlineplus/ency/article/003029.htm; and WebMD's Eye Health Center, http://www.webmd.com/eye-health/understanding-vision-problems-basics.

2. For more information on eye-teaming disorders see Children's Vision Information Network, "Vision and ADD/ADHD" (retrieved January 30, 2013, from http://www.childrensvision.com/ADD.htm.)

3. WebMD, Eye Health Center, retrieved January 30, 2013, from http://www.webmd.com/eye-health/understanding-vision-problems-basics.

4. Prevent Blindness America, "Vision Problems in the US," retrieved January 30, 2013, from http://www.visionproblemsus.org/.

5. Children's Vision Information Network, "Vision and ADD/ADHD."

6. R. Farrar, M. Call, and W. C. Maples, "A Comparison of the Visual Symptoms Between ADD/ADHD and Normal Children," *Optometry* 72, no. 7 (2001): 441–51.

7. W. C. Maples and M. Bither, "Efficacy of Vision Therapy as Assessed by the COVD Quality of Life Checklist," *Optometry* 73, no. 8 (2002): 492–98.

8. E. Borsting, M. Rouse, and R. Chu, "Measuring ADHD Behaviors in Children with Symptomatic Accommodative Dysfunction or Convergence Insufficiency: A Preliminary Study," *Optometry* 76, no. 10 (October 2005): 588–92.

9. Eric R. Eide, Mark H. Showalter, and Dan D. Goldhaber, "The Relation Between Children's Health and Academic Achievement," *Children and Youth Services Review* 32, no. 2 (February 2010): 231–38.

10. Detailed information about Lasik and other laser eye surgeries is available at sites like All About Vision, http://www.allaboutvision.com/visionsurgery/.

11. Newer laser-based surgery techniques such as monovision Lasik have been developed to correct presbyopia without corrective lenses.

## CHAPTER 6: SLEEP DISORDERS

1. "Sleep Deprivation Creating Nation of Walking Zombies," ABC News, November 8, 2006, retrieved July 23, 2012, from http://abcnews.go.com/Technology/story?id=2635961&page=1#.UA3FZGEhAuA.

2. This chapter focuses on the problems associated with too little sleep. But there is also evidence that people who sleep *too much* suffer from similar issues. More information on this topic is provided by Laura Blue, "How Much Sleep Do You Really Need," *TIME Health*, June 6, 2008, retrieved July 23, 2012, from http://www.time.com/time/health/article/0,8599,1812420,00.html.

3. Maggie Jones, "How Little Sleep Can You Get Away With?" *New York Times*, April 15, 2011, retrieved July 23, 2012, from http://www.webmd.com/sleep-disorders/guide/toll-of-sleep-loss-in-america. It's important to note that some people may be considered "short sleepers" or "long sleepers," who require less or more sleep than average, respectively, to function optimally. See, for example, American Psychiatric Association, *Diagnostic and Statistical Manual of Mental Disorders*, 4th ed. (Washington, DC: American Psychiatric Association, 1994). Anecdotal evidence suggests short and long sleepers represent only small minorities of the general population.

4. "Causes of Sleep Problems," WebMD, retrieved July 23, 2012, from http://www.webmd.com/sleep-disorders/sleep-disorders-causes.

5. American Psychiatric Association, *Diagnostic and Statistical Manual of Mental Disorders*, 5th ed. (Washington, DC: American Psychiatric Association, 2013).

6. American Sleep Apnea Association, "Sleep Apnea," retrieved July 23, 2012, from http://www.sleepapnea.org/learn/sleep-apnea.html.

7. *DSM*, 5th ed., p. 390.

8. Ibid., p. 795.

9. Stephanie Sajor, "Technology Leading to Higher Rates of Sleep Deprivation," ThirdAge.com, March 7, 2011, retrieved July 23, 2012, from http://www.third age.com/news/technology-leading-higher-rates-sleep-deprivation_3-7-2011.

10. Sharon Jayson, "Stress Levels Increased Since 1983, New Analysis Shows," *USA Today*, June 13, 2012, retrieved July 5, 2013, from http://usatoday30.usatoday .com/news/health/story/2012-06-13/stress-increase-over-time/55587296/1.

11. Jeanie Lerche Davis, "The Toll of Sleep Loss in America," WebMD, retrieved July 23, 2012, from http://www.nytimes.com/2011/04/17/magazine/mag-17Sleep-t.html.

12. Jeanie Lerche Davis, "The Toll of Sleep Loss in America," WebMD, retrieved July 23, 2012, from http://www.webmd.com/sleep-disorders/guide/toll-of-sleep-loss-in-america.

13. *DSM*, 5th ed.

14. Ibid.

15. "Causes of Sleep Problems," WebMD, retrieved July 23, 2012, from http://www .webmd.com/sleep-disorders/sleep-disorders-causes.

16. Jones, "How Little Sleep Can You Get Away With?"

17. "Sleep Deprivation Shown to Have as Much Impact on Reaction Time as Alcohol," Stanford University press release, September 28, 1999, retrieved July 23, 2012, from http://med.stanford.edu/news_releases/1999/sepreleases/reaction .html.

18. Eric Mick, Joseph Biederman, Jennifer Jetton, and Stephen V. Faraone, "Sleep Disturbances Associated with Attention Deficit Hyperactivity Disorder: The Impact of Psychiatric Comorbidity and Pharmacotherapy," *Journal of Child and Adolescent Psychopharmacology* 10, no. 3 (September 2000): 223–31.

19. As quoted by the Sleep Improvement Center, "ADD or Sleep Apnea," retrieved July 23, 2012, from http://www.sleepimprovementcenter.com/disorder_child .php.

20. Bonnie J. Kaplan, Jane McNicol, Richard A. Conte, and H. K. Moghadam, "Sleep Disturbance in Preschool-Aged Hyperactive and Nonhyperactive Children," *Pediatrics* 80, no. 6 (December 1, 1987): 839–44

21. "ADHD Linked to Sleep Problems in Adolescents," *ScienceDaily*, May 6, 2009, retrieved July 23, 2012 from http://www.sciencedaily.com/re leases/2009/05/090501090914.htm.

22. While prescription and over-the-counter sleep aids have become increasingly

popular, most practitioners and researchers agree that because of potential side-effect and dependence issues, the ideal approach to nonmedical sleep disturbance involves nonmedical treatments; hence, I've focused on these measures in this chapter.

23. Timothy Morganthaler, MD, "How Many Hours of Sleep Are Enough for Good Health?" Mayo Clinic, retrieved July 23, 2012, from http://www.mayoclinic.com/health/how-many-hours-of-sleep-are-enough/AN01487/.

24. Molly Webster, "Can You Catch Up on Lost Sleep?" *Scientific American*, May 6, 2008, retrieved July 23, 2012, from http://www.scientificamerican.com/article.cfm?id=fact-or-fiction-can-you-catch-up-on-sleep.

25. "Sleep Deprivation Creating Nation of Walking Zombies," ABC News, November 8, 2006, retrieved July 23, 2012, from http://abcnews.go.com/Technology/story?id=2635961&page=1#.UA3FZGEhAuA.

26. Webster, "Can You Catch Up on Lost Sleep?"

## CHAPTER 7: SUBSTANCE ABUSE

1. American Psychiatric Association, *Diagnostic and Statistical Manual of Mental Disorders*, 5th ed. (Washington, DC: American Psychiatric Association, 2013), p. 481.

2. Ibid., p. 481. This chapter will refer to substance use disorder, substance intoxication, and withdrawal (regardless of the substance in question) as "substance abuse"; all of these conditions/diagnoses can involve significant attention deficits and hyperactivity.

3. Centers for Disease Control and Prevention, "Alcohol Use," retrieved November 26, 2012, from http://www.cdc.gov/nchs/fastats/alcohol.htm.

4. NIDA, "Drug Facts: Nationwide Trends," retrieved November 25, 2012, from http://www.drugabuse.gov/publications/drugfacts/nationwide-trends.

5. *DSM*, 5th ed.

6. Ibid.

7. T. E. Wilens, "Attention-deficit/hyperactivity Disorder and the Substance Use Disorders: The Nature of the Relationship, Subtypes at Risk, and Treatment Issues," *Psychiatric Clinics of North America* 27 (2004): 283–301; F. R. Levin, S. Evans, and H. D. Kleber, "Prevalence of Adult Attention-Deficit/Hyperactivity Disorder Among Cocaine Abusers Seeking Treatment," *Drug and Alcohol Dependence* 52 (1998): 15–25.

8. Donald M. Dougherty, Dawn M. Marsh, F. Gerard Moeller, Reena V. Chokshi, and Valerie C. Rosen, "Effects of Moderate and High Doses of Alcohol on Attention, Impulsivity, Discriminability, and Response Bias in Immediate and Delayed Memory Task Performance," *Alcoholism: Clinical and Experimental Research* 24, no. 11 (November 2000): 1702–1711.

9.  Marvin R. Lamb and Lynn C. Robertson, "Effect of Acute Alcohol on Attention and the Processing of Hierarchical Patterns," *Alcoholism: Clinical and Experimental Research* 11, no. 3 (June 1987): 243–48.

10. J. Rosello, E. Munar, S. Justo, and R. Arias, "Effects of Alcohol on Divided Attention and on Accuracy of Attentional Shift," *Psychology in Spain* 3, no. 1 (1999): 69–87.

11. See, for example, N. Freeman, R. Friedman, B. Bartholomew, and E. Wulfert, "Effects of Alcohol Priming on Social Disinhibition," *Experimental and Clinical Psychopharmacology* 18, no. 2 (2010): 135–44.

12. See, for example, H. G. Pope Jr. and D. Yurgelun-Todd, "The Residual Cognitive Effects of Heavy Marijuana Use in College Students," *JAMA*, February 21, 1996.

13. American Council for Drug Education, "Basic Facts About Drugs: Marijuana," retrieved November 26, 2012, from http://www.acde.org/common/Marijuana.htm.

14. National Institute on Drug Abuse, "Treatment Approaches for Drug Addiction," retrieved November 26, 2012, from http://www.drugabuse.gov/publications/drugfacts/treatment-approaches-drug-addiction.

15. Ibid.

16. For an overview of many of the treatment approaches discussed in this section, see the *New York Times*, "Health Guide: Alcoholism and Alcohol Abuse," retrieved November 26, 2012, from http://health.nytimes.com/health/guides/disease/alcoholism/psychotherapy-and-behavioral-methods.html.

## CHAPTER 8: MOOD DISORDERS (BIPOLAR AND MAJOR DEPRESSIVE DISORDER)

1.  WHO International Consortium in Psychiatric Epidemiology, "Cross-National Comparisons of the Prevalences and Correlates of Mental Disorders," *Bulletin of the World Health Organization* 78, no. 4 (2000).

2.  R. C. Kessler, P. Berglund, O. Demler, R. Jin, K. R. Merikangas, and E. E. Walters, "Lifetime Prevalence and Age-of-Onset Distributions of *DSM-IV* Disorders in the National Comorbidity Survey Replication," *Archives of General Psychiatry* 62, no. 6 (June 2005): 593–602.

3.  See, for example, Paul Andrews and J. Anderson Thompson, "Depression's Evolutionary Roots," *Scientific American*, August 25, 2009, retrieved July 8, 2013, from http://www.scientificamerican.com/article.cfm?id=depressions-evolutionary.

4.  American Psychiatric Association, *Diagnostic and Statistical Manual of Mental Disorders*, 5th ed. (Washington, DC: American Psychiatric Association, 2013).

5.  Ibid.

6. Ibid.

7. D. G. Blazer, R. C. Kessler, K. A. McGonagle, and M. S. Swartz, "The Prevalence and Distribution of Major Depression in a National Community Sample: The National Comorbidity Survey," *American Journal of Psychiatry* 151, no. 7 (1994): 979–86.

8. *DSM*, 5th ed.

9. Lisa Cosgrove, Sheldon Krimsky, Manisha Vijayaraghavan, and Lisa Schneider, "Financial Ties Between *DSM-IV* Panel Members and the Pharmaceutical Industry," *Psychotherapy and Psychosomatics* 75, no. 3 (2006): 154–60.

10. See, for example, Jonathan Alpert, Anne Maddocks, Andrew Nierenberg, Richard Sullivan, Joel Pava, John Worthington, Joseph Biederman, Jerrold Rosenbaum, and Maurizio Fava, "Attention Deficit Hyperactivity in Childhood Among Adults with Major Depression," *Psychiatry Research* 62, no. 3 (June 1996): 213–19.

11. Barbara Geller, Betsy Zimerman, Marlene Williams, Melissa P. DelBello, et al., "*DSM-IV* Mania Symptoms in a Prepubertal and Early Adolescent Bipolar Disorder Phenotype Compared to Attention-Deficit Hyperactive and Normal Controls," *Journal of Child and Adolescent Psychopharmacology* 12, no. 1 (2002): 11–25.

12. Luke Clark, Susan Iversen, and Guy Goodwin, "Sustained Attention Deficit in Bipolar Disorder," *British Journal of Psychiatry* 180 (2002): 313–19.

13. Gina Kolata, "5 Disorders Share Same Genetic Risk Factors, Study Finds," *New York Times*, February 28, 2013, retrieved March 21, 2013, from http://www.nytimes.com/2013/03/01/health/study-finds-genetic-risk-factors-shared-by-5-psychiatric-disorders.html.

**CHAPTER 9: HEARING PROBLEMS**

1. For more information on hearing problems and their causes see online resources including the National Institutes of Health's Medline Plus, http://www.nlm.nih.gov/medlineplus/hearingdisordersanddeafness.html; and the Mayo Clinic's overview of hearing loss, http://www.mayoclinic.com/print/hearing-loss/DS00172/DSECTION=all&METHOD=print.

2. National Institute on Deafness and Other Communication Disorders, "Quick Statistics," retrieved January 30, 2013, from http://www.nidcd.nih.gov/health/statistics/Pages/quick.aspx.

3. Fred Bess, Jeanne Dodd-Murphy, and Robert Parker, "Children with Minimal Sensorineural Hearing Loss: Prevalence, Educational Performance, and Functional Status," *Ear & Hearing* 19, no. 5 (October 1998): 339–54.

4. National Institute on Deafness and Other Communication Disorders, "Quick Statistics."

5. Bess, Dodd-Murphy, and Parker, "Children with Minimal Sensorineural Hearing Loss."

6. Teresa V. Mitchell and Alexandra L. Quittner, "Multimethod Study of Attention and Behavior Problems in Hearing-Impaired Children," *Journal of Clinical Child Psychology* 25, no. 1 (1996): 83–96.

7. Joanne O'Connell and Kathleen Casale, "Attention Deficits and Hearing Loss: Meeting the Challenge," *Volta Review* 104, no. 4 (2004): 257–71.

8. American Speech-Language-Hearing Association, "Effects of Hearing Loss on Development," retrieved January 30, 2013, from http://www.asha.org/public/hearing/disorders/effects.htm.

9. National Institute on Deafness and Other Communication Disorders, "Quick Statistics."

10. National Institute on Deafness and Other Communication Disorders, "Cochlear Implants," retrieved January 30, 2013, from http://www.nidcd.nih.gov/health/hearing/pages/coch.aspx.

11. Encyclopedia of Surgery, "Cochlear Implants," retrieved January 30, 2013, from http://www.surgeryencyclopedia.com/Ce-Fi/Cochlear-Implants.html.

**CHAPTER 10: LEARNING DISABILITIES**

1. American Psychiatric Association, *Diagnostic and Statistical Manual of Mental Disorders*, 5th ed. (Washington, DC: American Psychiatric Association, 2013), p. 32.

2. Ibid.

3. National Center for Learning Disabilities website, retrieved September 28, 2012, from http://www.ncld.org/types-learning-disabilities/what-is-ld.

4. *DSM*, 5th ed.

5. National Center for Learning Disabilities website.

6. Learning Disabilities Association of America website, retrieved September 28, 2012, from http://www.ldanatl.org/aboutld/adults/index.asp.

7. Tina Stanton-Chapman, Derek Chapman, and Keith Scott, "Identification of Early Risk Factors for Learning Disabilities," *Journal of Early Intervention* 24, no. 3 (2001): 193–206.

8. Patricia Pastor and Cynthia Reuben, "Diagnosed Attention Deficit Hyperactivity Disorder and Learning Disability: United States, 2004–2006, Data from the National Health Interview Survey," *Vital and Health Statistics*, series 10, no. 237, abstract retrieved September 28, 2012, from http://www.eric.ed.gov/ERICWebPortal/search/detailmini.jsp?_nfpb=true&_&ERICExtSearch_SearchValue_0=ED502147&ERICExtSearch_SearchType_0=no&accno=ED502147.

9. Learning Disabilities Association of America website.

10. Martha Denckla, "Biological Correlates of Learning and Attention: What Is

Relevant to Learning Disability and Attention-Deficit Hyperactivity Disorder?" *Journal of Developmental and Behavioral Pediatrics* 17, no. 2 (April 1996), retrieved September 28, 2012, from http://journals.lww.com/jrnldbp/abstract/1996/04000/biological_correlates_of_learning_and_attention_.11.aspx.

11. R. J. Sternberg and E. L. Grigorenko, *Our Labeled Children: What Every Parent and Teacher Needs to Know About Learning Disabilities* (Reading, MA: Perseus, 1999).

12. IEPs are specialized education programs for children with specific special needs; public schools are mandated by U.S. law to provide IEPs from kindergarten through high school.

13. Sheryl Knapp, "Comprehension Skills for Kids with LD," retrieved September 28, 2012, from http://www.smartkidswithld.org/ld-basics/treatments-and-support/comprehension-skills-for-kids-with-ld.

14. "Understanding Dysgraphia," Wrightslaw, retrieved September 28, 2012, from http://www.wrightslaw.com/info/read.dysgraphia.facts.htm#act.

**CHAPTER 11: SENSORY PROCESSING DISORDER**

1. For a good overview of sensory processing disorder, including its diagnosis and treatment, see the Sensory Processing Foundation home page, retrieved March 4, 2013, from http://www.sinetwork.org/index.html.

2. Sensory Processing Disorder Foundation, "About SPD," retrieved March 4, 2013, from http://www.sinetwork.org/about-sensory-processing-disorder.html.

3. R. R. Ahn, L. J. Miller, S. Milberger, and D. N. McIntosh, "Prevalence of Parents' Perceptions of Sensory Processing Disorders Among Kindergarten Children," *American Journal of Occupational Therapy* 58 (2004): 287–93.

4. See, for example, A. Ben-Sasson, A. S. Carter, and M. J. Briggs-Gowan, "Sensory Over-Responsivity in Elementary School: Prevalence and Social-Emotional Correlates," *Journal of Abnormal Child Psychology* 37 (2009):705–716. Their parent survey results showed that 16 percent of children were bothered significantly by at least four auditory or tactile sensations.

5. Sensory Processing Disorder Foundation, "About SPD" (retrieved March 4, 2013 from http://www.sinetwork.org/about-sensory-processing-disorder.html)

6. Ibid.

7. Claudia Wallis, "The Next Attention Deficit Disorder?" *Time*, November 29, 2007, retrieved March 4, 2013, from http://www.time.com/time/magazine/article/0%2C9171%2C1689216%2C00.html.

8. Carol Kranowitz, "Two 'Look-alikes': Sensory Processing Disorder and Attention Deficit/Hyperactivity Disorder," *Beginnings* no. 15 (Summer 2010): 5. *Beginnings* is a publication of the National Alliance of the Mentally Ill.

9. See, for example, Batya Engel-Yeger and Daniella Ziv-On, "The Relationship

Between Sensory Processing Difficulties and Leisure Activity Preference of Children with Different Types of ADHD," *Research in Developmental Disabilities* 32, no. 3 (May–June 2011): 1154–62.

10. For more on occupational therapy, see the American Occupational Therapy Association, "About Occupational Therapy," retrieved March 5, 2013, from http://www.aota.org/Consumers.aspx.

#### CHAPTER 12: GIFTEDNESS

1. National Association for Gifted Children, "What is Giftedness?" Retrieved March 15, 2013, from http://www.nagc.org/index.aspx?id=574.

2. Ibid.

3. Mensa International, "About Us," retrieved March 16, 2013, from http://www.mensa.org/about-us.

4. Scott Barry Kaufman, "What Is Giftedness?" *Psychology Today*, May 16, 2008, retrieved March 16, 2013, from http://www.psychologytoday.com/blog/beautiful-minds/200805/what-is-giftedness.

5. See, for example, S. M. Baum, F. R. Olenchak, and S. V. Owen, "Gifted Students with Attention Deficits: Fact and/or Fiction? Or, Can We See the Forest for the Trees?" *Gifted Child Quarterly* 42 (1998): 96–104; and S. Lind, "Something to Consider Before Referring for ADD/ADHD," Counseling & Guidance 4 (1993): 1–3.

6. Table adapted/excerpted from James T. Webb, Edward R. Amend, Nadia E. Webb, Jean Goerss, Paul Beljan, and F. Richard Olenchak, *Misdiagnosis and Dual Diagnoses of Gifted Children and Adults: ADHD, Bipolar, OCD, Asperger's, Depression, and Other Disorders* (Scottsdale, AZ: Great Potential Press, 2004).

7. Janice A. Leroux and Marla Levitt-Perlman, "The Gifted Child with Attention Deficit Disorder: An Identification and Intervention Challenge," *Roeper Review* 22, no. 3 (2000): 171–76.

#### CHAPTER 13: SEIZURE DISORDERS

1. Ann Berg, Samuel Berkovic, Martin Brodie, et al., "Revised Terminology and Concepts for Organization of Seizures and Epilepsies: Report of the ILAE Commission on Classification and Terminology, 2005–2009," *Epilepsia* 51, no. 4 (2010): 676–85.

2. Keck Medical Center of USC, "Epilepsy," retrieved October 15, 2012, from http://www.doctorsofusc.com/condition/document/38390.

3. For an easy-to-understand overview of seizures, see for example "Seizures—Topic Overview," WebMD site, retrieved October 15, 2012, from http://www.webmd.com/epilepsy/tc/seizures-topic-overview.

4. "Aura and Seizures," WebMD, retrieved October 15, 2012, from http://www .webmd.com/epilepsy/aura-and-seizures.

5. Seizure occurrence rates from Susan Herman, "Single Unprovoked Seizures," *Current Treatment Options in Neurology* 6, no. 3 (2004): 243–55.

6. David Dunn et al., "ADHD and Epilepsy in Childhood," *Developmental Medicine & Child Neurology* 45, no. 1 (January 2003): 50–54.

7. Jane Williams et al., "Symptom Differences in Children with Absence Seizures Versus Inattention," *Epilepsy & Behavior* 3, no. 3 (July 2002): 245–48.

8. "Is It ADHD . . . Epilepsy . . . or Both?" Epilepsy Talk, retrieved October 15, 2012, from http://epilepsytalk.com/2011/02/19/ is-it-adhd%E2%80%A6epilepsy%E2%80%A6or-both/.

9. Williams et al., "Symptom Differences in Children with Absence Seizures Versus Inattention."

10. Gus Baker et al., "Quality of Life of People with Epilepsy: A European Study," *Epilepsia* 38, no. 3 (March 1997): 353–62.

11. Unfortunately, seizure disorders that first appear in adulthood tend to require long-term treatment—lifelong, in many cases.

## CHAPTER 14: OBSESSIVE-COMPULSIVE DISORDER

1. R. C. Kessler, P. Berglund, O. Demler, R. Jin, K. R. Merikangas, and E. E. Walters, "Lifetime Prevalence and Age-of-Onset Distributions of *DSM-IV* Disorders in the National Comorbidity Survey Replication," *Archives of General Psychiatry* 62, no. 6 (June 2005): 593–602.

2. American Psychiatric Association, *Diagnostic and Statistical Manual of Mental Disorders*, 5th ed. (Washington, DC: American Psychiatric Association, 2013).

3. The *DSM-V* includes much more detail on these and other psychiatric conditions from which OCD may be differentiated.

4. American Psychiatric Association, *Diagnostic and Statistical Manual of Mental Disorders*, 4th ed. (Washington, DC: American Psychiatric Association, 1994).

5. DSM, 5th ed.

6. R. C. Kessler, W. T. Chiu, O. Demler, and E. E. Walters, "Prevalence, Severity, and Comorbidity of Twelve-Month *DSM-IV* Disorders in the National Comorbidity Survey Replication (NCS-R)," *Archives of General Psychiatry* 62, no. 6 (June 2005): 617–27.

7. Bradley Peterson, Daniel Pine, Patricia Cohen, and Judith Brook, "Prospective, Longitudinal Study of Tic, Obsessive Compulsive, and Attention-Deficit/Hyperactivity Disorders in an Epidemiological Sample," *Journal of the American Academy of Child and Adolescent Psychiatry* 40, no. 6 (2001): 685–95.

8. Larry Silver, "Is It OCD or ADHD?"

9. Keith Ablow, "Could OCD start as ADD?" FoxNews.com, April 27, 2011, retrieved July 6, 2012, from http://www.foxnews.com/health/2011/04/26/obsessive-compulsive-disorder-start-attention-deficit-disorder/.

10. Mayo Clinic, "Obsessive-Compulsive Disorder," retrieved July 6, 2012, from http://www.mayoclinic.com/health/obsessive-compulsive-disorder/ds00189/dsection=treatments-and-drugs.

## CHAPTER 15: TOURETTE'S SYNDROME

1. R. Nass and S. Bressman, "Attention Deficit Hyperactivity Disorder and Tourette Syndrome," *Neurology* 58 (2002): 513–14. See also G. Erenberg, "The Relationship Between Tourette Syndrome, Attention Deficit Hyperactivity Disorder, and Stimulant Medication: A Critical Review," *Seminars in Pediatric Neurology* 12, no. 4 (2005): 217–21.

2. The other tic disorders, as per the *DSM-V*, are persistent (chronic) motor or vocal tic disorder (characterized by motor *or* vocal tics, but not both), provisional tic disorder (motor and/or vocal tics present less than a year), and unspecified or other specified tic disorder (both involve tic symptoms that do not meet full criteria for one of the other tic disorder diagnoses). American Psychiatric Association, *Diagnostic and Statistical Manual of Mental Disorders*, 5th ed. (Washington, DC: American Psychiatric Association, 2013).

3. Ibid., p. 81.

4. American Psychiatric Association, *Diagnostic and Statistical Manual of Mental Disorders*, 4th ed., rev. (Washington, DC: American Psychiatric Association, 2000).

5. National Alliance for the Mentally Ill, "Tourette's Syndrome," retrieved July 9, 2012, from http://www.nami.org/Template.cfm?Section=By_Illness&Template=/TaggedPage/TaggedPageDisplay.cfm&TPLID=54&ContentID=23053.

6. Centers for Disease Control and Prevention, "Prevalence of Diagnosed Tourette Syndrome in Persons Aged 6–17 Years—United States, 2007," retrieved July 9, 2012, from http://www.cdc.gov/mmwr/preview/mmwrhtml/mm5821a1.htm.

7. Mary Robertson, "Diagnosing Tourette Syndrome: Is It a Common Disorder?" *Journal of Psychosomatic Research* 55 (2003): 3–6.

8. Nass and Bressman, "Attention Deficit Hyperactivity Disorder and Tourette Syndrome." See also Erenberg, "The Relationship Between Tourette Syndrome, Attention Deficit Hyperactivity Disorder, and Stimulant Medication."

9. *DSM*, 5th ed.

10. See, for example, S. Olson, "Making Sense of Tourette's," *Science* 305 (2004): 1390–92. Also see Thomas Spencer, Joseph Biederman, Margaret Harding, Deborah O'Donnell, Timothy Wilens, Stephen Faraone, Barbara Coffey, and Daniel

Geller, "Disentangling the Overlap Between Tourette's Disorder and ADHD," *Journal of Child Psychology and Psychiatry* 39, no. 7 (October 1998): 1037–44.

11. National Institute of Neurological Disorders and Stroke, "Tourette Syndrome Fact Sheet," retrieved July 9, 2012, from http://www.ninds.nih.gov/disorders/tourette/detail_tourette.htm#201653231.

12. Erenberg, "The Relationship Between Tourette Syndrome, Attention Deficit Hyperactivity Disorder, and Stimulant Medication."

13. National Institute of Neurological Disorders and Stroke, "Tourette Syndrome Fact Sheet."

14. NYU Child Study Center, "Habit Reversal: A Treatment Approach for Tics, Tourette's Disorder, and Other Repetitive Behavior Disorders," retrieved July 9, 2012, from http://www.aboutourkids.org/articles/habit_reversal_treatment_approach_tics_tourette039s_disorder_other_repetitive_behavior_diso.

## CHAPTER 16: ASPERGER SYNDROME (AN AUTISM SPECTRUM DISORDER)

1. American Psychiatric Association, *Diagnostic and Statistical Manual of Mental Disorders,* 4th ed. (Washington, DC: American Psychiatric Association, 1994).

2. Ibid., p. 75.

3. Mayo Clinic, "Asperger's Syndrome," retrieved August 25, 2012, from http://www.mayoclinic.com/health/aspergers-syndrome/DS00551.

4. *DSM,* 4th ed., p. 77.

5. Mayo Clinic, "Asperger's Syndrome."

6. See, for example, NBCNews.com, "Proposed Autism Diagnosis Angers 'Aspies,'" February 11, 2010, retrieved February 28, 2013, from http://www.nbcnews.com/id/35348917/ns/health-mental_health/.

7. The *DSM-V* "gets around" this distinction between autism and Asperger's by requiring practitioners to code whether the autism spectrum disorder involves accompanying intellectual and/or language impairment; I maintain that maintaining Asperger's syndrome as a separate diagnosis is a more valid approach, for the reasons mentioned in this chapter.

8. American Psychiatric Association, *Diagnostic and Statistical Manual of Mental Disorders*, 5th ed. (Washington, DC: American Psychiatric Association, 2013).

9. Ibid., p. 52.

10. The amount of time children and adults spend gaming has risen dramatically over decades, to the point that there have even been deaths related to prolonged gaming; see, for example, Winda Benedetti, "Playing Video Games Without a Break Can Kill You," NBCnews.com, retrieved August 24, 2012, from http://www.nbcnews.com/technology/ingame/playing-video-games-without-break-can-kill-you-121765.

11. S. Ehlers and C. Gillberg, "The Epidemiology of Asperger Syndrome: A Total Population Study," *Journal of Child Psychology and Psychiatry* 34, no. 8 (1993): 1327–50.

12. Mayo Clinic, "Asperger's Syndrome."

13. *DSM*, 5th ed.

14. *DSM*, 4th ed., p. 76.

15. M. R. Woodbury-Smith and F. Volkmar, "Asperger Syndrome," *European Child & Adolescent Psychiatry* 18, no. 1 (2009): 2–11.

16. Daniel Rosenn, "Is It Asperger's or ADHD?" Asperger's Association of New England, retrieved August 28, 2012, from http://www.aane.org/asperger_re sources/articles/miscellaneous/aspergers_or_adhd.html.

17. Angelica Ronald, Emily Simonoff, Jonna Kuntsi, Philip Asherson, and Robert Plomin, "Evidence for Overlapping Genetic Influences on Autistic and ADHD Behaviours in a Community Twin Sample," *Journal of Child Psychology and Psychiatry* 49, no. 5 (May 2008): 535–42.

18. Gina Kolata, "5 Disorders Share Same Genetic Risk Factors, Study Finds," *New York Times*, February 28, 2013, retrieved March 21, 2013, from http://www .nytimes.com/2013/03/01/health/study-finds-genetic-risk-factors-shared-by-5-psychiatric-disorders.html.

19. C. Gillberg and E. Billstedt, "Autism and Asperger Syndrome: Coexistence with Other Clinical Disorders," *Acta Psychiatrica Scandinavica* 102, no. 5 (November 2000): 321–30.

20. Agneta Nydén, Eva Billstedt, Erland Hjelmquist, and Christopher Gillberg, "Neurocognitive Stability in Asperger Syndrome, ADHD, and Reading and Writing Disorder: A Pilot Study," *Developmental Medicine & Child Neurology* 43, no. 3 (March 2001): 165–71.

21. Mayo Clinic, "Asperger's Syndrome."

22. Ibid.

**CHAPTER 17: NEUROCHEMICAL DISTRACTIBILITY/IMPULSIVITY**

1.  Getting at a patient's brain chemistry is complicated, and can't be achieved by the standard blood tests most doctors administer. I send the blood samples of many of my patients to the Mayo Clinic's lab, to confirm levels of neurotransmitters and other chemicals in the brain. I've found that the Mayo Clinic is one of only a handful of U.S. medical facilities that provide highly reliable brain-chemistry reports.

2.  Those interested in learning even more about the role of serotonin and norepinephrine in brain chemistry could read the comprehensive *Neuropharmacology of Serotonin* (*Annals of the New York Academy of Sciences*, vol. 600, 1990), or

Gregory Ordway, Michael Schwartz, and Alan Frazer, eds., *Brain Norepineph-rine: Neurobiology and Therapeutics* (Cambridge: Cambridge University Press, 2007).

3. See, for example, Chantal Moret and Mike Briley, "The Importance of Norepi-nephrine in Depression," *Neuropsychiatric Disease Treatment* 7, supp. 1 (2011): 9–13.

**CHAPTER 18: SCHIZOPHRENIA**

1. Other diagnosable psychotic disorders, including schizophreniform disor-der, schizoaffective disorder, and delusional disorder, share symptoms with schizophrenia but differ from that disorder on dimensions of time (for example, shorter duration) or exact symptom picture. Those disorders may also be mis-taken for ADHD, but because schizophrenia is the most common and repre-sentative psychotic disorder, we will focus on that condition in this book. Full diagnostic criteria for schizophrenia and other psychotic disorders are presented in American Psychiatric Association, *Diagnostic and Statistical Manual of Mental Disorders*, 5th ed. (Washington, DC: American Psychiatric Association, 2013).

2. *DSM-V* removed the discussion of different types of schizophrenia, but it can still be useful to think about these general categories (including for treatment approaches to different patients) so I've included them here.

3. Merete Øiea, Kjetil Sundetb, and Bjørn Rishovd Rundc, "Contrasts in Memory Functions Between Adolescents with Schizophrenia or ADHD," *Neuropsycho-logia* 37, no. 12 (November 1999): 1351–58.

4. Research findings quoted in Jennifer Welsh, "Clearing the Mind: How the Brain Cuts the Clutter," LiveScience, April 13, 2011, retrieved November 15, 2012, from http://www.livescience.com/13690-brain-clutter-filtering-brain-cells-110413.html.

5. Gina Kolata, "5 Disorders Share Same Genetic Risk Factors, Study Finds," *New York Times*, February 28, 2013, retrieved March 21, 2013, from http://www.nytimes.com/2013/03/01/health/study-finds-genetic-risk-factors-shared-by-5-psychiatric-disorders.html.

6. National Institute of Mental Health, "How Is Schizophrenia Treated?" Re-trieved November 16, 2012, from http://www.nimh.nih.gov/health/publica tions/schizophrenia/how-is-schizophrenia-treated.shtml.

7. Elizabeth Walsh, Alec Buchanan, and Thomas Fahy, "Violence and Schizophre-nia: Examining the Evidence," *British Journal of Psychiatry* 180 (2002): 490–95.

8. Mayo Clinic, "Schizophrenia," retrieved November 16, 2012, from http://www.mayoclinic.com/health/schizophrenia/DS00196/ DSECTION=treatments-and-drugs.

## CHAPTER 19: FETAL ALCOHOL SYNDROME

1. For more information on the cause, symptoms, and prevention of FAS, see the National Library of Medicine, "Fetal Alcohol Syndrome," retrieved February 14, 2013 from http://www.ncbi.nlm.nih.gov/pubmedhealth/PMH0001909/; and the Centers for Disease Control and Prevention, "Facts About Fetal Alcohol Spectrum Disorders," retrieved February 19, 2013, from http://www.cdc.gov/ncbddd/fasd/facts.html.

2. Philip A. May and J. Phillip Gossage, for the National Institute on Alcohol Abuse and Alcoholism, "Estimating the Prevalence of Fetal Alcohol Syndrome: A Summary," retrieved February 14, 2013, from http://pubs.niaaa.nih.gov/publications/arh25-3/159-167.htm.

3. Keith Vaux, for Medscape, "Fetal Alcohol Syndrome," retrieved February 14, 2013, from http://pubs.niaaa.nih.gov/publications/arh25-3/159-167.htm.

4. Centers for Disease Control and Prevention, "Fetal Alcohol Spectrum Disorders: Data & Statistics," retrieved February 19, 2013, from http://www.cdc.gov/NCBDDD/fasd/data.html.

5. Vaux, "Fetal Alcohol Syndrome."

6. Amy Norton, "Fetal Alcohol Disorders Common in Eastern Europe Adoptees," Reuters, April 13, 2010, retrieved February 14, 2013, from http://www.reuterscom/article/2010/04/13/us-fetal-alcohol-idUSTRE63C39X20100413.

7. Ibid.

8. Centers for Disease Control and Prevention, "Fetal Alcohol Spectrum Disorders: Secondary Conditions," retrieved February 19, 2013, from http://www.cdc.gov/ncbddd/fasd/secondary-conditions.html.

9. Centers for Disease Control and Prevention, "Facts About Fetal Alcohol Spectrum Disorders."

10. V. Bhatara, R. Loudenberg, and R. Ellis, "Association of Attention Deficit Hyperactivity Disorder and Gestational Alcohol Exposure: An Exploratory Study," *Journal of Attention Disorders* 9, no. 3 (February 2006): 515–22.

11. Elizabeth Peadon and Elizabeth J Elliott, "Distinguishing Between Attention-Deficit Hyperactivity and Fetal Alcohol Spectrum Disorders in Children: Clinical Guidelines," *Neuropsychiatric Disease Treatment* 6 (2010): 509–15.

12. C. D. Coles, K. A. Platzman, C. L. Raskind-Hood, et al., "A Comparison of Children Affected by Prenatal Alcohol Exposure and Attention Deficit, Hyperactivity Disorder," *Alcoholism: Clinical and Experimental Research* 21, no. 1 (1997): 150–61.

13. Libbe Kooistra, Susan Crawford, Ben Gibbard, Barbara Ramage, and Bonnie J. Kaplan, "Differentiating Attention Deficits in Children with Fetal Alcohol Spectrum Disorder or Attention-Deficit–Hyperactivity Disorder," *Developmental Medicine & Child Neurology* 52, no. 2 (February 2010): 205–11.

14. For an overview of treatment approaches to FAS see the Centers for Disease Control and Prevention, "Fetal Alcohol Spectrum Disorders: Treatments," retrieved February 19, 2013, from http://www.cdc.gov/ncbddd/fasd/treatments. html.

15. For more on occupational therapy, see the American Occupational Therapy Association, "About Occupational Therapy," retrieved March 5, 2013, from http://www.aota.org/Consumers.aspx.

## CHAPTER 20: FRAGILE X SYNDROME

1. For more detail on the genetic basis of FXS, along with other features of the disorder, see the National Fragile X Foundation website, retrieved January 21, 2013, http://www.fragilex.org/.

2. K. Cornish, V. Sudhalter, and J. Turk, "Attention and Language in Fragile X," *Mental Retardation and Developmental Disabilities Research Reviews* 10 (2004): 11–16.

3. For more detail on the diagnostic criteria and features of autism, see American Psychiatric Association, *Diagnostic and Statistical Manual of Mental Disorders, 4th ed.* (Washington, DC: American Psychiatric Association, 1994).

4. National Fragile X Foundation, "Autism and Fragile X Syndrome," retrieved January 21, 2013, from http://www.fragilex.org/fragile-x-associated-disorders/ fragile-x-syndrome/autism-and-fragile-x-syndrome/.

5. Y. McLennan, J. Polussa, F. Tassone, and R. Hagerman, "Fragile X Syndrome," *Current Genomics* 12, no. 3 (2011): 216–24.

6. For more detail on hereditary aspects of FXS see National Fragile X Foundation, "Genetics and Inheritance," retrieved January 21, 2013, from http://www .fragilex.org/fragile-x-associated-disorders/genetics-and-inheritance/.

7. Centers for Disease Control and Prevention, "Fragile X Data and Statistics," retrieved January 22, 2013, from http://www.cdc.gov/ncbddd/fxs/data.html.

8. W. E. Kaufmann and H. W. Moser, "Dendritic Anomalies in Disorders Associated with Mental Retardation," *Cerebral Cortex* 10 (2000): 981–91.

9. Prevalence and other diagnosis information here from Centers for Disease Control and Prevention, "Fragile X Syndrome," retrieved January 21, 2013, from http://www.cdc.gov/ncbddd/fxs/data.html.

10. Centers for Disease Control and Prevention, "Fragile X Data and Statistics."

11. Randi J. Hagerman, Carey Jackson, Khaled Amiri, Rebecca O'Connor, William Sobesky, and Amy Cronister Silverman, "Girls with Fragile X Syndrome: Physical and Neurocognitive Status and Outcome," *Pediatrics* 89, no. 3 (March 1, 1992): 395–400

12. J. Turk, "Fragile X Syndrome and Attentional Deficits," *Journal of Applied Research in Intellectual Disabilities* 11 (1998): 175–91.

13. M. Tranfaglia, "The Psychiatric Presentation of Fragile X: Evolution of the Diagnosis and Treatment of the Psychiatric Comorbidities of Fragile X Syndrome," *Developmental Neuroscience* 35, no. 5 (2011): 337–48.

14. For an overview of treatment for FXS in children and adults, see National Fragile X Foundation, "Treatment and Intervention," retrieved January 22, 2013, from http://www.fragilex.org/treatment-intervention/.

15. Centers for Disease Control and Prevention, "Fragile X Data and Statistics."

16. An IEP sets customized educational objectives for a given student and includes approaches tailored to meet these objectives. The Learning Disabilities chapter in this book discusses IEPs in detail.

**CHAPTER 21: OTHER CONDITIONS**

1. For more details on iron deficiency, its causes, and its consequences see the Centers for Disease Control, "Iron and Iron Deficiency," retrieved March 12, 2013, from http://www.cdc.gov/nutrition/everyone/basics/vitamins/iron.html.

2. E. Konofal, M. Lecendreux, I. Arnulf, and M. C. Mouren, "Iron Deficiency in Children with Attention-Deficit/Hyperactivity Disorder," *Archives of Pediatric and Adolescent Medicine* 158, no. 12 (December 2004): 1113–15.

3. In this research study, the child participants did not have an iron deficiency, but the results suggest that improving iron levels can have a positive effect on attention-deficit/hyperactivity symptoms in general. Eric Konofal, Michel Lecendreux, Juliette Deron, Martine Marchand, Samuele Cortese, Mohammed Zaïm, Marie Christine Mouren, and Isabelle Arnulf, "Effects of Iron Supplementation on Attention Deficit Hyperactivity Disorder in Children," *Pediatric Neurology* 38 (2008): 20–26.

4. See, for example, National Library of Medicine, MedLine Plus, "Sugar and Hyperactivity," retrieved March 21, 2013, from http://www.nlm.nih.gov/medlineplus/ency/article/002426.htm.

5. See, for example, a review by Jennifer Warner, "Can Food Really Affect Your Child's Behavior?" MedicineNet.com, retrieved March 21, 2013, from http://www.medicinenet.com/script/main/art.asp?articlekey=52516.

6. This is from an unpublished study I helped conduct while working at Children's Memorial Hospital (Chicago) in the early 1980s.

7. For more information on the causes, consequences, and treatments of hyperthyroidism, see National Library of Medicine, PubMed Health, "Hyperthyroidism," retrieved March 13, 2013, from http://www.ncbi.nlm.nih.gov/pubmedhealth/PMH0001396/.

8. Miguel Alvarez, Ricardo Guell, Dana Chong, and Joanne Rovet, "Attentional Processing in Hyperthyroid Children Before and After Treatment," *Journal of Pediatric Endocrinology and Metabolism* 9, no. 4 (1996): 447–54.

9.  Julie P. Gentile, Rafay Atiq, and Paulette M. Gillig, "Adult ADHD: Diagnosis, Differential Diagnosis, and Medication Management," *Psychiatry* (Edgmont) 3, no. 8 (August 2006): 25–30.

10. For more on the causes, consequences, and treatment of pituitary tumors, see National Library of Medicine, PubMed Health, "Pituitary Tumor," retrieved March 13, 2013, from http://www.ncbi.nlm.nih.gov/pubmedhealth/PMH0001723/.

11. World Health Organization, "Preterm Birth," fact sheet, retrieved March 13, 2013, from http://www.who.int/mediacentre/factsheets/fs363/en/index.html.

12. For more on the early consequences of premature birth see the Mayo Clinic, "Premature Birth," retrieved March 13, 2013, from http://www.mayoclinic.com/health/premature-birth/DS00137.

13. National Institutes of Health, "Even Moderately Premature Birth Poses Risk of Developmental Delay," January 15, 2002, retrieved from http://www.nih.gov/news/pr/jan2002/nichd-15.htm.

14. As cited in James Randerson, "Premature Birth Has Long-Term Effects," *Guardian*, March 25, 2008, retrieved March 13, 2013, from http://www.guardian.co.uk/science/2008/mar/26/medicalresearch.children.

15. Karolina Lindström, Frank Lindblad, and Anders Hjern, "Preterm Birth and Attention-Deficit/Hyperactivity Disorder in Schoolchildren," *Pediatrics* 127, no. 5 (May 1, 2011): 858–65.

16. For more on the causes, consequences, and treatments of allergies, see National Library of Medicine, PubMed Health, "Allergies," retrieved March 14, 2013, from http://www.ncbi.nlm.nih.gov/pubmedhealth/PMH0001815/.

17. American College of Allergy, Asthma, and Immunology, "Allergic Rhinitis," retrieved March 14, 2013, from http://www.acaai.org/allergist/allergies/Types/rhinitis/Pages/default.aspx.

18. For more on heavy metal poisoning, see WebMD, "Heavy Metal Poisoning," retrieved March 14, 2013, from http://www.webmd.com/a-to-z-guides/heavy-metal-poisoning.

19. As cited in S. L. Baker, "ADHD Symptoms Caused by Lead Exposure, New Studies Claim," *Natural News*, February 16, 2010, retrieved March 14, 2013, from http://www.naturalnews.com/028175_lead_poisoning_ADHD.html.

**CHAPTER 23: EVALUATING AND MANAGING YOUR SYMPTOMS**

1.  To take the self-test, visit the Counselling Resource Mental Health Library, "Structured Adult ADHD Self-Test," http://counsellingresource.com/lib/quizzes/adhd-testing/adhd-test/.

2. M. Hamilton, "The Assessment of Anxiety States by Rating," *British Journal of Medical Psychology* 32 (1959): 50–55.

3. Examples of self-rating scales for anxiety and depression symptoms are provided by organizations including the Anxiety and Depression Association of America, http://www.adaa.org/living-with-anxiety/ask-and-learn/screenings.

4. See, for example, John Markoff, "Microsoft Examines Sources of 'Cyberchondria,'" *New York Times*, November 24, 2008, retrieved March 20, 2013, from http://www.nytimes.com/2008/11/25/technology/internet/25symptoms.html?_r=0.

# Index

**A**

"acting out," 21, 132, 220. *See also*
    hyperactivity/impulsivity

ADD (attention-deficit disorder), xiv,
    11, 19, 20, 25, 118, 244

    *DSM-III* and, 12

    history of, 2

    misdiagnosis of, 153, 155, 253–55

    normal inattention/distractibility
        misdiagnosed as, 253–55

    sleep-deprived teacher and, 52, 53

Adderall, 1, 22, 28, 193

    Adderall XR, 30, 194

    rising use and abuse, 25, 26, 27, 31

ADHD (attention-deficit/hyperactivity
    disorder)

    adult cases of, xvii, 1, 11, 20

    comorbid conditions, xvii, 14, 34, 60,
        89, 168

    cost of, 16–18

    cultural bias and, 19–24

    definition as outdated, 3, 4

    dietary changes ineffective for, 239

    as "excuse," 23

    "free spirit" stereotype and, 20–21

    gender and, 21

    genetics and, 3–4, 12, 34, 90

    history of, 10–13

    IQ and, 21

    managing symptoms, 270–72, 293n3

    media and, 22

    stimulant use and abuse resulting
        from diagnosis of, 1, 12, 16, 23,
        25–32

    subjectivity and bias in, 9, 20–21

    subtypes, 9

    symptoms, 7–8, 9, 20

    symptoms as normal for life phase or
        circumstances, 258

    as symptoms of another disorder, xiv,
        xvi–xvii, 1–2, 11, 33–36 (*see also*
        *specific disorders*)

    treatment, limited effectiveness of, 24

ADHD diagnosis

    assessing symptoms and, 260

    bias in, 20–22

    "checklist" of problems, 263

    *DSM-V* and, 7–9

    evaluating ADHD symptoms, 261–62

    evaluating other symptoms, 262–64

ADHD diagnosis (*cont.*)
  examination needed for making
    a sound diagnosis, xvi, 22–23,
    260–70
  evidence from teachers used in, 263
  four questions for evaluating patients,
    260–61
  hallmark signs of, xv, 46
  medical tests recommended, 268–70
  method for diagnosing, 7–9
  negative consequences of diagnosis,
    xiii, xvii, 3
  online "self-tests" and, 262, 294n1
  prevalence and growth of, 15–16
  rate of adults diagnosed, 1, 11, 21
  rate of boys vs. girls, 21
  rate of children diagnosed, 1
  self-diagnosing caution, 15, 21,
    257–58, 264–65
  subtypes, 9
  testing for other conditions and, 263,
    264
  in younger children, 20
ADHD misdiagnosis, xiii, xv–xvi, xvii,
    3, 11, 19, 22–23, 26, 31, 60, 95
  allergies mistaken for ADHD, 235,
    240–42
  Asperger syndrome mistaken for
    ADHD, 171–83
  bias and subjectivity in diagnosing
    ADHD, 20–21
  FAS mistaken for ADHD, 209–21
  FXS mistaken for, 223–34
  giftedness mistaken for ADHD,
    129–39
  hearing problems mistaken for
    ADHD, 93–103
  heavy metal poisoning mistaken for
    ADHD, 235, 248–50
  LDs mistaken for ADHD, 105–15

mood disorders mistaken for ADHD,
    79–92
NDI mistaken for ADHD, 185–95
OCD mistaken for ADHD, 151–60
overactive thyroid (hyperthyroidism)
    mistaken for ADHD, 235, 242–44
phase of life or specific circumstances
    producing symptoms mistaken for
    ADHD, 253–58, 271
pituitary tumor mistaken for ADHD,
    235, 244–46
poor diet consequences mistaken for
    ADHD, 235, 236–39
prematurity difficulties mistaken for
    ADHD, 235, 246–48
reasons for misdiagnosis, 20–23
schizophrenia mistaken for ADHD,
    197–208, 290n1
seizure disorders mistaken for
    ADHD, 141–49
SPD mistaken for ADHD, 117–27
sleep disorders mistaken for ADHD,
    51–63
substance abuse mistaken for
    ADHD, 65–78
Tourette's syndrome mistaken for
    ADHD, 161–70
vision problems mistaken for
    ADHD, 39–49
ADHD symptoms as normal behaviors
    for life phase or specific circum-
    stances, 253–58
  management of, 270–71
adolescence, life phase mistaken for
    ADHD, 253–55
Alcoholics Anonymous, 77
alcohol use. *See* substance abuse
All About Vision, 278n10
allergies, 235, 240–42
  distractibility/inattention and, 240

example, eight-year-old girl, 240–42
main symptoms, 267
prevalence of, 241
testing for, 269
treatment, 241
types of, 241
alogia, 202
American Academy of Neurology, xvii
review of "neuroenhancement," 32
American Academy of Pediatrics
on ADHD diagnosis exam, xvi
American Council for Drug Education
on adult marijuana use, 75
American Psychiatric Association
(APA). *See also Diagnostic and Statistical Manual* (various editions)
label of ADHD and, xi
reliance on *DSM-V*, 14
American Speech-Language- Hearing
Association, 101
anhedonia, 203
anti-anxiety medication, 180, 218, 231,
233
anticonvulsive medication, 90, 149
antipsychotic medication, 90, 168, 207
anxiety, 79, 154
Asperger syndrome and, 180
FXS patients and, 231, 233
generalized anxiety disorder, 151,
155
Hamilton Anxiety Rating Scale, 263
medication for, 180, 218, 231, 233
OCD and, 151, 157
panic disorder, 155
self-rating scales and, 270, 295n3
sensory processing disorder and, 117,
122
symptoms, assessing, 263–64
Anxiety and Depression Association of
America, 295n3

appetite loss
mood disorders and, 83, 265
stimulant side-effects and, 26, 28, 29,
32, 41, 95, 103, 118, 154, 193, 194,
212, 246, 256
Asperger syndrome, 15, 171–83, 288n10
age of onset, 177
anxiety and, 180
as autism spectrum disorder, 176–78
clues to look for (main symptoms),
174–75, 267
*DSM-V* classification as form of
autism, 171–72, 288n7
example, twenty-four-year-old man,
172–75, 178, 179, 182–83
genetics and, 179
hallmark signs of, 171, 172, 173
inattention/distractibility as symptoms of, 171, 172
obsessive interests and, 173, 174, 178
OCD and, 178
prevalence of, 178–79
relation to ADHD symptoms, 179–81
self-rating scales and, 270
social functioning and, 171, 172–73,
174, 175, 176, 177, 178, 179
SSRIs for, 180, 182
stimulants and, 172
symptoms, 176
Tourette's syndrome and, 178
treatment, 181–83
what it is, 175–78
autism/autism spectrum disorders, 13,
292n3. *See also* Asperger syndrome
FXS and, 228
genetics and, 179
hallmark signs of, 177
avolition, 202

**B**

Benzedrine, 12

bipolar disorder, 11, 13, 79–82, 90–91
  clues to look for (main symptoms),
    34, 81, 83, 265
  diagnosis, 83
  difference between bipolar disorder
    and major depressive disorder, 84
  *DSM-V* diagnosis of Bipolar I and
    Bipolar II disorder, 84, 86–88
  *DSM-V* prognosis, 91
  example, twelve-year-old boy, 80–83,
    87–88, 90, 91–92
  genetics and, 17, 83, 89, 90
  hyperactivity/impulsivity as symp-
    tom of, 34, 89–90
  hypomania and, 85, 87, 89
  impulsivity as hallmark symptom of
    mania in children, 89–90
  inattention/distractibility as symp-
    tom, 33, 79, 80, 81, 85, 86, 89, 90
  prevalence of, 88–89
  rapid cycling and treatment, 91
  relation to ADHD symptoms, 89–90
  self-rating scales and, 263, 270, 295n3
  treatment, 90–92
  typical age of onset, 89
boredom
  giftedness and, xvi, 129, 266, 132
  LDs and, 111, 113
  NDI and, 187, 195
Bradley, Charles, 2, 12

**C**

Centers for Disease Control and Pre-
  vention (CDC)
  ADHD, rate of children diagnosed
    with 16
  ADHD diagnosis, boys vs. girls, 21
  ADHD costs estimated by, 17

ADHD treatment, on limited effectiveness of current, 23–24
  on drinking during pregnancy,
    215–16
  on FXS occurrence, 228, 229
  on FXS prognosis, 232
  LDs and ADHD, 112
  report on alcohol use and substance
    abuse, 72
  Tourette's syndrome occurrence,
    167
Children's Vision Information Network, 46, 277n2
Concerta (methylphenidate), 27
Cylert, 12

**D**

depression (major depressive disorder),
  11, 13, 15, 79–82
  difference between bipolar disorder
    and major depressive disorder, 84
  *DSM-V* diagnosis of, 84–85, 87
  fatigue and, 72
  fidgeting as symptom, 85
  genetics and, 17, 89, 90
  inattention/distractibility as symp-
    tom, 33, 79, 80, 81, 85, 86, 89, 90
  main symptoms, 265
  pituitary tumor and, 244
  prevalence of, 88–89
  relation to ADHD symptoms, 89
  self-rating scales and, 263, 270, 295n3
  serotonin and epinephrine/norepi-
    nephrine levels and, 192
  SPD and, 117, 119, 120, 123
  substance abuse and, 71, 72
  treatment, 91
Dexedrine, 27
*Diagnostic and Statistical Manual*, 2
  insomnia characterization in, 56

"sleep-wake" disorders, 55, 56
"substance-related disorders" in, 69
*Diagnostic and Statistical Manual of Mental Disorders II (DSM-II)*, 12
*Diagnostic and Statistical Manual of Mental Disorders III (DSM-III)*, 12
    concept of ADD and ADD-H introduced, 12
*Diagnostic and Statistical Manual of Mental Disorders III-R (DSM-III-R)*, 12
    ADHD label introduced, 12
    criteria for ADHD in, 12
*Diagnostic and Statistical Manual of Mental Disorders IV (DSM-IV)*
    Asperger syndrome in, 171, 175–76, 177, 179
    compared to *DSM-V*, 13–14, 15, 16, 87, 168
    criteria for ADHD in, 9, 12
    criteria and features for autism in, 292n3
    depression criteria, 88–89
    as flawed, 14–15
    "short sleepers" or "long sleepers" in, 278n3
    self-diagnosing caution, 15
    Tourette's syndrome diagnosis in, 165, 168
*Diagnostic and Statistical Manual of Mental Disorders V (DSM-V)*
    ADHD, 7–8, 9, 20, 168
    ADHD diagnosis, changes from *DSM-IV*, 13–14, 15
    alcohol use disorder, 73
    Asperger syndrome disorder, 15, 171, 176, 177–78, 288n7
    autism/autism spectrum disorders, 179, 288n7

bipolar disorder, 82, 84, 85, 86–87, 89, 91
circadian rhythm sleep-wake disorders, 56
depression (major depressive disorder), 82, 84–85, 88
Internet gaming disorder, 57
learning disabilities, 108–9, 111–12
learning disabilities, three specific types, 109–10
mood disorders, 84–87
multiple personality disorder, 203
obsessive-compulsive disorder, 156, 157, 158, 286n3
parasomnias, 56–57
schizophrenia, 200–203
schizophrenia subtypes, 203, 290n2
substance abuse, 70–71, 74
substance-induced mental orders, 71, 72
on tic disorders, 287n2
Tourette's syndrome, 165–66, 167, 168
distractibility. *See* inattention/distractibility
disulfiram, 76
dopamine, 27, 269
*Driven to Distraction* (Hallowell and Ratey), 11

**E**
encephalitis, 12
endocrinological conditions. *See also* hyperthyroidism; pituitary tumor
    hyperactivity-impulsivity as symptom of, 34
    testing for, 244, 269
epilepsy, 145. *See also* seizure disorders
epinephrine, 27
epinephrine/norepinephrine, 189, 269, 289n2

epinephrine/norepinephrine (*cont.*)
NDI and, 185, 189, 190
testing for, 269

**F**

fatigue
depression and, 72
heavy metal poisoning and, 249, 268
iron deficiency and, 237, 267
life circumstances and, 52
mood disorders (bipolar and major
depressive disorder) and, 81, 85, 87,
91
OCD and, 152
overactive thyroid (hyperthyroidism)
and, 243, 267
pituitary tumor and, 244, 245, 268
sleep disturbance and, 265
fetal alcohol spectrum disorder, 215,
216, 217
fetal alcohol syndrome (FAS), 209–21
adoption and rates of, 216
attention problems, as differing from
ADHD, 217
clues to look for (main symptoms),
212–13, 267
example, nine-year-old boy, adopted
from Romania, 210–13, 215, 219–21
hyperactivity/impulsivity and, 209,
211, 212, 214, 215, 217, 267
inattention/distractibility and, 211,
214, 215
LDs and, 212
negative consequences of delayed
diagnosis, 218
over-stimulation, difficulty handling,
217
physical or occupational therapies
and training helpful for, 218–19
prevalence of, 215–16

relation to ADHD symptoms, 217–18
signs and symptoms, 209, 210, 211,
213, 214, 215, 216–17
stimulants and, 211–12
testing for, 214–15
treatment, 218–21
fidgeting
ADHD and, 1, 2, 8, 11, 20
adults and, 20
bipolar disorder and, 11, 34
endocrinological conditions (i.e.,
hyperthyroidism), 34
FXS and, 34, 230
hearing problems and, 94
learning disabilities and, 105, 106, 107
mood disorders (bipolar and major
depressive disorder) and, 11, 81
NDI and, 189, 190, 195
normal, 258
OCD and, 159
poor diet (iron deficiency and excess
sugar) and, 237, 238
self-tests and, 262
sensory processing disorder and, 118
"The Story of Fidgety Philip," 10, 11
Tourette's syndrome and, 11, 34,
161–65, 168, 266
vision problems and, 40, 46
fragile X syndrome (FXS), 35, 223–34
autism/autism spectrum disorders
and, 228
clues to look for (physical signs of
and main symptoms), 34, 225–26,
230, 267
diagnosis and undetected cases of, 229
effect of stimulants on, 230–31
example, fourteen-year-old boy,
224–25, 227–28, 232–34
hyperactivity/impulsivity as symptom of, 34, 223, 224, 230

inattention/distractibility and, 223,
224, 230
prevalence of, 228, 229
as prevalent among boys, 225
relation to ADHD symptoms, 230–31
social services and IEPs available to
patients, 231, 232, 293n16
testing for, 269
treatment, 231–34
in women and older adults, 227

**G**
genetics, 3
Asperger syndrome and, 179
autism/autism spectrum disorders
and, 179
bipolar disorder and, 17, 83, 89, 90
depression and, 17, 89, 90
FXS and, 223, 225, 226
hearing problems and, 98, 99, 100
NDI and, 191
OCD and, 155
patterns underlying ADHD are the
same as other disorders, 12, 34, 90,
158–59, 180
schizophrenia and, 205–6
symptoms of ADHD and, 11
testing to uncover disorders, 269
Tourette's syndrome and, 167
vision problems and, 45–46
giftedness, xv–xvi, 129–39
adult traits, 135
"asynchronous development" and,
133, 138
behavioral symptoms or problems
(table), 136
boredom and, xvi, 129, 132
clues to look for (main symptoms),
131–32, 266
example, nine-year-old boy, 130–32,

135, 136, 138–39
hyperactivity/impulsivity and, 129,
134, 136
inattention/distractibility and, 129,
135, 136, 266
misdiagnosis, costs of, 137
percentage of the population, 134
relation to ADHD symptoms, 136–37
testing for, 269
"treatment," 137–39
what it is, 133–36

**H**
Hallowell, Edward, 11
Hamilton Anxiety Rating Scale, 263
Harvard University
research on genetic overlap among
ADHD, autism, and other conditions, 180
research on patterns underlying
ADHD as the same as other disorders, 12
hearing problems, xv, 93–103
adults with attention-related issues
and, 100
causes, 97, 98
clues to look for (main symptoms),
95–96, 266
cochlear implants, 102
coping mechanism, 98–99
damaging consequences of misdiagnosis, 101
example, nine-year-old boy, 94–96,
99, 102–3
fidgeting and, 94
forms of, 97–98
genetics and, 98, 99, 100
hearing aids, 102–3
hyperactivity/impulsivity and, 93, 95,
96, 101

hearing problems (*cont.*)
  inattention/distractibility and, 93, 101
  lack of diagnosis, 93
  online resources, 282n1
  prevalence of, 99–100
  relation to ADHD symptoms, 100–101
  short attention span, impulsivity, and, 93, 94, 101
  stimulants and, 95, 103
  symptoms, 98
  testing for, 268
  treatment, 102–3
  what they are, 97–99
heavy metal poisoning, 235, 248–50, 269
  diagnosis, 249
  example, five-year-old boy, 248–50
  inattention/distractibility and, 248, 249
  symptoms, 249, 268
  testing for, 268
  treatment, 249–50
hyperactivity/impulsivity, 3, 11, 263
  adults and, 20
  as ADHD symptom, 2, 11, 19, 262
  Asperger syndrome and, 172, 173
  conditions causing, 14, 34, 46
  *DSM-III* and ADD, 12
  *DSM-V* and ADHD, 8, 9, 14
  encephalitis infections and, 12
  FAS and, 209, 211, 212, 214, 215, 217, 267
  FXS and, 223, 224, 230
  genetic basis, 11
  giftedness and, 129, 134, 136
  "growing out of," 20
  hearing problems and, 93, 95, 96, 101
  managing symptoms of normal levels without medication, 270–72

mania in children, impulsivity as hallmark symptom, 89
mood disorders (bipolar disorder and major depressive disorder) and, 79, 81, 82, 89–90
normal, for life phase or circumstances, 253–58, 260
NDI and, 185, 186, 188, 189, 190, 191, 194, 195, 270
neurological basis, 11–12
schizophrenia and, 197
seizure disorders and, 146
sensory processing disorder and, 118, 122, 124
sleep disorders and, 59
stimulants prescribed for, 25, 28
substance abuse and, 65, 74, 77
Tourette's syndrome and, 34, 161, 162, 163, 164, 165, 168
understanding of, 11
vision problems and, 39–41, 42, 45
hyperthyroidism, 192, 235, 242–44
  example, eleven-year-old girl, 242–44
  misdiagnosis of ADHD in adults and, 243
  symptoms, 34, 243, 267
  testing for, 269
  treatment, 243–44
hypomania, 85, 87, 89

I
inattention/distractibility, 2
  as ADHD symptom, 2, 7–8, 9, 10, 11
  adults and, 20
  allergies and, 240
  Asperger syndrome and, 171, 172
  boredom mistaken as, xvi, 129, 132
  conditions (other than ADHD) causing, 3, 14, 33, 263
  in *DSM-III*, as ADD symptom, 12

in *DSM-V*, as ADHD category of symptoms, 7–8, 9, 14
evaluating problem of, 262
FAS and, 211, 214, 215
FXS and, 223, 224, 230
genetic basis, 11
giftedness and, 129, 135, 136, 266
hearing problems and, 93, 101
heavy metal poisoning and, 248, 249
LDs and, 105, 106, 107, 108, 111, 113, 266
managing symptoms of normal levels without medication, 270–72
mood disorders and, 79, 80, 81, 85, 86, 89, 90
NDI and, 186, 188, 189, 190, 191, 192, 194, 195
neurological basis, 11–12
as normal behavior, 253–58, 260
OCD and, 151, 153, 154, 155, 158
overactive thyroid (hyperthyroidism) and, 242
poor diet (iron deficiency) and, 236, 237
prematurity and, 246, 247
schizophrenia and, 197, 198, 204
seizure disorders and, 141, 142, 143, 144, 144, 148
SPD and, 122, 124
sleep disorders and, 51, 52–53, 54, 59, 265
stimulants to treat, 2, 3, 25, 28, 194
"The Story of Johnny Head-in-Air," 10, 11
substance abuse and, 65, 71, 74–75, 77
Tourette's syndrome and, 161, 162, 163, 164, 165, 168
understanding of, 11
vision problems and, 39, 40, 42, 45, 46

impulsivity. *See* hyperactivity/impulsivity
International League Against Epilepsy, 144
IQ, xiv, 21
giftedness and, 134
learning disabilities and, 111
tests, 134
iron deficiency, 235, 236–39, 269, 293n3
example, thirteen-year-old boy, 236–38
inattention/distractibility and, 236, 237
relation to ADHD symptoms, 238
signs and symptoms, 237–38, 267
testing for, 268
irritability
depression and, 89
FAS and, 218
FXS and, 230
mood disorders and, 81, 82, 85, 87, 89, 90
sleep disorders and, 57
SPD and, 119
stimulant side-effects and, 29, 41, 193, 230

J
James, William, 11–12

L
Laufer, Maurice, 12
learning disabilities (LDs), xiv, 105–15
behavioral symptoms mistaken as ADHD, 110–11
clues to look for (main symptoms), 107–8, 266
*DSM-V* criteria, 109
*DSM-V* types of, 109–10
dyscalculia, 110, 114

learning disabilities (LDs) (*cont.*)
  dysgraphia, 110, 114
  dyslexia of fluency/dyslexia of com-
    prehension, 105, 108, 110, 114
  example, seven-year-old girl, 106–8,
    111, 112–13, 115
  FAS and, 212
  fidgeting and, 106, 107
  gender and, 112
  inattention/distractibility and, 105,
    106, 107, 108, 111, 113, 266
  individualized education plan (IEP)
    and, 114, 115, 284n12, 293n16
  IQ and, 111
  prevalence of, 111–12
  relation to ADHD symptoms, 112–13
  risk factors for, 112
  substance abuse misdiagnosed as, 75
  testing for, 269
  treatment, 113–15
  vision problems misdiagnosed as, 46
  what they are, 108–11
M
marijuana use. *See* substance abuse
Mayo Clinic, 189
  on Asperger syndrome, 176, 179, 181
  blood testing for neurochemical
    distractibility/impulsivity, 289n1
  hearing loss resources, 282n1
  prematurity, developmental conse-
    quences of, 294n12
  sleep tables, 61
MBD (minimal brain dysfunction), 12
MDMA, 27
medical tests, 268–70
  allergy tests, 269
  blood tests (CBC and specific tests),
    269, 289n1
  brain electrically activated mapping
    (BEAM), 269

CT Scans/MRI, 269
  electrocardiogram, 269
  electroencephalogram (EEG), 269
  genetic testing, 269
  intelligence/educational testing, 269
  self-rating scales, 270, 295n3
  urinalysis, 268
  vision/hearing tests, 268
Mensa, 134
mental illness, 290n1. *See also* mood
    disorders; obsessive-compulsive
    disorder; schizophrenia
  prevalence of, 79, 151
mood disorders, 15, 79–92. *See also*
    bipolar disorder; depression
  clues to look for, 82–83
  difference between bipolar disorder
    and major depressive disorder, 84
  *DSM-V* diagnosis of, 84–87, 88
  example, twelve-year-old boy, 80–83,
    87, 90, 91–92
  genetic link for, 89
  hyperactivity/impulsivity as symp-
    tom, 79, 81, 82, 89–90
  inattention/distractibility as symp-
    tom, 33, 79, 80, 81, 85, 86, 89, 90
  neurotransmitters and, 192
  OCD differentiated from, 157
  poor concentration as symptom, 33
  prevalence of, 88–89
  rates of mental disease and, 79
  relation to ADHD symptoms, 89–90
  self-rating scales and, 270, 295n3
  stimulants and, 27
  testing for, 269
  treatment, 90–92

N
naltrexone, 76
narcolepsy, 27, 55, 56

National Association for Gifted Children (NAGC), 133
National Center for Learning Disabilities, 111
National Center on Sleep Disorders Research, 58
National Education Association on "hidden" cost of ADHD, 17
National Fragile X Foundation, 228
National Institute of Mental Health (NIMH), on schizophrenia, 207, 208
National Institute on Alcohol Abuse and Alcoholism, 215
National Institute on Deafness and Other Communication Disorders, patterns and statistics related to hearing problems, 99–100
National Institute on Drug Abuse (NIDA)
    failure of abusers to seek treatment, 75
    prevalence of substance abuse, 72
    on treatment, 75–76
National Institutes of Health (NIH)
    Medline Plus, 277n1, 282n1
    on sleep disorders mistaken for ADHD, 60
neurochemical distractibility/impulsivity (NDI), 185–95, 270
    abnormal levels of neurotransmitters and, 185–86, 189–90
    blood tests for, 188, 194
    clues to look for, 187–88
    depression and, 192
    example, eight-year-old boy, 186–88, 190, 194–95
    genetics and, 191
    "growing out of," 194
    hyperactivity/impulsivity as symptom, 185, 186, 188, 189, 190, 191, 194, 195, 270
    inattention/distractibility as symptom, 186, 188, 189, 190, 191, 192, 194, 195
    norepinephrine reuptake inhibitors for, 193
    prevalence of, 191
    relation to ADHD symptoms, 191–92
    social functioning and, 187, 195
    SSRIs for, 185
    stimulants and, 185, 192–93
    testing for, 269, 289n1
    treatment, 192–95
    what it is, 188–90
neuroleptics, 168, 169
neurotransmitters, 27–28
    effect of stimulants on, 28
"Next Attention Deficit Disorder, The?" (Time), 124
norepinephrine, 27

O
obsessive-compulsive disorder (OCD), 151–60, 166, 286n3
    in adults, 158
    Asperger syndrome and, 178
    in children, 158
    clues to look for (main symptoms), 154–55, 159, 266
    differentiated from other disorders, 157, 286n3
    example, forty-two-year-old man, 152–55, 157–58, 160
    "exposure and response prevention," 160
    family history of, 155
    inattention/distractibility and, 151, 153, 154, 155, 158
    most common compulsions, 157

obsessive-compulsive disorder (OCD)
  (*cont.*)
  most common obsessions, 156
  obsessive-compulsive personality
    disorder and, 157
  prevalence of, 158
  relation to ADHD symptoms, 158–59
  ritualistic behavior and, 153
  self-rating scales and, 270, 295n3
  stress and worsening of symptoms,
    158
  testing for, 269
  "textbook" symptoms, 155
  treatment medications and therapy,
    159–60
  what it is, 156–58
overactive thyroid (hyperthyroidism),
    235, 242–44
  example, eleven-year-old girl, 242–44
  inattention/distractibility and, 242
  misdiagnosis of ADHD in adults
    and, 243
  symptoms, 34, 243, 267
  testing for, 269
  treatment, 243–44

**P**
phobias, 151, 157
pituitary tumor, 235, 244–46
  example, thirty-seven-year-old
    woman, 244–46
  symptoms, 244, 245, 267
  testing for, 268
  treatment, 245
poor diet (iron deficiency and excess
    sugar), 235, 236–39, 269
  example, thirteen-year-old boy,
    236–38
  hyperactivity/impulsivity and, 238,
    239

  inattention/distractibility and, 236,
    237
  relation to ADHD symptoms, 238–39
  signs and symptoms, 237–38, 267
  testing for, 268
prematurity, 235, 246–48
  definition of, 246–47
  developmental delay and, 247
  early consequences of, 247
  example, ten-year-old girl, 246–48
  inattention/distractibility and, 246,
    247
  interventions and therapies for,
    247–48
  main symptoms, 268
  rates of, 246–47
  relation to ADHD symptoms, 247

**R**
Ratey, John, 11
referral office, xvi
Ritalin (methylphenidate), 1, 12, 22, 27,
    28, 193, 194, 195
  rising use and abuse, 25, 26, 31
  Ritalin SR, 30

**S**
schizophrenia, 13, 168, 197–208, 290n1,
    290n2
  ADHD misdiagnosis and, 198, 290n1
  age of onset, 205
  "brain clutter" and, 207
  clues to look for (main symptoms),
    199–200, 267
  consequences of delayed treatment,
    204–5
  course of, 205
  diagnosis, 200–201
  example, ten-year-old boy, 198–99,
    204–5

genetics and, 205–6

hallmark symptoms (auditory hallucinations or persecutory delusions),
197, 199, 200, 204, 206

hyperactivity/impulsivity as symptom of, 197

inattention/distractibility and, 197,
198, 204

medical disorders with related symptoms, 203

multiple personality disorder and,
203

prevalence of, 205–6

psychotic disorders sharing symptoms with, 290n1

relation to ADHD symptoms, 206–7

self-rating scales and, 270

social functioning and, 198–99, 203

stimulants and worsening of, 198

suicide risk, 205, 206

symptom categories, 201–2

treatment, 207–8

violence associated with, 207

what it is, 200–205

seizure disorders, xv, 11, 141–49, 285n3

"absence" (petit mal) seizures, 144,
146, 147

adult cases of, 147, 286n11

"auras" and other symptoms, 146

categories of, 144–46

clues to look for (main symptoms),
143–44, 266

consequences of delayed treatment,
147

electroencephalogram (EEG) test for,
144

epilepsy, 145

example, nine-year-old girl, 142–44,
146, 147, 149

hyperactivity/impulsivity as

symptom of, 146

inattention/distractibility as symptom, 33, 141, 142, 143, 144, 144, 148

non-drug treatment, 149

one-time seizures, causes, 145

physiological process underlying, 145

prevalence of, 147

relation to ADHD symptoms, 147–48

short attention span, distractibility,
and, 141, 142, 144

stimulants erroneously given for,
146–47

surgical treatment, 149

temporal-lobe-based seizure, 145–46

testing for, 269

treatment using anticonvulsants,
148–49

what they are, 144–47

self-rating scales, 263–64, 270, 295n3

Sensory Integration and Praxis Tests,
122

sensory processing disorder (SPD),
117–27, 284n1, 284n4

adult cases of, 123

age of onset, 122

anxiety and, 117, 121

clues to look for (main symptoms),
120–21, 266

consequences of delayed treatment,
124–25

depression and, 117, 119, 120, 123

example, twelve-year-old girl,
118–20, 122–23, 124, 126–27

floppy babies and, 119, 122

hyperactivity/impulsivity as symptom, 118, 122, 124

inattention/distractibility and, 122,
124

prevalence of, 123

relation to ADHD symptoms, 124

sensory processing disorder (SPD)
(*cont.*)
self-rating scales and, 270
sensory integration therapy,, 125, 126
support groups for, 126, 127
symptoms, 121, 122, 124
testing and diagnosis, 122
treatment, 123, 125
what it is, 121–23
Sensory Processing Disorder Foundation, 121, 124
serotonin, 27, 189, 269, 289n2
NDI and, 185, 188, 189, 190
Short Sensory Profile, 122
sleep apnea, 55, 56
sleep disorders, 11, 35, 51–63
bipolar disorder and, 82, 83, 86, 87,
265
breathing-related sleep disorders, 55,
56
causes, 55
circadian rhythm sleep-wake disorders, 55, 56
clues to look for (main symptoms),
53–54, 83, 265
as comorbid ADHD condition, 60
consequences of, 58
depressive disorder and, 85, 265
example, thirty-six-year-old teacher,
52–54, 57, 58, 62–63
hyperactivity/impulsivity as symptom of, 59
importance of, 271
inattention/distractibility as symptom, 33, 51, 52–53, 54, 59, 265
insomnia, 55, 56, 59, 66
managing ADHD symptoms and,
271
minimum amount of sleep required,
55

minimum amount of sleep required
(table), *61*
mood disorders and, 83, 85, 86, 87,
265
naps for, 61
narcolepsy, 55, 56
NDI and, 187
parasomnias, 55, 56–57
practices to help, 62
prevalence of, 58–59
relation to ADHD symptoms, 59–60
self-rating scales and, 270
"short sleepers" or "long sleepers,"
278n3
sleep aids and medication, 279n22
"sleep debt," 61
sleep deprivation, 51, 54–55
"sleep hygiene," 61
sleeping too much (hypersomnolence), 55, 85, 278n2
"sleep-wake" disorders, 55
stimulant side-effects and, 26, 29, 32,
41, 95, 103, 118, 154, 193, 198, 212,
246, 256
stress and, 57–58
substance abuse and, 66
technology and, 53–54, 57, 58, 62, 63,
288n10
treatment (non-drug), 61–62
treatment delay consequences, 60
social functioning
ADHD and, 14, 20
asociality, 203
Asperger syndrome and, 171, 172,
173, 174–75, 176, 177, 178, 179
bipolar disorder and, 86
FAS and, 211, 219, 221
FXS and, 224, 232–33
giftedness and, 137, 138
hearing problems and, 95, 99, 101, 103

LDs and, 106, 112
NDI and, 187, 195
OCD and, 152, 157
schizophrenia and, 198–99, 203, 204, 206, 208
seizure disorders, 142
sleep disorders and, 56
SPD and, 117, 121, 123, 125, 127
stimulants and, 29
substance abuse and, 65, 70, 71
Tourette's syndrome and, 163, 165, 166
vision problems and, 43, 49
Society for Developmental and Behavioral Pediatrics, xvii
speech, accelerated. *See* talking, excessive
SSRIs (selective serotonin reuptake inhibitors), 160, 180, 182, 231
Stanford-Binet (IQ test), 134
Stanford University
    study on naps, 61–62
    study on sleep-disturbance and reaction-times, 60
Still, George, 11
stimulants, 25–32. *See also* Adderall; Ritalin (methylphenidate)
    addiction, 30
    alcohol and, as dangerous combination, 27
    Asperger syndrome and, 172
    development of tolerance, 26
    factors driving the problem, 31–32
    FXS worsened by, 230–31
    medical use, 27
    misapplication or abuse, 23, 25–26, 27, 31–32
    misdiagnosis of ADHD and, 95, 103, 142, 153–54, 159, 162–63, 164, 211–12, 236, 256

schizophrenia and, 198
side effects, 26, 28–29, 29n, 32, 41, 95, 103, 118, 142–43, 149, 154, 193, 194, 198, 212, 246, 256
time-release or long-acting, 30
Tourette's accelerated by, 164, 168
as treatment for ADHD symptoms, 1, 12, 16
"two-minute checklist" and, 32
what it is, 27–28
"Story of Fidgety Philip, The" (poem), 10
"Story of Johnny Head-in-Air" (poem), 10
Strattera, 193
stress
    breathing exercises and/or meditation to reduce, 62, 271
    diagnosis of ADHD and, 17, 124–25
    insomnia and, 56
    misdiagnosis of ADHD and, 218, 235
    of modern life, 55, 58, 256, 257, 271
    OCD and, 152, 158
    pituitary tumor and, 244, 246
    rise in, statistics, 58
    sleep disorders and, 55, 57–58
    technology and, 62
    Tourette's syndrome and, 163, 165, 166
substance abuse, 65–78, 280n2
    ADHD misdiagnosis and, 71
    alcohol use disorder, age range reported, 73
    clues to look for (main symptoms), 67–69, 265
    depression and, 71, 72
    *DSM-V* diagnosis of, 70–71, 74
    example, eighteen-year-old high school senior, 66–69, 71–72, 73–74, 77–78

substance abuse (*cont.*)
 families and, 73
 gender differences, 73
 hyperactivity/impulsivity and, 65, 74, 77
 inattention/distractibility and, 65, 71, 74–75, 77
 prevalence of, 72–74
 relation to ADHD symptoms, 74–75
 as "self-medication," 71–72
 ten classes of substances, 69
 testing for, 268, 269
 treatment, 75–78, 281n16
 treatment delay consequences, 75
 twelve-step programs, 77, 78
suicide risk
 alcohol use disorder and, 73
 schizophrenia and, 205, 206
 stimulant use and, 29

**T**

talking, excessive, 2, 9, 34, 81, 86, 90, 130, 186, 190
 bipolar disorder and accelerated speech, 86, 90
thalamus, overactivity of, 12
tic disorders, 287n2. *See also* Tourette's syndrome
 "tics of childhood," 166
Tourette's syndrome, 11, 161–70
 age of onset, 161–62
 Asperger syndrome and, 178
 clues to look for (main symptoms), 34, 163–64, 266
 example, eight-year-old boy, 162–64, 166, 169–70
 family history and, 161, 163, 164
 fidgeting and, 161–65, 168
 gender and, 167
 genetics and, 167

 habit-reversal training, 169
 hyperactivity/impulsivity as symptom of, 34, 161, 162, 163, 164, 165, 168
 inattention/distractibility as symptom of, 161, 162, 163, 164, 165, 168
 OCD differentiated from, 166
 prevalence of, 166–67
 relation to ADHD symptoms, 167–68
 short attention span and, 162
 stimulants and acceleration of symptoms, 162–63, 164, 168–69
 stress and worsening of symptoms, 163, 166, 169
 tics and, 161, 162–63, 164, 165, 168–70
 treatment, 168–70
 what it is, 164–67

**U**

University of Health Sciences in Chicago, xiv
University of Pennsylvania, attention sustainability and sleep studies, 59–60

**V**

Vanderbilt Assessment Scale, 7
vision problems, xv, 11, 34, 39–49
 changes over time, 44–45
 clues to look for (main symptoms), 41–42, 265
 errors of "refraction" as most common problem, 43–44
 example, seven-year-old girl, 40–42, 43, 44, 45, 48–49
 eye diseases, 43, 44
 "eye-teaming" disorders, 44, 46
 forms of, 43
 genetic link, 45–46
 inattention/distractibility as symptom, 33, 39, 40, 42, 44, 46

injuries and, 44
Lasik surgery and, 48, 278n10, 278n11
macular degeneration, 44, 45, 48
misdiagnosed as learning disabilities, 46
online resources, 277n1
prevalence of, 44–45
relation to ADHD symptoms, 46–47
retinal detachment, 44, 48
testing for, 268
treatment, 47–49
treatment delay consequences, 47

undiagnosed, cognitive and behavioral symptoms occurring, 39–40
Vyvanse, 27, 30, 193, 194

**W**
WebMD, 189
　Eye Health Center, 277n1
　on heavy metal poisoning, 294n18
　on seizures, 285n3
　on sleep, 287n3
　on stimulants, 277n1
Wechsler (IQ) scale, 134

# About the Author

D r. Richard C. Saul is a professor, clinician, researcher, and radio personality. For more than thirty years Dr. Saul has incorporated his clinical and academic experience into the practice of Behavioral Neurology and Development.

Dr. Saul has served on the Boards of Highland Park and Lurie Children's Hospitals, and was past Chairman of the Department of Pediatrics at Highland Park Hospital. While working with the Healthy Systems Agency, a federal program, he was responsible for containing healthcare costs in Illinois. He is the past medical director of the HMO in North Suburban Chicago.

Dr. Saul has been a Castle and Connolly Best Doctor in Chicago for the past ten years. His work has been applauded in *US News and World Report*. He is a member of the American Academy of Pediatrics, the American Academy of Neurology, and the Society for Behavior and Development. He lives with his wife outside of Chicago.